By the same author:

Testament of the Third Man: Rants from the Sidelines of Faith

Exiles at Home: Jamaican Chronicles

BY THE WAY...

To Will

Best wishes for the New Year and beyond

from

Derek

BY THE WAY...

Essays and Atavisms

Dereck C. Sale

Trafford Publishing
Bloomington, IN

Order this book online at www.trafford.com
or email orders@trafford.com

Most Trafford titles are also available at major online book retailers.

© Copyright 2017 Dereck C. Sale.

All rights reserved. No part of this publication may be reproduced, stored in a retrieval system, or transmitted, in any form or by any means, electronic, mechanical, photocopying, recording, or otherwise, without the written prior permission of the author.

Scripture quotations marked NIV are taken from the Holy Bible, New International Version®. NIV®. Copyright © 1973, 1978, 1984 by International Bible Society. Used by permission of Zondervan. All rights reserved. [Biblica]

Print information available on the last page.

ISBN: 978-1-4907-8413-7 (sc)
ISBN: 978-1-4907-8415-1 (hc)
ISBN: 978-1-4907-8414-4 (e)

Library of Congress Control Number: 2017912954

Because of the dynamic nature of the Internet, any web addresses or links contained in this book may have changed since publication and may no longer be valid. The views expressed in this work are solely those of the author and do not necessarily reflect the views of the publisher, and the publisher hereby disclaims any responsibility for them.

Trafford rev. 11/20/2017

North America & international
toll-free: 1 888 232 4444 (USA & Canada)
fax: 812 355 4082

For: Birgitta, on our fiftieth

Vanity is an atavism
Friedrich Nietzsche

CONTENTS

Introduction   xv

RUMINATIONS

Romancing Sweden	1
The Age of Youth	11
Mind and Cosmos	19
Science & Its Limits	25
Those Social Animals	31
A Rose by Any Other Name	35

DAYS IN THE SUN

An Island Entire of Itself?	41
The Company We Keep	51
The Stock Market: Fiscal Incentives Needed	61
Corporations and the Community	67
Aspects of Underdevelopment	73
Nationalism and the New Elite	79

ISSUES

Have Gun, and an Excuse to Use It	87
On Values: Freedom	89
Multilateral Agreement on Investment	99
Subliminal Contradictions	109
War and Pieces	119
Thatcher's Enduring Legacy	127

CONUNDRUMS

Why I'm Not Born Again	133
Pre-Vatican II Catholicity	143
Christianity From Below	163

A Case Appealed (revisited)	169
In Deference To Mark	187
Women Priests?	191
Interview on *Love or Logic*, with Jeff Selver	199

PROFESSION THAT LOST ITS WAY

The Reluctant Profession	217
On the State of the Profession	221
The Auditor's Responsibilities	225
Falling on Our Swords	245
Accountant, Where is Your Soul?	255
The Small Practitioner: Virtual Casualty?	259
Requiem for a Profession	263
Dubious Resurrection	267

Books Read, Enjoyed & Recommended	273
Bibliography, Sources & Endnotes	329
About the Author	337

INTRODUCTION

There comes a time when mortality gets the better of us. We recognize that many years have elapsed when we weren't looking and, without warning, we become conscious of having little to leave behind when we go. As egotistical as the idea may be, exiting without even a small footprint is disquieting. But then we ask ourselves, who cares? Why should future generations remember us? It dawned on me that what would bring my grandparents back to life, so to speak, would be evocations of things that were important to them—what they *thought* about the world. There was much I could have learned from and about them. As it turned out, I only knew the Williamson grandparents; the older Sales had migrated to Canada leaving Noel, my father, behind when I was five years old. Problem was the Williamsons were too large a family (twelve children, one of whom, my mother, Gertrude, would have eleven of her own) to allow me much access to other than uncles and aunts. Grandpa Williamson, before he in turn migrated to Canada, left me four books: two from the 1920s on great games of chess—he was a chess master of his day; a copy of Henry George's *Progress and Poverty* (1879); and *The Importance of Living* (1938) by Lin Yutang. None iconic or sentimental, but together they are for me the apotheosis of things that forever will remain unsaid.

What follows is a collection of published papers, reflections, and speeches delivered over many years. I am heartened in thinking that one day, if only out of curiosity, my grand-children may reach for, and find even vaguely interesting, this potpourri of vanities.

BY THE WAY...is divided into sections, each with a theme of sorts. *Ruminations*, is the most introspective—I'll say no more. The second, *Days in the Sun*, covers my involvement in Jamaica's affairs during the 1970s. The third, *Issues*, contains writings and presentations on topics I could not shut up about as the years went by; while the fourth section, *Conundrums*, is devoted to questions of a religious nature. Which leaves *A Profession That Lost Its Way*, for me the most difficult section.

At nineteen, having graduated from St George's College in Jamaica, I decided to follow in my father Noel's footsteps. Unlike lawyers who could be called to the Bar in Jamaica, one could aspire to the most coveted CA qualification - that of an English Chartered Accountant - only through study and work-experience *in England*, where I spent five years of January.

Returning to Jamaica I began rooting surreptitiously for the profession to step out of its ultra conservative box and speak to societal issues within its purview. (Surprisingly, today the English Institute leads the way in that direction.) Today, at a stage in life when illusions and the future are behind me, I am opening the box. If you don't get a rise out of the tortured history of well-healed professionals, or teary-eyed over their missteps, feel free to skip section five.

The last section is not a section, per se. It was prompted by the usual question. In that vein it's a list of books read and enjoyed over many years, and my recommendations to book-lovers who have left fiction behind for greater challenges.

I wish to thank my friend and colleague Robert Robson, who spent weeks ferreting out misspellings and other typographical demons that appeared in the manuscript from who knows where. I banished as many as I could; the obstinate ones that remain are all mine. Many thanks also to my friend, Gerry Jackson, for his kindnesses in writing and installing the computer program for the book-list. And, last but not least, heartfelt thanks to Will Lewis for his help in formatting the draft and especially for his creativity and insights in designing the book-cover.

RUMINATIONS

Romancing Sweden

The SAS Caravel comes in high over Stockholm, then rapidly loses altitude, so that ears ache with the increasing pressure. Visibility is nil. The clouds seem to cling to the ground that for the most part is lost from view as the plane makes its approach to Ärlanda airport. We step out in wet, windy 60° weather; behind me is Birgitta, holding infant Joanna; yours truly carrying the stroller. We shuffle down metal stairs to the tarmac. In the airport building we have our passports stamped and collect our bags. Going through customs consists of walking with the bags through a nothing-to-declare door, beyond which grandma (mormor) Marianne is waiting to greet us with fearsome hugs and kisses. She is on holiday from teaching English at home to the south. A short bus ride and we are in Marsta, where we catch the train for Stockholm.

The countryside is lush green in pastures, except when we rumble through fields of wheat, interspersed with clusters of pine forest that dwarf the next expanse of green. The farm buildings are painted red with white windowsills and a roofs like the top half of an old copper thrupence. The clouds are fast disappearing so that a reluctant sun appears, throwing dark shadows of pine forests across wet fields. The serenity of the eastern countryside creeps into my bones.

Sweden's capital, a city of about two million people, stands partly on islands near the coast, where Lake Malaren has its outlet to the Baltic. Although very modern, picturesque Stockholm has its history preserved in the Old City, which nestles on the island of Gamla Stan. Unlike many European capitals, during the summer this stately metropolis is

An edited version of a paper published in *Touche Ross (Jamaica) Newsletter* - September 1969

BY THE WAY...

noticeably free of the rush and crush. Almost everyone is on holiday. Walking along the broad boulevards, traveling by subway, or riding the buses, we experience a distinct airiness that belies the fact we are in a large city and surrounded by high-rise buildings. I leave Birgitta, Joanna, and Marianne to explore a mall, and take off to keep an appointment.

There is a truism that a country's living standards are directly connected with the amount of paper it consumes. The greater the consumption, the higher the standard of living, so it goes. Sweden is probably the highest consumer of paper in the world. One can't help noticing the high incidence of books and printed matter in the shops and in Swedish homes and offices. The conference room of a noted firm of Swedish Chartered Accountants in Stockholm is no exception. Bookcases line the walls, bindings new and expensive looking - a feast to the eyes of an amateur bibliophile. The partner I have arranged to meet speaks perfect English; his name is Hans and he is around forty-five years, bald, pragmatic, and to the point. A member of the Swedish Institute of Authorized Public Accountants, members of which are able to audit listed public companies, he spent eight years qualifying.

Hans is unequivocal: No, Sweden does not as a rule protect locally produced goods against competition from abroad. This *laissez-faire* policy adversely affects certain sectors of the economy because Swedish products are often more expensive and therefore less attractive to the consumer than imported goods. Yes, the unions aggravate the situation in these sectors in that they tend to force up the cost of wages which cannot be passed on in the form of higher prices. The philosophy is simply that if a particular company goes under, its workers can do as well elsewhere. Corporate taxes are not regarded as excessive in Sweden. On average, companies pay about 50% in taxes (including wage related levies) on taxable earnings, but calculated net of fairly generous allowances. A rather novel allowance is that given on trading inventories, which, according to my understanding, may be written down substantially for tax purposes.

But individual taxpayers are not so fortunate. The tax summit of 80% is very soon reached in executive salary hikes. To add insult to injury, having paid one's dues to society one is not allowed to suffer in private. The higher the tax bill, the more likely one will come under the ever vigilant eye of the pundit. For pay-packets are not shielded from public view. There is such a thing as the "Tax Calendar," the annual issue of which is much heralded by the media, which take great delight in pouncing on some of those who have had the dubious honour of paying into the public coffers the greater part of their income. These individuals can be criticized for their high (gross) earnings, without anything being written about their contributions to Government coffers, and even less about their take home pay.

The train we catch to Uppsala is modern and roomy enough to walk around in. The track veers inland through the province of Upland. Through fertile fields and wooded countryside north-west of Stockholm we cover the 40 miles to the City of Eternal Youth, as it is called, where stands not only the oldest university (founded in 1477) in the country, but one of the most beautiful Gothic cathedrals in Scandinavia. A mixture of the old and the new in architecture and monuments, Uppsala is situated on the banks of the Fyrisan, now, I am told, less of river than it was in the past, that flows into Lake Malaren.

Professor Andersen is greying on top, but youthful of face and slim of body. We are welcomed into his study, where he treats us to coffee, bullas and scintillating conversation. He is happy paying 60% of his salary in taxes. He thinks that Swedish people work too hard. Work becomes a therapy, a religion, and there is an alarming number of children who suffer for the greater glory of material wellbeing. They are sometimes called "key children" because they are sent to school with the house key around their necks. Yes, it is a paradox that a country which enjoys one of the highest standards of living in the world also has one of the highest suicide rates. Yes, it is possible that Swedish people, in having everything, have nothing to fight for; maybe they live too well ordered lives, have too much done for them by a paternalistic government. But then, they are not ashamed of ending their lackluster lives either. Like the trees which bear fruit in season and finally die, so with them.

Continuing north for some 65 miles, we pass through forest-country where one never tires of the sight of majestic pine and spruce, book-ending long stretches of yellow Cenolla fields and small farms. Some 55% of the country's land area is in forest. Gävle is a coastal city of about sixty thousand, situated not far from where the river Dalälven flows into the Baltic.

Father Kowalski, who is Polish and speaks English falteringly, is the only Catholic priest in town and is pastor of the only Catholic church for many a mile. Welcoming us into a small room beside the sacristy, he explains that there are few Swedes among the Catholic clergy. The Lutheran Church, funded by the government, sidelines all other congregations. After we have tea, the women leave to look after the baby, and Kowalski becomes disarmingly forthright, even if hard to understand. He laughs ruefully when he admits that getting through to the youth is difficult, a problem he would not face in Poland. For Swedes are basically irreligious. They are

Romancing Sweden

practical rather than theoretical; truth must be capable of demonstration. Before the others return we speak at length about the State religion. He repeats what someone else has told me - the Lutheran Church is "above" the common man, who paradoxically is not averse to baptism and automatic membership in the church. All very strange when one learns that a sizable number of Swedes equate religion with superstition.

Be that as it may, no one can deny that Swedish churches have a charm all their own. Throughout our journey we are seduced by their simple elegance and style. With black domes and black window-sills against white walls, they dot the countryside and decorate every town we pass through, relics of long ago, each with its model graveyard in full bloom, ritually attended by family and friends who take pride in the memory of those who had nowhere else to go.

Not far from Gävle we get off the train to stay a few days in the picturesque village of Älvkarleo. Situated walking distance from the Dalälven, stands Birgitta's grandparents' old family residence. A rambling two-story house, it is furnished as they left it - from crystal chandelier in the spacious dining room, to decorated porcelain goblets (to catch water from the well) in the bedrooms, even to carefully cloistered love letters in the oak cabinet in the reading-room. The river makes for refreshing baths and the weather is good, except for the cold mists of a morning when the pit-toilet outside beckons. Birgitta's father and younger sister arrive. He is a physician and her sister is in school in the southern town of Falköping where they live. Not long afterwards, Birgitta's two brothers appear. It's a joyous time with long days, and friends dropping in.

Booked to visit other family, we leave Älvkarleo and head further north by car. The coastline, punctuated by inlets in the Gulf of Bothnia, is spectacular. Another hundred

BY THE WAY...

and fifty miles and we pass through the industrial city of Sundsvall; still another hundred and eighty and we are in Örnsköldsvik, a smaller community on the coast, off of which is an archipelago of many islands and atolls. Here, close to the Arctic-Circle and a stone's throw from Finland across the Gulf, is the privately developed island of Malmo, with its summer houses overhanging the water's edge and boats moored to front doors. The air is fresh and white seagulls plentiful. Uncle Pelle, short, wiry and sun-burnt, meets us with his boat and transports us across placid waters, to the front door of the main house where Aunt Karin, who is almost as short as her husband, is waiting to welcome us. Famished, we sit down to dinner, along with two of Birgitta's cousins who have their own houses on the property and who join with their parents in making us feel at home.

The next evening, university students holidaying next door insist we join them for a traditional meal of Surströmming. This is raw fish harboring a smell so high it requires a strong stomach to sit at the table, much less to eat it. Served with large thin squares of bread called Tunnbröd, the Surströmming needs several pints of beer and "Snaps" (like whiskey) to wash it down. There's no doubt about the real reason for the party.

A lively conversation switches from holidays to politics and Swedish society. These students are basically socialist in outlook. They don't mind the government as "Big Brother" so long as it improves the lot of the people. They feel strongly about the free education and healthcare they enjoy. The thought of poverty alongside riches is abhorred. All governments should provide for those who can't work, as is the case in Sweden. Many of them seem past university age. Study for study's sake appears sufficient. Even university education is free – except that students who can't afford to pay living expenses usually borrow from the government to do so. (Such loans are repayable in easy installments out of income after university.)

Sweden is one of two neutral countries west of the Soviet Union. Not being involved in WWII meant that the country was neither destroyed nor the population traumatized by five years of turmoil. Unlike many countries throughout Western Europe, Sweden is not a member of NATO. Neutrality depends on self-preservation, which in turn requires national self-confidence and vigilance. The latter is evident, so I am told, in the number of no-go military-protected areas such as Boden-Lulea and Kalix in the far north; and, equally, in Sweden's manufacture of sophisticated weaponry, including home-spun jet-fighters, tanks and warships that are the envy of countries with economies much larger than that of Sweden - to say nothing of its relatively small population of eight million. In this context, it is not surprising that all the male students holidaying with us on pristine Örnsköldsvik have served in the military for up to fifteen months after leaving high-school. If they had refused on pacifist grounds, and some young people do refuse to serve each year, they would have elected to go to prison for a similar term - an alternative apparently considered "respectable".

Another bright evening and six of us have reconvened, growing in number to eight when two blond young ladies from Stockholm join us. There is Snaps available, but thankfully, not even the smell of Surströmming. As we have come to expect, the discussion is far-reaching, involving as it does independent minded twenty-one year olds who are free of taboos and display a casualness towards life peculiar to the completely secure. Generally, the Swedish government takes full credit for the high standard of living - for some reason under-playing the importance of the industrial sector, which in turn is not beyond complaining that fiscal policy without hard work is not an arbiter of wealth. But there is little question that socialism permeates the society: from the rich, to the merely comfortable; doubtless there are the poor, but not in the sense that the word is used in most other countries. One can't help being impressed by their empathy for the under-dog. At the same time, considering the rising tide of discontent with immigrants in England between the Notting Hill Gate riots of the 1950s, before which it was almost non-existent, and today fifteen years later, one wonders whether the Swedes will not have their own winter of discontent in years to come. I am conscious of conflating, unfairly no doubt, the mindset of these students with a psychology born of political neutrality, a mindset that translates into a penchant for seeing the world from a great height, especially with regard to the United States.

Criticism of US foreign policy is instinctive. The consensus seems to be that Americans never do anything, whether it be fighting in Vietnam or aiding South America, unless a monetary return is expected. This gut-reaction to wealth we are told is even more prevalent among so-called working-class Swedes. There is a distrust for American politicians who happen to be rich - as if the latter necessarily begets the former. Such ethnocentric rationale makes for bizarre conclusions. For example, the opinion of at least one person, that poor, black Americans constitute the majority of the population and are oppressed by a white minority. This type of misinformation doubtless makes for other distorted views among what must be regarded as very educated and well-meaning young people.

Inevitably, in a society so far advanced, there is much rooting for the underdog, real or imagined. For example, it is well known that Sweden grants asylum to American soldiers

Romancing Sweden

who refuse to serve in Vietnam. The fourteen year old kid wears a NLF pin on his shirt; the monthly pamphlets he reads tell of the glorious struggle for "liberation". The map on the wall in his den illustrates the many areas of South Vietnam, "liberated" by the Vietcong. And yet this vision of helping the underprivileged strikes one as rather ironical, given Washington's long-standing claim that US motives for the war are bound up in liberation for the oppressed - avowedly with no ulterior motive.

We must leave Örnsköldsvik with its mid-night sun, flocks of white sea-birds, and, of course, its charming young people. Our journey north is at an end when we board morbror Pelle's fishing canoe and are transported across the short stretch of water to collect the car.

Having seen and heard much about this great country I can appreciate that the hallmarks of Sweden are order and, yes, rules. Things must not only be done well, they must be done according to what is tried and true. Efficiency is not only an aim, it is a passion: the uniformity in architecture, the cleanliness of parks, the well-tended churchyards. From the tidy stacks of firewood outside each farmhouse, to the street signs governing pedestrians, to the fanatical preoccupations with behind-the-wheel regulations over wearing seat-belts, switching on head-lights in the daytime, the striving for exactitudes is almost inquisitional. There is an old Swedish story about the man who is attacked by a bear. He is carrying a rifle but fails to use it. When asked why, he replies, "I didn't know if it was allowed."

We retrace our drive south, stopping to visit friends in Stockholm, and thence by train to Älvkarleo to say goodbye to the old people; finally stopping for a day in Falköping where Birgitta spent her teen years. The last leg of our journey takes us through the province of

BY THE WAY...

Västergötland, with its many towns, wooded areas, and farms with expanses of red clover, through the forests of Halland, to the coastal city of Hälsingborg, where we board the boat-train for Denmark. Among many other insights, we leave with the knowledge that emblematic of modern Sweden is nostalgia for the past and cognizance of the debt owed to the aged and infirm, those who are the "conscience of the nation...who have given us all we have". As we watch the city lights fade against the night sky, we have no doubt that this country's debt has been paid.

Kingston, Jamaica 1969

The Age of Youth

Whether or not we justifiably can say that today's youth are too dogmatic, that they think they know all the answers, we have to admit that the world can no longer ignore what they have to say. In every sphere of life the call of youth for a better world is heard loud and clear. In every country youth have had their say on social justice, the arms race, war, pollution, politics, religion and many other important issues too numerous to mention. No longer are they seen and not heard, no longer do we refer to them as rebels without a cause.

Never before have adolescents caused such an upheaval, started such a chain reaction of soul searching by so many governments in so many countries as is happening right now. Consider the present preoccupation of politicians in the U.S.A., with the youth vote next year. In many European countries the same thing obtains. From now on it seems youth will have a very important veto at the polling booths. Not only the United States and Europe are caught up in this new age - we have only to consider the effect of the Red Guards on China's Cultural Revolution between 1966 and 1969 to realize how much the phenomenon of youth in the twentieth century crosses national boundaries and ignores political ideologies.

In matters of religion too, both inside and outside the Church, youth are in the forefront of change. This is the age of the Holy Spirit, the Great Awakening - like the first great Age of Faith between the eleventh and thirteenth centuries, when Gothic cathedrals lifted man's eyes to the Heavens, youth today are rejecting horizontal attitudes, adopting vertical ones. Up to the Second Vatican Council, the twentieth century witnessed the Church becoming rather

A paper delivered before the district convention of *The South Florida District of Serra International*, December 1971 utilitarian in outlook. Even today, especially in developed countries, this tendency manifests itself in the accent on comfortable, rather than challenging, Christian values. In a sense church buildings are furnished in that image - you know what I mean - the cushioned kneelers, carpeted aisles, air-conditioning - reflecting the inward looking, self-satisfied, closed shop attitudes that still exist among many who consider themselves Christians.

These are the attitudes young people have rejected. To them, anything that seeks to bottle up the Holy Spirit is anti-Christian and questionable. Today their religion must be a personal experience rather than an intellectual exercise. It must reflect Christian brotherhood rather than the "holier than thou" norms of fifteen years ago. Today young people swell the ranks of the Jesus People, the Straight people, the Catholic Pentecostals. Other Christian crusades, like the Cursillo and Search Movements, have also made their mark on Catholic thinking and the Church is accommodating many changes of emphasis inspired by these movements. Only this morning we attended a guitar youth mass - unheard of ten years ago.

So there is a lot to learn from the young in this Age of Youth. We cannot afford to turn a deaf ear - we must consider what they are trying to say and not reject it out of hand. Too many of us have allowed ourselves to think that the values handed down to us, the values which we have grown accustomed to, the convenient norms of yesterday, are the only ones worth having. Many of our young people are saying they are not. To them, established values have fallen on hard times. It is not enough, they say, to do what Dad did merely because he did it. They want more than security and a comfortable home, and a grey flannel suit; and they want it now - life is

The Age of Youth

too short to worry about fulfillment tomorrow. The price the world demands for a moderate pension is too high - in the end what has one achieved? We will merely have grown fat at the expense of our brothers wherever they may be. We will have contributed to the double standards of the establishment with all its pretensions of Justice and Service.

These are some of the things youth are saying. We may agree or disagree; the important point is that if youth are questioning our values, then maybe we will be forced to look at ourselves more closely. Just as the ban-the-bomb marches, and the civil rights demonstrations of the sixties bore fruit in their time, so are many youth crusades bearing fruit today in areas as far apart as Vietnam and Washington, D.C. It is probably true to say that young people under twenty-five play a greater role in demanding racial tolerance and social justice than their elders over forty.

But nothing is ever as simple as that, is it? Like every other social and religious rethinking, this age has its grey areas. Not everything that youth stands for is worthy of our respect and adoption. In all fairness we should not whitewash their shortcomings. Today, all over the world many of our young people have taken to drugs; even for teenagers, this is becoming a real problem. The high incidence of pre-marital sex and illegitimacy is also reaching alarming proportions, reaching down as it does to high school level. What of the growing tendency of some towards Satanism and the occult with all the perversions these entail? What of the university radicals who preach and practice violent revolution and subversion of one kind or another - the rioting on campuses and destruction of public property in countries as far away from each other as Canada and Japan, in cities as different as London and Calcutta. Today if we live in an age of enlightenment, it is also an age in which all restraints have been overthrown. Never before have the basic truths of life been thrown out and trampled on to such a great extent by the very young. Today the Pope is never criticized because he is a man with human failings. His integrity is not questioned; it is rather because he is Pope that he is attacked, because he is a spiritual leader who presumes to be able to tell me what to do. After all, I attend university; what right has anyone to tell me what to do or think?

Out of all the contradictions we find in young people today, some anomalous situations emerge: it is taken for granted that they are more independent, yet more than ever before, many of them cling to each other in closed communities all over the world, quite unlike their counterparts of a generation ago. Often regarded as knowing their own minds, youth often prove otherwise by a desperate search for identity. Again, their reputed ability to face up to life quite frequently dissolves into escapism and psychedelic fixes. So many demand political recognition while rebelling against lawful authority; democracy becomes anarchy, and love of neighbor rejection of parents.

These things represent the other side of the coin, which often we do not want to see. Indeed it becomes difficult or impossible for many of us to reconcile the three sides - to sift the good from the not-so-good, and what is decidedly bad. The question is, can youth reconcile them? For myself, at what for many of you may be the tender age of thirty-one, I see the confusion of many of today's young people who have not had the benefit of growing up in a world that shaped our values. When I went to school the possibility of students changing school policy was unheard of; obedience grew out of the shock of a master's bamboo cane; what was not done out of love was done out of fear. Today we have completely abolished the cane, and when rules are broken various psychological correctives are resorted to. I can't help but question whether the substitute is better than the original. Then again, we pride ourselves in the freedom of expression we allow our children. But how much of this new found freedom for kids is coming from a real desire on our part to help them grow into mature adults, and how much of it is really the result of irresponsible parenthood. In European countries like Sweden, where I spoke to a university professor recently about youth, there is the phenomenon known as "key-children" - those who are sent to school with the house key around their necks so they can let themselves into the empty house after school. In America I believe these children are called "latch-key kids." How often as parents do we abandon the young for worldly pursuits, or in order to keep up with the Joneses. We try to buy them off with material goods and bodily comforts. How convenient it is to bring up rich heirs rather than rounded individuals.

I believe that what is happening more and more today in our homes, in our schools and universities, is that the youth are jumping off the high board before learning to swim. How can we stop them, when we threw them in at the deep end in the first place? It is easier to justify a situation that has developed, than try to do something about it. So children run wild; and when parents find that they cannot control them any longer, they say it's better for the children they cannot. We tend to rationalize everything to suit ourselves, don't we? And there is no lack of radical thinkers and quack psychologists to give us all the assurances we need to do just that.

If the breakdown of family life is taking root in the developed countries, it is firmly established in many developing countries. When we look at the situation in Jamaica, where upwards of 50% of the population is under 21, the problems are enormous. The vast majority of young people, especially in the cities, have no family life at all - often never knowing their fathers, probably brought up by their grandmothers. Coupled with the squalor of their surroundings, sparse clothing, and not enough in their stomachs, this makes for a rough passage through childhood and adolescence. These children, like their counterparts in ghettos all over the world, are today very aware of the "good life" that many other people enjoy. In many instances the only education they have awakens in them false goals impossible of achievement. This leads to frustration, which in turn often results in crime and delinquence.

I am one of those who believe very strongly that this generation has been denied what the last took for granted. This generation has not been given that grounding in certainty and internal peace which is essential for proper development of a person. Instead this generation has had foisted upon it the convenient notion that children and adolescents, left to themselves, are better at deciding what is good for them than are their parents. The notion that children can somehow grow up by instinct, has found great favor with modern intellectuals who would have us believe that the ills of human nature are coincident with adulthood. The trouble is that many of these romantics are as divorced from youth as their ideas are from reality. For surely one of the outstanding features of man is that his development from childhood depends on a slow process of learning rather than animal instincts. It is by virtue of man's prolonged youth that he comes to maturity, guided not by instincts but by adults who have come up before him.

There is no denying that the years, between, say, thirteen and twenty-three, can be very trying ones of adjustment - even in the most ideal circumstances. These are crucial years when many decisions affecting one's whole future are made. During this time one usually decides on a profession or course of study,

The Age of Youth

or not to study. One often finds God or rejects Him during this time. Many choose a partner before twenty-three. None of these decisions can be made in an atmosphere and with a background of complete uncertainty. There has to be some basis - some vantage point from which reflective judgments can be made. Discipline is what we are talking about; not the discipline that stunts growth, but rather that which puts things in some perspective. It is amazing how many parents have forgotten this word and what it means. They have forgotten it because they have forgotten what parenthood really means. If children have rejected their parents, it is because parents have rejected self-sacrifice and a true dedication to their children. Without self-sacrifice and dedication on our part, there will always be a crisis in authority, if only because there is no authority in the family anymore.

I do not believe there has been a time in history when there has been a greater need for strong adult guidance of the young. The world is overfull of brinkmanship and economic pressures. The resulting malaise is not lost on the young, in fact it has had a devastating effect on idealistic young minds. How often have we observed a small child walk into a strange room, and immediately his attention is riveted by an object on the floor. He makes a beeline for it; nothing can distract him from it. Whether it is a needle that may injure him, or a harmless piece of thread, he sees it immediately - why? Because he is so close to the ground, maybe. In the same way, young people tend to see many things which we completely overlook - some of them very important things. But it is only with our help, and by our example, that some sense can be made of an imperfect world. To this end we have got to shake ourselves out of the self-righteousness we have often passed off as Christianity.

When across from the dinner table the television moves

BY THE WAY...

among the starving in East Pakistan, what do sensitive young people think? We present them with man's inhumanity to man and without thinking, lead them in Grace, which in the circumstances sounds something like the prayer of the Pharisee, "I give you thanks God that I am not like the rest of men - I am not grasping or unjust, or adulterous or even like those have-nots on the television screen over there. I fast on family fast days and drop a dollar in collection every Sunday." How many of us pray like that without realizing what we are doing to our children? But the young see it and are turned off - disillusioned. They are unable to understand what they find in a harsh world. On the one side man's phenomenal technological achievements - on the other, impending disaster, famine and dispossessed peoples. How long can the imbalance last? Many experts are now saying the world will not see the end of this century.

And so, during the summer time, the big cities are besieged by the dropouts, the hippies who come to present their credentials to the establishment. Straggly, dirty, often barefooted, these pathetic figures prefer to live on the dole rather than compromise their convictions. Can despair have taken root so early? These young people, many of them, have had all the material goods given to them, yet today they scrape the bottom of the barrel and we give them a wide birth. Like the young man who takes his inheritance and squanders it, will they not realize one day that there is important work to be done in their father's house? Will they not one day lift their eyes and turn towards home? And when they do, where will we be? Will we see them coming from afar, and be on the road to embrace them?

Kingston, Jamaica - December 1971

Mind and Cosmos

Mind-body questions have been around for centuries, if not millennia; certainly, since Descartes in the seventeenth century. At the risk of over simplifying the history of a debate that has roots in antiquity, it seems that the Ancients were not particularly disturbed by the issue. For them mankind was an integral part of the cosmos. Absenting insignificant differences between Plato's terrestrial and celestial realms, and Aristotle's idea of one world combining matter and form, the Stoics sum up the thinking of the Ancients with their devotion to pantheism. According to Cicero (in his Stoical mode):

> "nothing is more perfect than this world, which is an animate being, endowed with awareness, intelligence and reason." But, in his Tusculan Disputations he claims that "to the soul comes that knowledge prescribed by the god at Delphi that the [human] mind… is linked with the divine mind…."

This position is not far from the Judeo/Christian tradition wherein the godhead is transcendental to, rather than permeating nature, and speaks through, rather than being one with, the human mind (or soul). In Christian Europe the latter view prevailed for fifteen hundred years, until Descartes postulated separation between inner-mind and external-world. The mind produces consciousness, which is the "essence" of human beings, whereas the essence of matter is "spatial extension" —shape, size, and motion – as pertain to a stone. Matter and mind are different in kind as well as nature; the two have no common properties.

A review of *Mind and Cosmos: Why the Materialist Neo-Darwinian Conception of Nature Is Almost Certainly False*, Thomas Nagel, 2014

BY THE WAY...

Therefore, the issue becomes: if we assume we know about matter, wherefore mind? At its core, modern science is materialist in nature: evolution by natural selection is a scientific theory. Therefore, consciousness must be explicable in materialistic terms if it is to be part of the evolutionary process as ordinarily understood. Even if they are not compatible? Descartes knew nothing of evolution, but, as to the mind-body separation that for him was a permanent divide, he would hold that reconciliation between the two must lie with God. After all, it was God who placed the idea of his very existence in his mind at its "creation" (Meditations 3). Thus, the chasm between mind and body is conveniently spanned by a *deus ex machina*: the Christian God landing on the stage to resolve the actors' dilemma.

Cartesian dualism, with or without divine intervention, persisted into the twentieth century and beyond. It posed (and still poses) so many problems that the scientific community has simply wished them away, or rationalized them out the door. For example, in the late 1930s, A. N. Whitehead wrote that "Consciousness is the triumph of specialization... the evolution of sensory experience." For him it was a form of "upward evolution." Therefore, "the idea that mental functioning is not part of science is false." As cited by John Searle and Thomas Nagel, the decades that followed saw many theories emerging to ground such rationalizations in biological formulations such as "neural firings" (Crick); "mapping" (Edelman); "functional organization of the brain" (Chalmers); "side effect without functionality" (Sobers); "certain brain processes are extra-physical" (Sorell); "intentional motivation" (White); to John Searle himself.

Searle posits that consciousness is a product of the "lower-level neural processes in the brain and is itself a feature of the brain.... As such it is an emergent property of the brain....

causally explained by the behaviour of the elements of the system, but not a property of any individual elements...." His example is the behavior of $H2°$ molecules explaining liquidity without themselves, individually, being liquid.

Thomas Nagel finds this rationale wanting. The fact that we can discern obvious connections between the brain as a physical organ, and mental processes as immaterial "awareness" resulting from brain activity, does not mean that materiality is reducible to consciousness. *Mind and Cosmos* is his chiseled refutation of axioms surrounding materialist reductionism. While focused on the human mind, its author is not afraid to venture into the stratosphere. For him there is something missing in the idea that the physical sciences can explain everything. If science would have it that life is "the product of chemical processes governed by the laws of physics," how does this account for what is not part of the physical world?

Then, nature's plot thickens. After all, consciousness is not confined to humans: all sentient creatures possess it to some degree - the "higher" animals more than others. For humans, consciousness is in the end-zone, and the end-zone is open-ended; while at the baseline, the "lesser" sentient creatures react to stimuli - exhibiting instinctive behaviours. These attributes allow them to feed and protect themselves, as well as nurture their young; but their narrow starting-point is also their end zone. Once a cow, always a cow. Unlike baseline animals, humans possess cognition: the ability to grow intellectually and understand complex issues. Beyond cognition, they grapple with value-judgements: matters of justice, morals, ethics, and the like. According to Nagel, how these higher human attributes could have purely materialistic foundations is a mystery that Natural Selection, in its current form (based on pure chance), does not explain.

BY THE WAY...

So, what may provide the rest of the story? Those of a religious persuasion call it Intelligent Design, bandied about by deists as scientific, replacing the shopworn, fundamentalist, expression "Creationism" but not the Biblical foundation behind it. Whether in its "strong" or "weak" form, ID holds that God provides the *modus operandi* for the world in general and life in particular. God is the mover and shaker, much as a watchmaker constructing a watch (an idea borrowed from Paley). This is the "intentional" alternative "theory," that relies on God to create life and consciousness out of matter, with or without evolution by natural selection. In this scenario, outside of material reductionism, we are stuck with a deity filling the Darwinian gaps.

It is not for me to argue for "God's foot in the door," and not being religious Nagel doesn't buy it anyway. His position is down to earth, centered mostly on the human attribute of value, which he sees as the litmus test for anyone attempting to validate the materialist version of evolution. It is hard enough to have ethereal consciousness emerge from the physical brain; it is more difficult to imagine that the much more complex human attribute of reason could emerge by chance from that organ. Might not reason, assuming it to have appeared later than consciousness itself in our evolutionary development, be a product of "the universe waking up and becoming aware of itself?"

If, as must be assumed, there was a time when consciousness had not yet become attached to chemical processes, it follows that at some point it emerged in primordial organisms and later evolved into the super-rational states peculiar to primates, especially humans. How did this come about? For Nagel, the answer to the puzzle may lie in a natural teleological bias in the universe that is a constant, and is independent of the evolutionary processes or blind chance.

This "element" would be the missing link in an otherwise materialist environment. Absent a cosmological mind, he holds that modern science cannot cut through the vicissitudes of the mind-body dichotomy. Far from an explanatory thesis wherein mental processes are shown to be connected to the physical brain, his purpose is to elucidate a causation underpinning consciousness that is not so attached.

He is fully aware that "in the present intellectual climate recognition of [a natural teleological hypothesis] is unlikely to be taken seriously." At the same time he charges the scientific community to demonstrate how, in the absence of some form of teleology "a staggeringly functionally complex... self-producing cell...could have arisen by chemical evolution alone from a dead environment." Scientists of the *Stardust* ilk, among others, are not averse in positing that humans are made up of the same elements as the universe writ large. If we assume they are correct, consciousness by definition must be one of those elements, embedded - or pan psychic, in the cosmic nervous system. Indeed, as Nagel intimates, must not "survival of the fittest" itself be dependent on that element, which purely materialist evolution overlooks?

Mind and Cosmos is a tightly constructed argument for a new approach to the mystery of human consciousness. With a penchant for academic detachment, Thomas Nagel succeeds admirably in making his case.

November, 2015

Science & Its Limits

Evangelicals have come out swinging in recent years against what they see as their enemy at the gate. In broad terms that enemy is secularism. In narrower terms it is the rise of atheism in western countries, aided and abetted by the likes of Dawkins, Grayling, Hitchens, Harris, and others. But at its root is a visceral distrust of science. Christian disavowal takes the form of dismissive non-interest. As one Evangelical put it to me, "Scientists merely repeat what they were told in university." If this is a one-line rejection of science, Del Ratzsch's rejection is 189-pages long.

The easiest way to discredit a proposition is to cite known reservations that proponents have about it. The theory that all ravens are black satisfies reasonableness. That is, until the objector cites the fact that the argument is inductive, a posteriori, and experiential - its veracity contingent upon the discovery of a non-black raven. Immediately, the proponent is put on the defensive. After all, inductive truths are prone to refutation in ways that analytical truths based on *a priori* verities are not – here, refutation equals contradiction. So, "All bachelors are unmarried men" is not refutable, in the sense that "All ravens are black" is. If the limits of science are judged according to the limits of inductive theory, that is a position with which most scientists would agree; if science is dismissed on that ground the judgment appears ludicrous.

I make no claim to the high ground in looking askance at *Science & Its Limits: the Natural Sciences in Christian Perspective*. However, even to a non-scientist like myself, this book's arguments against science are disingenuous. First of all, they have more to do with dismissals of selective scientific *theories* than with science itself. Ratzsch's approach is first to recall

A review of *Science & Its Limits* by Del Ratzsch, (2nd Ed.), 2000

BY THE WAY...

his version of the underpinnings of science's "traditional views": empirical basis thereof, rationality, objectivity, predictability, and the rest; and then to explain to readers that in the development of theories each of these criteria has drawbacks - conveniently allowing him to discount scientific "truth." He makes short thrift of scientific advances in the modern era, preferring to pour cold water on the philosophy that supposedly lies behind them. Towards this end he next focuses on positivism (Francis Bacon to Auguste Compte and beyond) with its bases in empiricism and abhorrence of such as metaphysics or religion. For Ratzsch, the "empiricist principle" inherent in positivism "fails when applied to... moral truths..." (p31). Indeed, throughout the early chapters of the book religious "truth" is alluded to as science's unattainable goal when it has nothing to do with science.

As for Karl Popper (1902-1994) and his falsification principle, according to which no theory can be credited as scientific unless it is open to falsification should evidence therefor be found, Ratzsch is very happy that the principle is an attack on positivism. This appears to be why he mentions the falsification principle at all, seeing that, otherwise, he affords it little creditability. Yet, Popper, as elaborated on by Alexander Bird in his famous book *The Philosophy of Science*, (pgs. 167-177), did not deny the importance of empirical evidence and inductive processes. He sought to overcome the indeterminacy of induction (the Hume Problem) by inferring a *deductive* process that would provide a degree of certainty. Bird finds wanting Popper's attempt to side-step uncertainty through the falsification method (p.246), while Ratzsch is bent on dismissing, or at least belittling, empirically-based science itself. After all, his gaze is fixed on heavenly perspectives, yet to be revealed. Meanwhile, does genuine science not require predictability, which means looking to the future even if it is forever uncertain? Ratzsch, like many people of the Good Book, is no friend of uncertainty embedded in scientific solutions. The dichotomy between predictability as a requirement of the genuine variety, and uncertainty as a necessary evil of that science, is therefore grist for his mill as he seeks to grind scientific half-truths into pious imaginings.

It turns out that the staged dismissal of positivism is a side show. For Ratzsch, the real villain of his book, his *casus belli*, is Thomas Kuhn. Copious attention is paid to *The Structure of Scientific Revolution* (1962), the reason for which is not clear given that the work is historical, not prescriptive. Kuhn makes his appearance on page 38 of *Science & Its Limits*, and thereafter is cited regularly, becoming the arbiter of everything scientific. His contributions are adumbrated in a manner that a cursory reading of *Science and Its Limits* would suggest Kuhn's history of science is somehow normative for the scientific community rather than descriptive of how the profession developed over time. Readers are led to believe that once Kuhn's book was published, paradigms became a reality, threatening the "purity" of scientific research. Was modern science ever free of some form of paradigm within which practitioners operated? In 1687 Isaac Newton wrote, "In experimental philosophy (natural science) we are to look upon propositions collected by general induction...as accurate... till such time as other phenomena occur by which they may be made more accurate...." At what stage was the purity of research threatened by this process?

The ensuing discussion is stranger still. According to the author "the Khunian movement has placed humans and human subjectivity...firmly in the center of science... [which] is no more ruggedly and rigidly objective and logical than the humans who do it" (p.50). Supposedly, Kuhn's paradigms "prevent one from seeing counter instances to one's theories...

obscuring perceptions...and blocking access to "perfectly neutral database(s)" (as if such things exist). In the end the real problem is that the "beliefs of scientists determine what truth is" (p.52). And so on and so forth (pgs.61/62). One is driven to ask, what of Christianity? Is it not true that the Reformation arose out of Lutheran and Calvinist paradigms which embodied new ideas about biblical supremacy, worship, and salvation? Today there are hundreds of Christian communities that have grown out of those paradigms, such that their originators would be at a loss to recognize some of them. Does that invalidate the Reformation, or Protestantism as practiced today? Rather than relying on Mr. Ratzsch's book, readers should explore Kuhn's for themselves.

At various junctures the discussion becomes confused. We are told there is no formal definition of "natural" science (p.122), which seems to leave the door open for additions and/or substitutions. Except that the author provides no definition, formal or otherwise, for his version of science. This leaves him struggling either to equate theology with science, or to assure readers that differences don't matter? According to Ratzsch, one theory (by any name?) is as good as another because either or both might be incorrect, subject to later revision, or merely "human" and therefore lacking of absolute truth. Is this how science works: competing paradigms in dances of the seven veils, driving scientists to distraction?

At its heart, *Science & Its Limits* has little to do with concrete examples, either of scientific achievements or scientific failures. Its author is bound and determined merely to point fingers at scientific *theory* - again with examples in short supply. The result is empty rhetoric, with Christianity as the ulterior motive. Simply put, generalities and academic nomenclature do not an academic discussion make. If their proponent had lived in the sixteenth century his bottom line probably would have been that of the Vatican: "Burn those starry-eyed heretics and give us back our God."

That approach seems to underlie much of what the second half of the book preaches, relying as it does on questionable assertions, false analogies, and obfuscations in order to placate readers' fears and trepidations about the threat that science poses to Biblical precepts. In the end, the purpose is to put religion on a par with science in formulating objective truth about nature and the world. Beliefs are all the evidence one needs for this, which brings us to the crux of the matter at hand: dressing religion in scientific clothing. For Evangelical and other embattled Christians, it is the fulcrum that raises God's plan above "natural science." It is called Intelligent Design (ID), which has been at the heart of Bible-Belt opposition to the exclusivity of Darwinian evolution.

Ratzsch devotes 32 pages (then some), to elaborating on the subject, the premise being that ID "should be given a fair scientific chance" in secular schools (p.130). That, of course, presents problems of his own making. Has he not devoted many pages to denigrating everything scientific? How then can he advocate that ID should have a rightful place in the scientific field? Has he not placed all scientific hypotheses on the same plane – unprovable, lacking certitude, one no better that another, etc.? Hoisted on his own petard, he wriggles out of the noose by implying that ID is on a level *above* science - the supernatural variety. Apparently conscious of the box in which he finds himself, he carefully avoids the word "theory" in reference to ID – replacing that berated word with benign references to "the concept of" and "the argument for." After all, if ID were just another scientific theory his dismissals of paradigms would discredit the proposition, and, if *falsifiable*, that would mean God could be fired.

Since maybe the seventeenth century it has been difficult

BY THE WAY...

for most people to see what love, sin, morality, and yes, Scripture, have to do with science. In the case of Scripture, the books that Christians refer to as such were written two to three thousand years ago. They were an important part of the underpinnings of Western civilization for most of that time. But what contribution to scientific advances did these books, and the learning they represented, make during that time? Is it not abundantly clear that significant advances were achieved only *after* strict adherence to religious versions of the world and the cosmos went into decline?

Science & Its Limits reads like a desperate attempt to turn back the clock, presumably in the interests of those who live in the past. In many respects the book is nineteenth century Christian apologetics in its reductionism and naivety. The last chapters represent the author's vain attempt to compress the wide boulevards of science into the narrow lane of creationism, a sycophantic genuflection to the supposed paucity of intelligence in Bible-Belt States. Do closeted people still exist who seek security away from the world, instead of opening their eyes and educating themselves to live in it? If Del Ratzsch really believes what he has written, is it facetious to suggest he dump his car and hitch up a horse and buggy?

Winter, 2016

Those Social Animals

Going back to the Ancients, there have been many variations on the theme of man as necessarily a social animal. Modern thought on the inter-relationships of humankind has roots in the writings of seventeen and eighteen century luminaries such as Thomas Hobbes and Jean-Jacques Rousseau. Together they gave new meaning to the idea of a societal *contract,* which they saw as inherent in the state for the common good. For Hobbes, the primary reason for government was to keep the people safe. Absent safety and the government should be thrown out. For example, Hobbes was prescient in advocating the need for *societal* care for the poor, whereby it is the responsibility of the commonwealth, not the individual, to look after those unable to care for themselves. His dictum was overlooked in Victorian England in so far as *charity* was prominent in social welfare, largely the result of anathema on the part of the wealthy towards income taxes and big government. A century and a half later, this is today part of Libertarian ideology.

For Rousseau, the Social Contract reflects the General Will of a free society (thus overcoming man's self-alienation), even if at the same time it denies freedom to dissenters. Here, the dichotomy between the rights of the majority and those of the minority becomes a problem, given that everyone should be subject to the dictates of reason. Each person is obliged to obey the General Will in his or her own interest. Having been forced to be free, every man obeys himself.

The nineteen century saw the emergence of individualistic preoccupations of thinkers such as John Stewart Mill, for whom self-interest was a virtue, a la Adam Smith before him. Liberalism put individual gratification and fulfillment at the centre of utilitarianism. Everything was allowed to the individual so long as self-indulgence brought no harm to others. In that sense, individual liberty is sacrosanct and responsibility for another person essentially tenuous: One forbears from doing something only in so far as it impinges on another's rights. In this restrictive sense, what is good for the individual is good for society. The obverse is Marxist/Leninist philosophy, which places the individual at the feet of the proletariat, whose "moral and political authority" the masses will recognize "until classes are abolished" (*Selected Essays of Lenin*, 1919). Essentially, what is good for the state is good for the individual.

Whether we see "collective" man as temple of God and centre of the universe, immortalized by history, or stranded as pebble on a beach about to be washed away by superior forces, he or she must live with other people. For Saint Augustine, as Arendt avows in *Between Past and Future*, the Latin phrase "to live" is synonymous with *inter homines esse* - "to be in the company of men." Indeed to conceive of life without interaction with other human beings is almost impossible. In many respects we are reflections of others who have touched our lives. Could this be otherwise?

We might assume that when prehistoric humans roamed the forest they were closer to dumb animals than to fellow human beings. Given more time, Robinson Crusoe was more likely to have descended into savagery, than been ennobled by splendid isolation. According to Rousseau, "it is one of the idiosyncrasies of man that in order to enjoy himself, indeed to be fully human, he requires the company and the help of other men." Why then the apparent obliviousness of so many people we meet, to those around them? So often we observe from a distance those who seem to live only for themselves, those who value privacy over friendship – who cluster in nuclear families with bars on windows and bolts on doors.

Apparently, such people do not need the company of others. Or do they? The psychologists tell us that the greatest killer of modern urban men and women is loneliness, that is, in reference to the industrial First World with particular reference to North America. Here, anxiety brought about by wealth, or more by the lack of a living wage, saps life of real meaning and puts us out of touch with the cosmos. In *The Question Concerning Technology*, Martin Heidegger posited that the illusion attached to man as "lord of the earth" leads to the delusion that "man everywhere and always encounters only himself." But is this a delusion? Or is the alienation we experience a mirror held up to our technological age?

For those who traverse this continent in a vain search for the counterfeit god of fortune, the toing and froing is never seen for what it is: our return to a primitive condition, a denial of most of the tenets of a caring community. If as Rousseau contends, "no citizen should be wealthy enough to buy another and none poor enough to be forced to sell himself," indeed, if our highest purpose is achieved when we consciously agree to accept responsibility for our fellow human beings, modern capitalist society based on individual advancement deprives us of that humanity.

Self-indulgence is synonymous with North American consumerism. The youngest kids are left in no doubt about this the very first time they view television or listen to the radio. Accumulation of and attachment to possessions are inherent attributes of their formative years, intensify in adulthood when making a living becomes paramount, and in the end are necessities for the enjoyment of a consumer-capitalist retirement.

Is it when one takes responsibility for a partner and children that introversion born of alienation first becomes chronic? To eat bread one must look over one's shoulder at

BY THE WAY...

the person who might snatch it out of one's mouth. Sounds too dramatic? Why then is mainstream North America so careful about rocking the boat - in any calling, be it workplace, church, profession or dinner party? The answer is vulnerability, real or imagined - an insecurity that leaves tenured professors speechless and news-paper carriers fearful of asking for their wages. At the level of the closeted family, one's partner, one's children, are always threatened by something and need to be protected. The most natural thing is to leave the night-latch in lock position. The unwritten commandment is give not of yourself, lest you be taken for a ride. Friendship? Brotherhood? The gatekeeper of Jericho pulls back in disbelief as the biplane soars over the wall and crashes in the desert beyond.

Extracted from *Reflections on our times,* September 1983

A Rose by Any Other Name

The period spanning the twelfth through fourteenth centuries found the Church going through difficult times: administratively - declining revenues occasioned by reduced benefices; pastorally - dealing with the result of Gregorian reforms, especially those combatting corruption among the clergy; but also theologically - agonizing over new ways of seeing the world through the eyes of emerging academia.

From around 1150 there arose itinerant sects, groups of dissident clerics and laity, who stood against the traditional Church. The more radical movements were not only reform minded, but preached heresy with a dualistic bent: spiritual things seen as Godly, the material world evil – indeed, created by the Devil. These groups also inveighed against the priesthood, the Church's sacraments, infant baptism, procreation, and meat. Chief among the sects were the *Cathars* with foundations in the Manichean heresy dating back to the third century. But there were others such as the *Publicani*; and the *Albigensians* against whom the Fourth Crusade was launched; and the *Bogomiles*, who the experts say originated in Bulgaria.

Over time, these sects, seen as part of "Satan's Army" from as early as the third century (Russell, p.86) were denounced by Church authorities. The movements flourished at one period or another in the region spanning the Rhineland, Lombardy, Taulouse, and the Langueduc in southern France, even into northern Italy. Many myths and legends grew up about their practices and beliefs. Although some noble families became adherents, especially in Milan, the sects were by and large comprised of the poor and the ignorant at the margins of society, and easily fed into nefarious

BY THE WAY...

"reputations" for incest, cannibalism and demonology, fueling pogroms to eradicate them.

At this time, on the side of the Church, there arose the Franciscan Order of mendicants, who were blessed by Rome in the early thirteenth century. Beginning as wandering "holy men," *qua* apostles, these friars were committed to living a life of poverty and service among the poor. But after Francis's death in 1226 the Order grew wealthy and rationalized more materialistic and academic pursuits. As a result a schismatic minority, seeking after original ideals, broke off the trunk as the *Spirituals*, and in turn gave rise to the radical *Fraticelli* who were eventually ostracized by the Church (Norman Cohn, pgs.61&62).

Traditional Franciscan belief is that Christ and the Apostles lived in poverty, owning no property whatsoever. Rome came to regard this position with alarm, especially in view of its implications *vis a vis* the Church's worldly possessions. The debate raged. Finally in 1323 Pope John XXII declared that to believe that Jesus practiced absolute poverty was heretical (ibid.)

Coexistent with these developments was the reconciliation of Aristotelian philosophy with Christian theology, or vice versa, in the centuries after the writings of the Greek philosopher were introduced to the West by Averroes in the eleventh century. The assimilation was a gradual process (much as capitalist economic thought has been assimilated with or assumed into Christian beliefs over the last 150 years) and had its detractors for many years. The principal "assimilator" was Thomas Aquinas, himself a Dominican monk, in his *Summa Theologica* (1266-73). He was canonized by John XXII.

All of which brings us to *The Name of the Rose*, Umberto

A Rose by Any Other Name

Eco's great medieval novel that was made into a movie in 1986, starring Sean Connery. The story is set in 1327 in a Benedictine monastery in northern Italy. Connery is cast as a Franciscan intellectual who journeys to the monastery to take part in a debate over ecclesiastical poverty, and becomes embroiled in a murder mystery. But the latter is merely a backdrop to Eco's brilliant elucidation of a forgotten time, and the ideas that drove good men to do bad things.

There are many evocative scenes set in authentic surroundings with memorable performances by a host of characters cut exactly to fit an apocalyptic era. Seeing the world through their eyes is an exhilarating, though sometimes disturbing, experience. Bernard Gui, the story's colorful inquisitor, although hammed up in the movie, was a real historical figure much feared in his day. Notorious as its author was, apparently Gui's manual for inquisitors (fourteenth century) is silent on witches *per se*; the practice of *magic* was more the target then (Cohn). For anyone hot on medieval history and even if one is only lukewarm, *The Name of the Rose*, especially film, is not to be missed.

From *Reflections on Our Times* July 2002

DAYS IN THE SUN

An Island Entire of Itself?

When I accepted your club's gracious invitation to speak about recent developments in Jamaica, I thought at first that I had a relatively easy task. I would just relate what has happened there in the last year or two, and that would be sufficient. The more I thought about it, however, the more I felt it necessary to dig deeper, even if that meant taking advantage of the exalted position you have bestowed on me as District Governor. So I beg your patience, as well as your forgiveness, if by having me here tonight you will have enjoyed a fabulous dinner but eschewed an ear-full.

We live in a world where events taken out of context manifest themselves in sensational headlines serving neither worthwhile information nor understanding. Such has been the case, I think, with international reports about Jamaica in the past few years. One such article recently appeared in the London Daily Telegraph: "The United States [has] pin-pointed among Cuba's neighbours in the Commonwealth Caribbean the island of Jamaica as the country most ripe for unrest and subversion. There are real fears that the island under the government of Prime Minister, Michael Manley, is now in the grip of an economic and political crisis which is heading Jamaica for the most serious upheaval in the Caribbean since the Castro revolution".

This is just one example of the position taken by many foreign journalists in recent times and doubtless you are familiar with the point of view. From relative obscurity Jamaica has emerged a country worthy of lengthy articles in almost every newspaper one can think of, including the New York Times, the Wall Street Journal, the London Observer,

A paper presented in West Palm Beach, Florida, during the author's term as Governor of the South Florida District of Serra International – 1976. Title from *No man is an Iland, intire of it selfe* by John Donne

BY THE WAY...

the London Financial Times, and the Vancouver Sun - to say nothing of the Miami Herald. Most of the articles have been so-called in depth analyses of current events from the pens of professionals who have the enviable ability to select certain facts and make them sound like the whole truth. Worse than this, however, is their ability, on occasion, to fabricate events and present them as fact-based. For example, two weeks ago a prominent New York daily published the story about an assassination attempt on the life of the leader of the opposition Jamaica Labour Party, when no such attempt had been made.

In the short time I have with you this evening it is not my intention to castigate the foreign press which would be a pointless exercise, but rather to try to place some of the facts which have been presented as the whole truth in some perspective. Unlike the professional journalists, however, I would like to confess serious shortcomings as a historian and political commentator. Almost anything I say can be found wanting by the Miami Herald.

This being your bi-centennial year, you have been looking back to 1776 and the Declaration of Independence, with some amount of nostalgia. It might interest you to know that Jamaica was very much behind the American colonies two hundred years ago. In fact, the Jamaican House of Assembly, representing for the most part 13,000 sugar planters, already in December 1774 had sent a petition to the King of England concerning what it regarded as the right of the American colonies to self-determination. This was in spite of the fact that self-determination for America would probably be detrimental to Jamaica and the other British possessions, given that the American colonies had already shown a preference for trading with the French dependencies. Indeed, such trade was an integral part of their claim to be independent

An Island Entire of Itself?

of British rule, which had saddled them with the Stamp Act that protected the likes of Jamaica and the other British Sugar colonies. It is worth remembering that in 1776 those small Caribbean islands with Jamaica front and centre, were equally, if not more important to Britain than the thirteen American ones. Protecting her Caribbean interests was then at the root of Britain's intransigence on trade issues and thus one of the prime causes of your War of Independence.

But maybe I am jumping a bit ahead of myself. For those of you who may not know much about Jamaica I should point out that the island has a population of about two million, is 4,400 square miles in size, 144 miles long, and approximately 50 miles wide. If I can remember my geography correctly, two-thirds of the island is over 2,000 feet with the central mountain range rising 7,400 feet. Columbus, who discovered the island in 1494, described it as "the fairest island that eyes have beheld; mountainous and the land seems to touch the sky...all full of valleys and fields and plains"

Held by the Spanish for 160 years the island still boasts a few romantic Spanish names, but not much else of a Spanish heritage. In 1655 a small British naval force, having failed in its commission to take the island of Hispaniola for Cromwell and fearing for their heads, decided to capture Jamaica as a kind of consolation prize for him. This they did with some dispatch, thus beginning 300 years of British colonization. During the first 200 years Jamaica was not a full Crown Colony (as was the case with many other British possessions), in that island laws were not automatically imported from England. They emanated in right of the local House of Assembly which was extremely jealous of its independence - hence the anomaly of that petition referred to above supporting the American colonies against England. In the 1700s sugar became King and Plantation owners (many

BY THE WAY...

of whom lived in England) became very rich. By 1739 there were 430 sugar estates on the island which for a time was the leading sugar producing country in the world. For this reason the West Indian islands, with Jamaica the most productive, were major sources of Britain's wealth, and in many respects more important to England than is commonly acknowledged.

In 1776 there were 200,000 African slaves working on the Jamaican plantations. During the eighteenth century and beyond there were numerous uprisings. In 1790 the French revolution manifested itself 100 miles away from Jamaica in Haiti, where a slave revolt unprecedented for its size and ferocity left some 12,000 dead in the first two months of the war. This event did not go unnoticed in Jamaica, giving rise to the bloody Maroon War waged against establishment forces by runaway slaves in mid-western parishes. The last major slave uprising in Jamaica was in 1823 when it became clear that the status quo, wherein a small minority of mostly white planters, many living in England and presiding over the black majority on the island through resident agents, was under serious threat. The rebellion hastened an end to slavery, an end effected by British law but bitterly opposed by members of the Jamaican House of Assembly who naturally saw it as the death knell for the island's economy. When the Emancipation Act was passed in England in 1834 the sugar planters adopted it only after certain conditions covering reparations for lost profits (really the opportunity cost of emancipation), along with an interregnum during which slaves were not allowed to abandon plantations (a policy itself prematurely abandoned), were met. Of course, no reparations for the slaves were considered. In the end so-called freedom did not prevail for them until 1838, a freedom which was illusionary because the former slaves had no representation in the Assembly.

All through these years we find a local minority legislative

An Island Entire of Itself?

assembly fiercely opposed to British rule and reluctant to introduce reforms, which even London 5,000 miles away could see were necessary. Over time, the population grew to some 300,000, the large majority being completely without democratic rights or property. For twenty seven years after emancipation, grievances among these former slaves festered as "Free Trade," adopted by Britain, militated against the island's exports, forcing many sugar estates to close. Sugar prices declined, unemployment soared, and destitution became widespread.

When things got really bad in 1864/65 two voices were raised against the suffering of the poor. One was George William Gordon, the illegitimate son of a slave girl and her white master, who rose to become a member of the Assembly. He pressed for peaceful protest. The other was Paul Bogle, a Baptist preacher, an activist, and eventually a revolutionary advocating violence. Of the two, Gordon actually succeeded somewhat by getting a petition to Queen Victoria, asking for her assistance on behalf of the suffering masses. But to no effect. Dressed in homespun economic justice of the day, the queen's letter in reply advocated that the disaffected "should work harder and look to their own efforts and wisdom to improve their lot."

Paul Bogle thought otherwise, leading what came to be called the Morant Bay Rebellion of 1865, wherein some of his followers killed a handful of planters and a few British troops in a rather tragic incident at the eastern end of the island. As a deterrent against further terrorism there was an overkill of suppression on the part of Governor Eyre, who instituted a State of Emergency over the area and let loose the army to ravage the country-side, killing 400 peasants including women and children, and burning 1,000 homes. A bewildered Gordon, who had sided with the peasants' cause but had taken

BY THE WAY...

no part in the violence, was dragged from his bed in Kingston and shipped to Morant Bay, where he, along with a defiant Bogle, was summarily hanged under martial law.

The long term effect of this tragedy was far reaching. It spooked the minority in power and panicked the House of Assembly into surrendering the island's constitution and the independence which had been cherished for 200 years. Largely because of an inordinate fear of a bloody revolution similar to the one in Haiti generations before, Jamaica became a full crown colony of England in 1866. Today, one hundred years later in 1976, there is a minority of people ready to give up our new-found independence from Britain, this time because of a fear of a Cuban-style revolution.

The paradox is that the island remained peaceful, and progressed fairly well as a Crown Colony, during the century after the Rebellion. There was a certain stability which was reassuring, and also development of sorts in the categories of roads, agriculture, the legal system and even the arts. But the lot of those at the bottom of the social scale remained much the same. It was only when full adult suffrage was introduced in 1944 that opportunity was given to two newly formed political parties to build from the grass roots, with Jamaica as a sovereign country in mind for the future. But build with what? Public school education beyond primary grades was almost non-existent. True, labour in certain sectors had become better organized, and minimal advances in economic prosperity were thereby achieved. Apart from that no real progress in societal reforms was realized during the rest of the colonial years. In 1962, England, an imperial hegemon no more, walked away from any responsibility by granting Jamaica independence.

I have tried to provide an insight into the background of modern Jamaica. But what are the effects of the type of

An Island Entire of Itself?

development I have described? Like many other Third World countries, for centuries Jamaica's economy had been predominantly agricultural with large foreign interests. Because of the lack of locally manufactured goods these had to be imported. Thrifty and enterprising merchants very early cornered available foreign exchange earned in the canefields and applied it to the importation of consumer goods, expensive cars, and appliances from the US and England. For the most part this was an uncontrolled redistribution of wealth that merely prolonged the poverty of the many.

Beginning mostly in the early 1950s tourism grew exponentially. Then suddenly bauxite was discovered and Jamaica became one of the world's largest exporters of this valuable resource. Sadly, it was an industry encouraged by our British overlords but very poorly framed in contractual terms. As expected, the capital came from outside. The upshot was that for the first two decades much more wealth was taken out of the island than was ever invested in it. Secondly there was very little spin off from primary development seeing that the huge profits made in the secondary stages of production were all made in the developed countries. Needless to say, the reinvestment and diversification which emanated from those profits remained abroad while the pollution stayed at home.

In 1973 the Government decided that after 25 years the pittance being earned out of what was a wasting asset was not enough. For all these years, exports of extracted ore had been priced per ton, at minimal amounts bearing no relation to market value of the minerals, and even less to the cost of aluminum imports into the island. In the last year of the old basis the island earned $24m. In the year after the selling price was increased as a result of the Manley "cartel", which became *The International Bauxite Association*, the island earned $174m. It befuddles the mind when one considers what such

BY THE WAY...

earnings could have accomplished over the previous decades. Of course, the bauxite companies screamed blue murder, and then went on to increase their profits in the years to come.

But even if we were to discount all of this, there remains the fact that if the sugar on this table is to pay for the tractor which Jamaica needs for its production, the island must get a fair return for its exports. Sugar earnings must keep pace with tractor prices. Otherwise, more and more sugar will have to be produced to purchase fewer and fewer tractors, leading eventually to bankruptcy. When it is recognized that world production of sugar is at present ninety million tons, of which 95% is produced by the EEC, US and Australia. Together these countries hold the handle in fixing market prices; who holds the blade?

On the other hand developed countries like the United States have enjoyed relatively stable prices in basic commodities purchased from third world countries like Jamaica. So the rich get richer and the poor poorer. A recent survey showed that 12% of the population of the U.S. was considered poor, that is, in relation to their ability to purchase a weekly bag of groceries at basic services. I believe the poverty line is $4,000 per annum. But poverty is relative. The cost of food and shelter is relative. An income of $4000 per year would keep the average Jamaican labourer in luxury. At present she has no social-welfare underpinning, few if any affordable services. Early this year in rural Jamaica some twenty people died of food poisoning. A shipment of bulk flour, which is the only kind of flour that a poor woman can afford for her children, was contaminated with Parathion, a deadly insecticide. In one of the cases a family of six infants and children ate their main meal of contaminated flour dumplings. When the contortions started there was no hospital nearby and the vehicle tracks into the bush where

An Island Entire of Itself?

these people eked out their existence were inaccessible. All died without medical attention.

At present our gross domestic product is about 2.6 billion dollars and our population over 2 million. This means on an average of roughly $1,000 per capita per annum. However when the disequilibrium between rich and poor is taken into account the picture is much worse. If 20% of the population enjoys 80% of the wealth, I estimate four-fifths of the people have an annual per capita income of some $300. If added to this is an unemployment rate of 25% and an inflation factor of 15 - 20% per annum, what is left is desperation amounting to festering city slums, children with legs like pencils and stomachs like balloons, shacks of zinc, cardboard and mud, over which an acrid pall of smoke from burning garbage hangs like the shadow of death.

But let me end by looking again at the Daily Telegraph report with which I began. It criticizes the Jamaican Government's "stubborn determination to push ahead with a policy of radical social and political changes at a time of acute recession in the Caribbean." The question is: does the present Government, or any other for that matter, have any option but to introduce radical reforms and hope for the best? The period of 14 years since independence in 1962 has been an extremely short time in which to bring about meaningful change. In many respects nation building had to start from ground level in that, for most of the people, there was no national commitment to begin with. At the bottom of the economic divide many aspired to "going back to Africa;" at the top many lived as if in Florida in Kingston. In the centre were the ones who had been rocked to sleep by mother England. Until I was twenty-one Jamaica had no national flag, no national anthem. My generation grew up British, much as Virginians born in 1740 grew up British.

BY THE WAY...

When Paul Bogle and William Gordon, whom Mother Country buried as traitors, were raised up as newly minted Jamaican heroes, those at the top of the society turned up their noses, while those at the bottom simply remembered. Patriotism was something one learned about by watching British or American movies. After 500 years as a member of the new world we found ourselves a nation with no money and an illiterate mass of people living in seventeenth century conditions with little confidence and less self-respect. The few said, forget the past and build for the future; the many felt they were living the past and had no future.

The overarching problem of living so close to the richest nation in the world is that life styles are patterned after those with abundance across the water. Progress becomes synonymous with the accumulating of material goods. Of course only a small minority can afford to live like rich Americans. So please forgive me if I wish to leave you with one proposal, if nothing else. There has to be an awakening of conscience among rich nations, and that includes the media which often seeks to destroy rather than build, in order to stem the rising tide of revolution that is fast engulfing countries like Jamaica. Thank you for having me.

West Palm Beach, Florida, November 1976.

The Company We Keep

Company law is not a subject that usually generates much interest outside of the legal and accounting professions. But, as in most countries of the free world, the limited liability company is the dominant form of business enterprise, owning most of the private wealth, employing the majority of the working population and producing the majority of the nation's goods. Indeed, because corporations are the most prominent form of business enterprise their incidence within society may be taken as a litmus test for economic advancement. My purpose today is to discuss in general terms the origins and rise of corporate law in the British tradition, and to put before this conference certain reforms in the legislation that I as a practitioner see to be necessary going forward.

Any review of the history of company law in our tradition naturally must begin in England. In medieval times trading associations in England were quasi partnerships, even though incorporation had already been recognized for purposes other than trade. By the sixteenth century the Crown was granting Royal Charters (albeit to a limited extent) to merchant adventurers for trading overseas, eventually superseded by Acts of Parliament such as the charter granted to the East India Company in 1600. Even so, at first, these effectively were trade-protection associations, wherein each member invested in the capital stock of the corporation and was paid out at the end of a voyage or other adventure in trade.

Eventually, loose business arrangements of this sort solidified into so-called permanent joint stock companies, wherein investors could purchase transferable "rights" to stock that remained on the books, much as obtains today. Limited

Paper presented before the *Conference of Accountants*, at Kingston, Jamaica - December 1974 liability, the most important advantage of incorporation, did not exist in the early stages of the corporation, at least not in the sense it exists today. Indeed, it began in a back-handed way: limited liability was first seen to be valuable in protecting the assets of the company from seizure in the event of calls on the members' separate debts. Any limitation of a member's liability was therefore illusory, given that the company could make calls on its members as it saw fit.

By the end of the seventeenth century the idea of the corporation as a marriage-bed occupied by adventurers and other investors was already seen as one of the main advantages of incorporating a business or an *adventure*. In the beginning of the eighteenth we witness significant growth in corporations and the buy-out of dormant charters for purposes of respectability. Many bogus and speculative companies flourished and dealers in worthless securities became rich. The ringleader among these questionable corporations was the South Sea Company (or as it came to be known, the South Sea Bubble) which embarked on various ventures, the most notorious being a plan to acquire the National Debt of England. As one writer put it, the company "was formed for scheming rather than trading." Founded in 1711 the company collapsed in 1720 and with it the economy of England, resulting in widespread loss of confidence in corporations by landed and commercial interests.

The Bubble Act of 1720 was in reality an "Anti-Bubble" Act. However, instead of restoring confidence in the economy it stuck a knife in the side of many companies already in financial trouble in this downturn. Far from protecting investors, the Bubble Act stifled company formation. Public confidence in the economy was destroyed for the next seventy-five years. And yet it was not until 1825 that the Act was repealed, largely through the action of the Board of Trade,

The Company We Keep

which came into its own at that time and thereafter has occupied a front seat in overseeing British company law ever since.

From then on, there has been several revolutions in company law. In 1844 following an epoch making Company Law Report by a committee he had chaired, Gladstone, as president of the Board of Trade, introduced The Joint Stock Companies Act. Henceforth companies were to be incorporated by mere registration; there would be clear distinctions between them and partnerships; publicity would be enhanced to protect against fraud; and liquidation provisions appeared for the first time. One thing was missing: limited liability with teeth. Eleven more years went by before this was granted in the momentous Limited Liability Act of 1855 (allowing for limited liability where there were twenty shareholders), and which was amalgamated with the Joint Stock Companies Act in the following year. Modern company law in the British tradition was born, especially after its successor Act in 1862, when the short title of *Companies Act* was introduced. As an aside it is worth mentioning that the short-lived *Limited Liability Act* required that corporations be audited. Although rescinded in the following year, this stipulation would remain as one of the back-drops to a fledgling accounting profession.

So far as Jamaica is concerned, it is worth remembering that only the Common Law of England applied automatically (unless overruled). In other words, enactments in England post 1655 when the island was "settled" under Oliver Cromwell, did not apply unless formally adopted in Jamaica. None of the early Companies Acts were adopted prior to 1864 when we find a short act of 51 Sections providing for incorporation and patterned off the 1862 British Act. Without going into detail the process culminated in the Jamaican

53

BY THE WAY...

Companies Act of 1965, which is a carbon copy of the British Companies Act of 1948.

Before leaving this section, there are matters that are hangovers from the past and require our attention. At the heart of corporate law is the company as legal person, separate from its shareholders. Yet, this matter is not spelled out in Companies Acts down to the present time. Indeed, it was first adjudicated in the now famous court case of *Solomon vs. Solomon* (1897). Solomon was a leather merchant who had incorporated his business and had lent the company ten thousand pounds secured on assets of the company. After the company went bankrupt the liquidator claimed that Solomon was not entitled to repayment of his loan before other creditors were paid because, *inter alia*, incorporation had changed nothing in regard to his former business arrangements. The House of Lords disagreed, finding that the company was a person in its own right. Solomon's liability was therefore limited to the purchase price of his shares.

Whatever advances in corporate law Jamaica has made in recent years, there are outstanding issues I believe our legislators should address. At present, company directors owe a fiduciary duty only to shareholders as a whole. This may have been acceptable in 1902 (*Percival vs Wright*) but certainly not in 1974. Under this rule individual shareholders are given little consideration, and non-shareholders none at all. Legally therefore the interests of employees, consumers, and the nation writ large, are virtually irrelevant so far as company law is concerned. Equally important is the matter of insider trading. Of course, the foregoing shortcomings (and I am sure there are many others that this conference will raise) are not confined to the Companies Act, but extend to the general body of corporate law as it relates to modern conditions. I am not suggesting there are easy solutions; however I believe there is room in the legislation for a general code of ethics regarding companies and their directors.

Probably, the most noticeable aspect of company legislation in this century has been recognition of the necessity for more and better financial and other information for shareholders, creditors, and the public at large. In spite of this the legislation has lagged far behind standards developed by accounting professions in the UK and US. Indeed as one observer put it, "Our dedication as accountants is not so much compliance with a set of rules - with their inevitable ambiguities and alternatives - but attention to a reliable and informative portrayal of a company's affairs." In providing for adequate disclosure, organizations such as the Institute of Chartered Accountants and the Stock Exchange have important roles to play. But in the final analysis Governments have the responsibility to ensure legislation reflects public opinion, the stage that financial development has reached within the country, and the social and economic policies that they have been elected to pursue.

The matter of public accountability is nowhere more controversial than the current requirements, both in England and Jamaica, that annual financial statements be filed with the Registrar of Companies. That mandatory filings should be retained for large, especially publicly quoted, corporations is obvious. That it should apply on the basis of seven (or more) shareholders is not. The criteria should be any two of: gross revenue, number of employees, and liabilities in excess of a certain amount. The same criteria should apply for annual audits to be mandatory.

New philosophies: Recent decades have seen the emergence in the West of new schools of thought regarding the bases upon which company law is structured. As we

BY THE WAY...

have discussed, the company began as an association of adventurers, and/or adventurers and investors, under the banner of trade. Over many years these relatively small "voyager" operations evolved into multi-nationals, wherein owners (shareholders), are entirely divorced from those doing the work and are subject to change by means of names on a register. For the behemoths that bestride the world the original concept of the company as an association of persons is long dead. Where a primitive charter company might have enjoyed exclusive trading rights bestowed on it by the Crown or Act of Parliament, today the large corporation is often in a position to arrogate to itself very similar privileges. In terms of people employed, goods produced, resources controlled, the large company wields enormous power. The wheel has come full circle. Instead of corporations being subject to government, governments are often in hock to corporations.

Questions that come to mind include: What responsibilities are inured in such power? And, is company law broad enough to ensure, directly or indirectly, that the community's interests are protected? (At the other end of the scale, is the law flexible enough to accommodate the small company?) To the first point, I would suggest that, just as publicity is the price of limited liability, accountability to the community is the price of economic power. We have to remember that corporations are much more wary of economic blow-back from issues such as pollution, environmental degradation, product worthiness, than they used to be. Even labeling is more important than it used to be. Sweden insists not only on seat-belts in cars, but also cars having head-lights on all day! In the US, the recent crackdown on cigarette advertising is another case in point. These developments are complementing older constraints built into old laws such as anti-trust laws in the US and the *Monopolies and Mergers Act* in the UK.

Allied to these developments have been: (a) talk of more state control or participation in key companies, as part of public policy. Such "partnerships" are used in France and Italy and gaining ground in Third World countries; (b) growing calls for more and effective control by shareholders; and (c) activism towards the recognition of workers' rights in sharing ownership and control of corporations in which they are employed.

Focusing on (c), the theory derives from the control, in small companies, that shareholders have over the election of directors and therefore the input they have in the running of the company. That control grows weaker the bigger the operation, and wider the spread of shareholdings, all but disappearing in the end. In the final analysis, all that is left to the shareholder is property rights in shares held. For practical purposes he or she is relegated to the position of a contributor of loan capital, one who waits patiently for his or her interest (or dividend) cheque. In order to regain some modicum of control, various forms of organizational structure have emerged in different countries, particularly the two-tier system of management described below. This is all part of a brave plan on the part of shareholders to regain something of the ground they have lost. But achievements have not been spectacular. For their part employees have been gaining recognition at almost the same rate as shareholders have been losing control. It is important to remember that, in ex-colonial countries like Jamaica, employees traditionally have been at a distinct disadvantage in this struggle. Until very recently they were subject to a time-warp called the *Master and Servant Act* of 1842.

Today's advocates for change dismiss the absurdity

of Victorian verities dictating labour policies. They posit that employees constitute the *core* of any operation; indeed, especially in large corporations they are the only visible "association" of people worthy of the name "company". For company law to completely ignore this, to entirely overlook the fact that employees are members of the company in their own right, is unrealistic - if not unjust. Accordingly, employees have a right to some control over the assets they have helped to create. This right is beyond wages earned. Put another way, they have invested capital in the form of their labour, just as valuable, if not more so than capital investors provide in the form of money. (The irony is that money that changes hands on a stock-exchange seldom reaches the company.)

In an attempt to solve the anomalies surrounding shareholder control, and the need for employee participation therein, various models have been adopted. Principal among these has been the two-tier Board system that takes account of worker representation. In West Germany, for example, public companies have a Supervisory Board comprised of shareholders (2/3) and employees (1/3), under whose surveillance a Board of Managers - elected by the Supervisory Board - has the responsibility of looking after day to day operations. Terms of service for these two boards are four and five years respectively. In France a similar sharing of control obtains in a company's Directorate, where 1/3 may be comprised of employees. These are but two of many examples of "worker participation" in developed countries - examples which, after careful consideration, countries like Jamaica may be wise to follow.

Meanwhile, Jamaica is entering a phase of more and more involvement by the state in key industries. This is part of the Manley Government's plan for a *mixed economy*. Whatever benefits may be derived from such involvement in corporate affairs (the bauxite industry as a case in point) the ground-rules will have changed radically. Instead of shareholders in their own behalf appointing Directors, the Government will occupy the position of the public at large doing the same thing. Some of these hybrid corporations will cease to be listed on the Stock Exchange, and ironically will be tempted to reduce rather than increase public accountability – tragic for the new economy, unless there was a commitment to expand existing checks and balances that foster and maintain confidence in the system. After all, is this not the whole purpose of company law?

Redacted from this transcript are some sixteen pages covering technical issues, which were part of the original presentation.

Kingston, December, 1974

The Stock Market: Fiscal Incentives Needed

Recent weeks have seen much probing among the rubble of this island's economy. In concert with that various beating-sticks have been applied to the exposed nerve-ends of our Stock Exchange in a falling market. Whether or not some of the negative criticisms levelled at the Exchange are justified at this time, I believe we have room for suggestions on the positive side. There are two major problems facing the economy, as embodied in the Exchange. The first is the lack of direct investment, due mainly to the fact that available funds are revolving in the short-term deposits commanding interest rates that are attractive, or are being funneled into speculative ventures and/or hard assets, mainly for the purpose of hedging against inflation. The other problem is that the risks attendant on equity investment are greater in times of uncertainty. For the last few months our paralyzed economy has been anything but inspiring of confidence.

Of course, it is true that both the high interest rates and the severe restrictions on imports in effect are meant as stop-gap solutions to the greater problem, which is declining foreign reserves, but no one can deny that something has to be done very quickly to free-up the economy if the country is to go forward. Like the insolvent company with the potential to turn around, Jamaica has to find the means to refinance the business sector before suppliers cut us off. The end result must be reactivation of the economy that is focused on greater production.

We are all waiting anxiously for the revenue section of the budget. Not knowing what fiscal measures the Government is about to introduce in order to raise the extraordinary amounts

Paper published by *The Daily News*, April 15, 1974

BY THE WAY...

of money it proposes to spend in the coming year, leaves us in a quandary, especially given that we also are in the dark whether or not the budget will reinforce the deflationary policy presently being pursued to combat soaring inflation. Maybe the stops will be pulled out, if only partially. My guess is that the Government will have to take the chance of pumping money into the economy, and more than this, getting more involved in certain areas (the announced expansion of AMG retail outlets is a case in point) in order to take up the slack now rearing its ugly head in the jobs market. The challenge is getting as much production as possible out of every dollar it spends. Clearly too, it is of paramount importance that, quite apart from new measures introduced to bring down interest rates, new fiscal incentives are necessary if capital is to be attracted out of the short-term market and into long-term investment in the industrial and agricultural sectors.

Far from being a luxury, as some people would have us believe it is, the Stock Exchange is a vital necessity in the mobilization of funds. I do not see any other medium through which this can be accomplished. According to my research some thirteen million dollars have been raised on the local market in new issues since the inception of the Exchange five years ago, and this by only fourteen out of forty-one listed companies - that is, absent substantial sums subscribed mostly by foreign parent companies over that period. Surely, it is a mere token of what could be raised if the market were given a long overdue shot in the arm.

What we need are fiscal incentives for a broader-based lineup of stocks, meaning a substantial increase over the forty-one corporations presently listed on the Exchange. Each major sector of the economy should be represented, each with its own index. At present, agriculture, tourism and mining are for the most part unrepresented. In order to encourage

The Stock Market: Fiscal Incentives Needed

smaller companies to apply for listings the minimum capital requirement should be reduced from $100,000 to $50,000. There must exist an atmosphere of confidence, with assurances not only that the Government is behind efforts of the corporate sector to expand, but also that the veil of uncertainty surrounding our mixed economy will be lifted.

At present most publicly listed companies pay income tax at 45% of profit, as against 50% paid by most private companies. The 5% differential is negligible and, for prospective listings sitting on the fence, provides no incentive to come and play. This issue requires immediate review by Finance. One solution may be to exempt qualifying companies from paying additional profits tax (now 15% of taxable income). This would mean that the private company coming on board would pay tax at around 30%. An ameliorating factor for the loss of public revenues could be that listed companies enjoying the lower tax rate be required to remit to the Government tax deducted from dividends paid. An extension of this could be the imposition of a dividend premium tax not recoverable by shareholders. One of the benefits of either strategy would be the incentive for companies to plough back profits rather than distribute them to shareholders. At the same time companies that can afford to pay dividends [or are seeking to raise capital] would still do so in the new era, wherein corporate taxes would be less than at present, provided dividends paid were not excessive.

At this time companies operating "basic industries" enjoy investment allowances against profits calculated at 20% of cost for new equipment--40% for companies in the agricultural sector. The Government should replace such allowances with cash grants at a reduced rate. Because grants would be more costly in terms of Government revenues the number of industries regarded as "basic" may have to be reviewed.

BY THE WAY...

However, if the Government intends direct injection of money into the economy, investment grants replacing investment allowances bear consideration.

But why, one might ask, should listed companies be the only ones favoured by fiscal incentives? To begin with, the exigencies of our present situation do not allow for a general reduction of tax revenues. That can be effected only on a selective basis, and probably only at the expense of increases at the personal level. Therefore, much will be expected of companies that benefit from changes, and in fairness to everyone, they should be accountable to the public. The Stock Exchange is a natural choice for ensuring this. If the economy is going to turn around, where is equity capital to come from except from savings through a revitalized capital market? In this regard we cannot include fully paid shares bought on the Exchange. These transactions, though the most numerous on a day-to-day basis, merely represent transfers from one pocket to another. Apart from democratizing ownership they have no effect on production.

Finally, there are those who point to the low savings rate in the country. They are correct, but I don't know that the building societies, the cooperatives, or the life assurance companies - to say nothing of the tourist industry - have had anything to grouse about raising money down the years. In order to compete the Stock Exchange doubtless will have to substantially increase its promotional efforts. This will mean support from the Government or from the listed companies themselves. But it will be money well spent.

Kingston, April 1974

The Stock Market: Fiscal Incentives Needed

Postscript: The author was instrumental in setting up the office of *Stock Exchange Auditor*, whose duty it was to monitor stock brokers' adherence to Stock Exchange Rules in their dealings with the public.

Corporations and the Community

It is a great honour for me to be able to discuss with your club aspects of Jamaican company law, which many, especially those in the business community, feel are important, but which the government has been slow to address. Suddenly, the media are on board! The result has been a general upsurge in interest in this area of the law. Indeed, storms have been blowing up around the bauxite companies, banks, public utility companies and especially Crown corporations, whether operating or in the works. Matters that have given rise to concern and comment affect a wide range of issues in the community, touching, as they do investors, creditors, customers and the proverbial man in the street.

The reports and commentary have covered a wide range of concerns that beg the questions. Why has company law not been broadened to accommodate at least some of them? Is it a fact that we were duped into believing various protections were in place that did not exist? The most recent case in point was the legislation proposed to protect bank depositors. More often than not company law reform is sidelined because the company is viewed as an appendage of the shareholder, which was true up to a point a hundred years ago. No longer. If one owns a share in a publicly listed company in 1975 one is not identified with the company for practical purposes, having no say in what it does or how it is run. Further, those that do hold the reins cannot be challenged so long as they act within their powers, and cannot be removed by minority shareholders for any reason at all. Of course, a few exceptions obtain; but in general, these do not obviate the helplessness of small shareholders when it comes to the *management* of large corporations.

Paper presented before *Kiwanis Club of Kingston* – March 1975

BY THE WAY...

Effectively, we have less control over the large, listed company than we do over the government itself.

The corporation is the dominant form of business enterprise. Together, corporations own most of the wealth, employ the majority of the working population and produce by far the greater part of the nation's goods, which together speak to Jamaica's expansion in industry and commerce, as well as the island's growing sophistication in business acumen, especially evident in our very active stock market.

In 1969 the local stock exchange was born out of a desire of the public to own shares in local companies. By the end of 1974 there were forty one companies listed on the exchange. These companies had net assets in excess of a half-billion dollars at *book value*. Now, this represents but a small part of corporate wealth, most of which is in the hands of multinationals that are not listed. Clearly, company law must take into account an extremely wide range of stakeholders' interests; at least it must set the tone or provide the philosophy for detailed legislation outside of the corporate remit. We may be shocked to discover that it does not.

For there is much that the *Companies Act*, for all its hundreds of pages, does not include. What is there revolves around formation of companies, governance in the interests of shareholders, liquidations of companies, and basic accounting/financial disclosers - the latter likely to lag far behind advances being made internationally in financial reporting. One alternative is for the Legislature to delegate responsibility for improvements in reporting standards to an independent body capable of doing the job, much as obtains in the United States. How else will the required research ever be achieved? In other areas also, legislation lends to inflexibility. For example, the requirement that all companies whatever their sizes must be audited on an annual basis. Together with the requirements

Corporations and the Community

for holding meetings and for annual filings of documents with the *Registrar of Companies*, rules that correctly apply to large companies, are costly when imposed on thousands of small ones, especially those having no public footprint whatever. The answer may be to exempt those companies from such red-tape. For example, companies where (a) turnover is below $250,000; (b) liabilities are less than $100,000, (c) employees less than 30/shareholders less than 10, or (d) a combination of the foregoing.

The sad fact is that company law in the English system of law was not designed to cope with the complex developments in corporate affairs that have arisen since the late nineteenth century. The underlying philosophy has not advanced beyond that of protecting capital: shareholders first, creditors some distance behind - depending on how "protection" is viewed. When they opened for business, Smith & Sons sold basic foodstuffs to the locals, had three employees, and owed bank and suppliers modest amounts. But, what happened after they incorporated as *Smith & Company Ltd.?* Not much. They continued to operate primarily in their own interests, provided they paid their way. But what has happened to companies since those early days?

As far back as 1932 two Americans, Burle and Meins, in their book *The Modern Corporation and Private Property*, wrote:

> "The rise of the modern corporation has brought a concentration of economic power which can compete on equal terms with the modern state.... Where its own interests are concerned, it even attempts to dominate the state.... [Indeed], business practice is increasingly assuming the aspect of economic statesmanship."

In the meantime, corporate law, especially in the UK and colonies, had not progressed beyond mid-nineteenth thinking focused on corporate capital interests. Recently

BY THE WAY...

there was a case of alleged insider trading on the part of a director of a certain cigarette manufacturer. A big hue and cry ensued in the media about the paucity of legislation to protect investors against such wrongdoings. We can't argue with that. But what about legislation to protect *consumers* against the use of such products? Not a word. And not one section out of 379 in the Companies Act addresses such matters. So, how do you quantify the cost of ill health? What warnings to the public at large are to be found in Directors' glowing remarks at the annual general meeting of shareholders? Is their report of millions of dollars profit not, in many cases, a net loss to the community writ large?

A fundamental flaw in all of this is that directors owe *fiduciary duty* exclusively to the shareholders of their company. Of course, they have other duties under company law, but these, for the most part, are technical rather than ethical responsibilities, found maybe in case law, which may or may not be specific in addressing a particular wrong-doing. Even where a law exists, difficulties arise. For example, there is no minimum standard of care and skill, arising out of the limited fiduciary relationship directors have to their company, expressly required of them by the Companies Act, not even a statement of basic principles governing their actions or duties - much less principles involving ethics that should obtain in their dealings with *third parties*. The implication to be drawn from this is that profits, however earned, will compensate for the ills that they cause the community. When directors consider expansion or diversification of business social costs are often ignored. All we need to do in this country is drive by the lakes of red slime left behind by bauxite mining.

Recently, Malcolm Sharp of *The Daily Gleaner* deplored the amount of pollution over Kingston. In the region around the industrial estate the extent of it is reaching

Corporations and the Community

alarming proportions. But when the annual reports are read at general meetings no mention will be made of the men, women and children whose lives will have been shortened for the greater glory of higher share prices. And, if Kingston Harbor becomes another Dead Sea in the next ten years, the companies owning the ships and those businesses responsible for the dumping of industrial waste in the sea, will say pollution the inevitable cost of progress.

The upshot is that the narrowly defined "fiduciary rule" may have been acceptable at the beginning of this century – but not today. Employees, consumers and the public at large are not irrelevant in formulating corporate philosophy. Countries as different as Canada and Ghana have taken steps to redress the many injustices that boardroom fiat imposes on Third World communities. So should we.

Kingston, Jamaica – March 1975

Postscript: For readers who may be curious about Jamaican politics in the 1970s, newspaper reports of the December 1974 *Conference of Accountants* were generally supportive. The left-leaning *The Jamaica Daily News* became almost ecstatic in reference to the paper on company law (p. 51 above), which it went overboard in claiming "may well be the single most important document that has emerged from the regular sessions held by a variety of professional institutions over the years." Of course, the uptick was worker-participation, alluded to in the conference paper (and the follow up) in support of which the *Daily News* championed. But it was not until the foregoing presentations on suggested reforms were made that the conservative *Daily Gleaner* referred to the conference. This was followed in early April 1975 by what, presumably, was intended as an editorial *coup de grace* dismissing what was seen as impractical suggestions.

The left would have none of it. Less than a week passed before a two-part article by Stanley Reid appeared in the *Daily News* using my paper as a base for radical criticism of inequality and other aberrations in Jamaican society, special attention being given to "the proverbial worker." Whether these developments had anything to do with the Prime Minister's setting up of an Advisory Committee on the subject in May 1975 is doubtful, but the committee's findings, published in February 1976 and entitled *Report on Worker Participation in Jamaica*, quoted from the paper and proposed the implementation of worker participation under the aegis of a commission established by the Government, involving where necessary amendments to the Company Act to facilitate the process.

Aspects of Underdevelopment

Ladies and gentlemen, as your chairman mentioned in his very kind introduction, our subject today is Jamaica's failing economy, and the various solutions on the table before us as a society. We are all aware that 1977 has begun with dire warnings of serious problems ahead. Yesteryear's bleak prognostications are today's realities. The business sector is reeling from the financial squeeze: capital controls are in place, government spending is curtailed, and those of us who must travel are faced with onerous restrictions on foreign exchange. At the same time the great majority of people throughout the island is at subsistence level. Everyone is awaiting with trepidation the details of the economic package which Finance will lay before the country tomorrow. The problems we know. It is the posited solutions that are confounding. If I may venture to recount the prominent ones among them, which I hope we can discuss today, they are - not necessarily in the order of importance: (1) devaluation, (2) production, (3) foreign investment and loan capital, (4) the New World Economic Order, and (5) societal motivation.

There are so many conflicting views about (1), I am reluctant to comment on it. However, I will venture to say that a wait-and-see policy may not be as crazy as it first appears. There is some protection in the home-made ban on unnecessary imports that would otherwise be attractive given the favourable exchange rate at the moment. In any case, to say that devaluation would solve our problems would be to delude ourselves. The real problem with the status quo is so-called under-the-table capital flight. No doubt, tomorrow we will hear the government's position on this important issue.

The second item is "production." No one can deny that

From a paper before the *St. Andrew Rotary Club*, January 1977 production must increase. And yet the questions remain. More of what? How? At present, I believe the estimate is 15,000 employed in the manufacturing sector, if sugar is excluded. The average per capita investment is about $12,000. As is the case in most other developing countries we face the reality that any increase in industrial production will require capital, which if local, must come from agriculture, mining and tourism, together commanding 85% of export earnings. Industrial expansion will require capital equipment from abroad, as well as worker training, not forgetting manufacturing inputs, all financed by access to foreign currency. If, for most countries at our stage of development, two-thirds or more of expenditure abroad goes to importing industrial components and capital goods, our exports must be sufficient to keep pace with the rising cost of those imports. Given current level of unemployment we simply cannot afford the expansion needed to significantly reverse that situation unless we resort to borrowing abroad. The IMF looms before us.

The third solution is tied to the second: We hear a lot about free trade and foreign direct investment. According to this theory, what Jamaica needs is a complete opening up of the economy, with no restrictions on capital flows into, or out of the island. More specifically, we are told that economic salvation lies in foreign capital developing local industry. I believe this requires more thought. We cannot ignore the downsides. Foreign investments are not permanent implants. In case we devalue, the island must standby ready to repatriate old inflows at unfavorable rates of exchange. As history makes plain, foreign investments are not altruistic gestures on the part of foreign corporations. They come under various guises and sometimes at high costs: to extract raw materials or minerals for the home country, to take advantage of

Aspects of Underdevelopment

monopolies (including low wages) not otherwise available at home, or simply to increase market share for shareholders; and finally to remit profits in hard currency on an annual basis (or earlier).

This does not mean that foreign investment is always inimical to the host country; it's just not a solution to all the latter's ills. Apart from the negatives already mentioned, if we look at a sample of technology agreements governing the production of goods using foreign brands, what we find are restrictions on the ability of the local factory to *export* finished products, thus compromising one of the main reasons for the investment in the first place. Some agreements even specify the countries to which products may not be exported, and still others will specify that production is only for the Jamaican market. Such restrictions curtail or eliminate our ability to earn the foreign exchange that must be found elsewhere in order for us to pay the investor.

Another aspect of inward foreign investment is double-dipping that often accompanies it, such as the chicanery around local use of home-based technology in manufacturing processes. One example is that of a local subsidiary paying a foreign parent for use of technology, which the parent owns. Here, we are not referring to a *purchase* of technology for our local needs going forward, but instead specious rent transfers between two entities under common control. It is rather ironic that we are said to be paying for technology we so desperately need, but are denied ownership, thus adding to our underdevelopment.

On the other hand, the old (colonial style) industrialization, with its preference for agriculture, is all but dead. World prices do not promise self-sufficiency in food. I recently found myself in a cane field surrounded by and having to inform a large group of men and women carrying machetes, that their sugar-cane cooperative was facing bankruptcy. Today, growers cannot stand idly by for long, before the receivers move in. For many, the future is bleak. Something must be done to salvage what remains of the capital investment in this sector that traditionally has been heavily indebted to the banks. As you know, recent years have seen many farmers coming out of cane and going into cattle rearing. This process might have to be reversed in the national interests of foreign exchange earnings and employment. Concerning bauxite extraction and the mining sector generally, more emphasis needs to be put into research in order to promote more efficiency, especially in the area of waste management.

The fourth solution, or issue, at hand is that regarding the New Economic Order. We are all familiar with the UN Declaration that seeks to level the playing-field between developed and developing nations. I made the point at a conference in Florida recently that Jamaica was exporting sugar at subsistence prices, over which we have no control whatsoever. (Very roughly, the total sugar production of ACP countries is three million tons, as against world production of ninety million.) During the discussion period, a prominent businessman got up and asked how Jamaica could expect the U.S. to pay more, when New York was floundering. Fair point, maybe. But then he went on to remark that if Jamaica put sugar lands into marijuana, the US would pay a huge price for it. Joking or serious, whether he knew it or not, he had hit on the head the reason for a new world economic order. Without it the third world sells not its products but its soul. Call it economic prostitution.

Mr. Chairman, I began by listing the five areas that pundits see as solutions to Jamaica's economic woes. The fifth is the issue of motivation. There is no doubt that something

Aspects of Underdevelopment

must be done to bring people together for the common good. But this must involve the *whole* country. At present, minority groups have become whipping posts. As the situation deteriorates, invective against them increases. This is not motivation, but intimidation. The effect has been dejection and cynicism on the part of those who feel the earth shifting beneath their feet. There is growing disaffection among so-called classes. What we have been talking about over the past five years, what has given rise to so many heated arguments setting fathers against children, brothers against sisters, what is driving so many from our shores, is at its root the history of the island and the societal injustices it embodies. The difficulty is that a few are being tarred for injustices not of their making, for a tragedy that has been systemic over many centuries.

Out of the current finger-pointing, out of the accusations about one being a capitalist or a socialist, has emerged destructive branding that creates rifts among friends and acquaintances alike. A Red Guard mania - self-righteous, self-serving, and undemocratic - is abroad in the country. And if burning of witches is in the offing, the politicians will have stoked the fires. This does not mean there is no truth in what has been said. After 500 years as a member of the New World we find ourselves a sovereign nation with few resources and a mass of poor people living in seventeenth century conditions. As I believe I told our friends in Florida, the few in Jamaica say: forget the past and build for the future; while, for the many it is: we are living in the past and have no future.

Among all the uncertainties there is one certainty facing us: all of us will have to do with less. A reduction in our standard of living is imminent. Using the new import limits as a rough guide, we will have to be satisfied with life-styles equivalent to 60% of what obtained at the best of times. Even this scenario may be an understatement. For middle and

BY THE WAY...

upper-income groups the availability of many luxuries, now regarded as necessaries, will no longer be available. For lower-income folks rising prices will have dire consequences. This impending catastrophe looms out of the island's hazy future, and anxiety fills our subconscious. This is a time for a national commitment. We must rise above the consumerism to which we have grown accustomed.

St. Andrew, Jamaica, 1977

Nationalism and the New Elite

In recent times, beginning maybe with the last election campaign, the political intelligentsia of the Peoples National Party, comprising revolutionary romantics, government hardliners, and sycophantic freeloaders, have been the core of the island's new elite. They sit in their ivory towers promoting propaganda against so-called "fascists" who they claim are seeking to overthrow the Manley Government. These so-called fascists are presented to us in all shapes and sizes. There is the local threat from militants in the parliamentary opposition, who, if we read certain columnists, are the strong-armed few brandishing mailed fists behind their bosses' every word and action. Then, of course, forever before us is the CIA as arch conspirators with hands in every act of violence. Finally, there is the mysterious "Big Man" who is hatching all manner of nefarious plots with, if you please, elements in the army.

As an example of what-could-happen-here, the spectre of the Chilean coup four years ago has been kept vividly alive by television documentaries, discussion groups, interviews, recorded speeches and "solidarity" visits by Cuban dignitaries and the like. By these means, even "housewife" demonstrations - except those in support of the Government - are being labelled as fascist-oriented. Through subliminal messaging and political bombast, the perverse condition now is accepted by many who do not know what it means, except that it is the hand-maiden of capitalist interests, and the principal enemy of much vaunted "Democratic Socialism." As usual, it is easier to identify enemies without,

Published by *The Daily Gleaner*, October, 1977. This is an edited version of a paper written by the author under the pseudonym, Courtney DeSeyle

BY THE WAY...

than those within the country. We all commiserate with our Chilean friends, but this does not justify manipulation of their tragedy for our political ends. Chile notwithstanding, it must be remembered that in the 1930s a fascist was head of a movement called National Socialism. At the same time across the border, a communist was claiming to be one of the fathers of socialism. And more recently, we have the Red Book in China, and its contribution to yet another, this time Maoist, version of socialism. Indeed, almost any political tribalism can be so described.

Closer to home, between 1944 and 1962 the awakening of what may be described as a *Jamaican* conscience was predominantly liberal in character. Such tribalism that existed was economic and class-oriented, not ideological. This is not forgetting that below the surface were racial tensions, endemic to a large segment of the population for whom slavery was easy to remember and is at the root of our convivial motto, "Out of many, one people." Yet, the lead-up to Independence Day in August 1962 was relatively free of bitterness and "struggle," unlike many other countries, especially in Africa, that gained their independence through blood and the sword.

Today, the Government would have us believe that it was a bloodless revolution that brought us out of the colonial wood and gave us Mr. Manley's version of socialism. The facts are more sinister. For having won their independence under the banner of a liberal philosophy, having travelled some distance along the bumpy road to self-determination, Jamaicans suddenly stumbled over the bankside and rolling down the slope, ended up in a road too narrow for pacifist socialism, but wide enough for activist *nationalism*. Stunned and not very sober, we mistook this road for the highway and resolutely set off, oblivious of the precipice on our left. Thus, have we ended up where African revolutions began. One has

Nationalism and the New Elite

only to look at Nigeria, Pakistan, Cyprus and even Guyana for confirmation. It is painfully obvious that nationalist movements may be societally cohesive in demanding, and obtaining, independence, but are divisive in maintaining it. This is because nationalism is elitist.

In his *Notes on Nationalism* (1945) George Orwell defines nationalism under several headings, the two most relevant to our discussion are (1) the classification of citizens in terms of their allegiance or otherwise to a country; and (2) the obsession with power on the part of politicians whose *raison detre* is staying in power.

Far from a nirvana of inclusiveness that our Prime Minister preached and wrote about on coming into office, what obtains today is Big-Man baiting by various members of the political elite, whose tirades against "capitalists" have fanned the flames of violence against minorities. Across the suburbs of Kingston, house-holders have resorted to padlocks on bedroom doors and metal gates in passages, for security *within* the confines of their homes. Those we still can name as friends or acquaintances, and those who have been attacked, or threatened, are now the subjects of macabre conversations. Predictably, an exodus of middle-class citizens whom the country cannot afford to lose, is now underway, aided and abetted by our Prime Minister egging them on - even reminding them that there are "five flights to Miami every day." What he means, of course, is that dissidents are not wanted. If you can't control them, if you can't trust them, help them to disappear. What began as a hug-in has ended in good-riddance to thousands who once had hopes of contributing towards nationhood.

Shortly after he assumed office Mr. Manley published *The Politics of Change* (1974), in which he eloquently expounded on the importance of national *inclusiveness*, especially for countries like Jamaica fresh out of colonialism, and even more so for those that had experienced the ravages of slavery. For him, the Peoples National Party was already working towards that end, and further, was the only political party "capable of organizing mass political response, mass understanding and mass involvement in the process of change" that would be required to move the country away from its blighted colonial past and towards self-reliance. Three short years later, where are we?

Today, the ideal of Democratic Socialism, or the so-called "mixed economy" it favours, has been supplanted by a political appeal to the more emotive nationalism, and thence, with vitriolic twists, to emotionally driven patriotism. If the argument is that only the new elite are responsible for the growing divisiveness throughout the island, it only serves to emphasize the weakness at the centre of Mr. Manley's government. On the other hand it cannot be denied that there are other people seeking government approval by mouthing what has become PNP prejudices and hates. The growing discrimination against "enemies," the witch-hunting of "economic criminals," the head-bashing and general intimidation tactics of Party thugs, are manifestations of a snowballing militancy aimed at extending the power-base.

What is more subtle, though no less disturbing, is the suggestion that support for this new thinking is the prerequisite of being "Jamaican" – an aberration at the core of the latest thinking, typified recently in a television interview wherein the moderator opined that one of our leading newspapers was "more patriotic" than its competitor. The ease with which otherwise intelligent people are joining the crowd voicing Party rhetoric is disturbing. Meanwhile, demonstrations are brutally put down, poor people and their

Nationalism and the New Elite

belongings are thrown into the street, and election candidates are jailed on spurious charges.

So, the facts are that Democratic Socialism morphed into nationalism, which then morphed into patriotism, which now is fast declining into fascism. Wherefore the inclusiveness and sharing Mr. Manley promised? Are his cherished beliefs in tatters? Jean-Francois Revel (*The Totalitarian Temptation*) may have the answer, and for those determined to hang on, provide some hope, when he postulates: "The facts of life do not penetrate to the sphere in which our beliefs are cherished; as it is not they that engendered those beliefs, so they are powerless to destroy them."

Kingston, October 1977

ISSUES

Have Gun, and an Excuse to Use It

Yesterday, President Reagan attacked Libya in retaliation for Colonel Khadafy's alleged terrorism in recent times. Today's news is full of the world's reaction to these "defensive" strikes and the threats of revenge pouring out of Tripoli. While one television network takes viewers into the city's rubble-strewn districts, another network zooms in on Reagan's triumphant smile as reporters gather. After all, this is the sort of excitement on which the media thrive – brinkmanship, teach-him-a-lesson strong-man tactics.

Yet the diplomatic shambles of the last few days is cause for concern. As the full impact of this strike against sleeping Tripoli sinks into the consciousness of people all over the world, the "tough-beans" attitude presently in vogue in Washington may yet upturn in the President's lap. The neighborhood "bad-boy" is harassing the kids and becoming a real nuisance. Dad loses his temper and confronting the fellow in the street slaps him across the face. Therapy it may be for Dad to vent his spleen thus, but solution it most probably is not. Should he be surprised if at night a rock finds its way through his bay window?

This six-gun approach to terrorism is likely to take us down a very rocky road indeed. How could it be otherwise? Any rational person must be able to see the shortcomings of such dubious diplomacy. This attack was without doubt aimed at Khadafy himself. However, what would success have accomplished except to make the man a martyr? Instead, worse than this likely has been achieved. With children of his household killed, Khadafy is now a hero, as well as a martyr. But let us suppose that he and all his advisors had been killed: is it not inconceivable that, in the wake of American

Extracted from: *Reflections on Our Times*, April 1986

BY THE WAY...

violence against the embodiment of the Libyan state, the new regime would do other than continue where Khadafy left off? So what did Reagan's bravado achieve? The answer can lie only in the larger than life image he has of himself. Such is the stuff that Messianism is made of – the will to act that becomes an end in itself. If the President needs reassurance that by irrational acts he does right for his country, let him ask Khadafy.

Prince George, BC, 1986

Note: Readers may remember that on December 18, 1988, Pan Am Flight 103 was downed over Lockerbie, killing 270 people. The bombing was blamed on the Khadafy regime.

On Values: Freedom

The discussion by Peggy Noonan and her guests in their recent television program is interesting for what it includes, but distressing for what it omits. Many people would agree that the questions she raises reflect general concerns and should be discussed; however, I for one am disappointed that the interlocutors seek only to raise issues, not examine them, and, accordingly, found their arguments having little value in terms of viewers' enlightenment. The subject of Freedom is dealt with rather obliquely, if at all. Therefore, I ask forgiveness if I stray from that topic myself in what follows.

As with most of what claims to be "intellectual" television in the U.S., contributors are carefully chosen to support "responsible" and therefore safe positions on any given subject, more so for avoiding criticism of public policy or touchy issues like gun control. Not for discussions to be too focused on ghetto poverty and human degradation in the "Land of the Free." This would not be good manners when one's sponsors are Corporate America and elite viewers. Programs chaired by establishment figures are particularly careful to skirt around in-depth critiques of money in politics, crime and punishment, credibility of the media, police brutality and foreign policy.

Any one of these subjects, examined objectively and without fear or favour, would challenge received truth - a very bad thing for those who pull the strings of the society. Accordingly, real issues may be alluded to in order to add "high seriousness" to a particular debate, but participants are always conscious of the rules. The situation is very much like what obtained for the portrayal of sex in American movies forty years ago. In 1955, both producers and the public knew and respected the fact that sex was taboo. Sometimes,

Comments on PBS Presentation: *On Values-Freedom*, June 1995

BY THE WAY...

vague references to that subject were made, maybe to lend gravity, certainly to contribute titillation regarding plot or character. But dealing with the matter openly, whether in words or actions, was totally against regulation. It was not unusual to have separate beds provided for married couples on honeymoon.

Today, grassroots socio-political, economic, and foreign policy issues are more or less taboo subjects, so far as the mainline U.S. media are concerned. These topics are more often than not overlaid with propaganda based on accepted wisdom. The players always know the limits of their remit. In a totalitarian state propaganda is disseminated through direct control over the message. In a democracy even more effective propaganda is achieved by indirect means, that is, by selection of the messengers.

This is particularly true of the U.S. media. For example, in the months leading up to the Gulf war, the main US war coverage, both Public Television and the national networks, carefully avoided anything that could be described as "unpatriotic," that is anything that questioned the correctness of what was happening, or the official computer-game versions of massacres of women and children. According to Laura Flanders in *Beyond the Storm*, 1991, p 162, the nightly news invariably relied on guests "overwhelmingly pro-Pentagon and pro-war and also predominantly white and male. ABC and CBS devoted 0.7% of total Gulf coverage to the war's opponents." Then there was the *Izvestia* style disinformation, like Ed Bradly's report on CBS on January 16, 1991 that it was "eerie" that "there's no one on the streets of New York," on the same night that thousands of protesters were marching in the city. (ibid. 164) Through connivance such as this, the U.S. media outlets waltz with the power brokers, helping to keep the country safe for democracy.

On Values: Freedom

The obvious question is: can "values" be discussed in a vacuum? Can "freedom" be discussed when reference to embarrassing facts is prohibited, or when the rules forbid criticism of structural institutions and conditions which go the root of people's lives? With very little knowledge of life in South Georgia in 1795 one can imagine a mainstream television "anchor" of that era interviewing three establishment intellectuals of the day. One respondent expresses concern about rising unrest among the field "workers," who he says are looked after much better than their fathers were in 1755. He can't help remembering how respectful workers were when he was a boy. Today, he says, in spite of public floggings and incarcerations of criminal types, the roads are not safe for decent plantation folk. Another respondent feels strongly about falling church attendance, and a general lack of morals among younger workers. What is necessary, he believes, is a return to a principled way of life among these people, a moral re-awakening. A third warns that, if the present trend of abusing plantation privileges continues, he can foresee public hangings replacing the cat-o-nine tails for most offenses. He regrets this of course, but thinks it inevitable unless....

Clearly, these 1795 responses and observations are mere propaganda of a "plantocracy" running scared: the message is designed to support the status quo, to dress up a system that inures to the benefit of elites. The various comments tend to deflect attention from core issues, indeed to deny them entirely. The United States is a country which consumes maybe thirty percent of the world's resources yet has some thirty to forty million people, mostly black, living in poverty. Run by an oligarchy in the State Department/Executive Office, who daily thumb their noses at Congress and who

BY THE WAY...

traditionally represent moneyed interests in general and the military industrial complex in particular, that society has much to answer for in its disregard for the sacred values which Noonan and company promise to explore.

Steel puts racism at the root of the "evil" he sees in the American psyche. But he is careful to relegate the problem safely to the past. This makes the subject rather academic and therefore inoffensive to sensitive ears. When he offers the view that society owes nothing to the black man because of his blackness, this must come as a great relief to viewers who were reaching for their channel-changers. Discussing American racism, as it affected him forty years ago, what Steel fails to mention is that it is still very much alive today in his backyard. But of equal concern, it has now shifted overseas. Beginning with the atom bombs dropped on the Japanese (never considered for Germans) racist overtones have marked all major foreign US adventures of recent decades. In the early fifties the bomb was seriously considered for use against the North Koreans.

As for the genocidal Vietnam War the level of Napalm and fire bomb atrocities against an almost defenceless population was shocking in the extreme and can be attributed at least in part to the dehumanizing of yellow-skinned peasant under-classes. But racist intent reached its peak in 1990 against Arabs, followed by thousands of tons of high explosives dropped, once more, on a defenceless population of "lesser breeds" in Iraq. In the decades between these wars of liberation, the U.S economy became more and more dependent on the sales of arms to poor countries (which used them to kill other poor people). These are the "values" which should be discussed and critiqued in the public forum. Who has paid the price for the American dream? Whose nightmare is it?

On Values: Freedom

The Noonan interviews represent "Traditional America." The Founding Fathers are ever present in the background, and in the foreground sentimental, simplistic slogans which promote mindless patriotism. All four participants bemoan in his or her own way what is seen as a loss of innocence in the broader community. But for each of them, the world is viewed from the standpoint of the individual drawn in his or her own image. After all, narcissism is the corner stone of all right-wing thinking, whether in the person of a Rhode Island tycoon, fundamentalist dirt farmer or Jamaican "white man."

If I believe that my success derives from my own moral rectitude, hard work, and good citizenship, it follows naturally that if only other people were like me their problems would disappear. This is the old story of the two men who go up to the Temple to pray. One, a Pharisee stands in the front pew and prays, "God I thank you I am not like other men, or like yonder publican, I tithe, I observe the Law and do not commit adultery." At the same time the publican, a tax collector, stands at the back with bowed head and prays: Lord have mercy on me, a sinner." We are told only the publican's prayer was heard. It is when we stand in the latter's shoes that we are able to see that we are not blameless but share some responsibility for the evils we bemoan.

The common enemy of all establishment elites is "the Left," real or imagined. The left lurks behind everything they detest and is identified with any position not to their taste. In the U.S., generations of vilifying socialism make the left an easy hook on which to hang every piece of political or religious garbage. Like Adam of old, if you can give it a name you are in control. One often hears fundamentalist Christians describe the media as being "on the left." This conclusion is tied to one-issue obsessions, such as the subject of abortion, which a libertine media largely supports. But it is gross

BY THE WAY...

ignorance of how the world operates to hold that big business, as represented by and even embodied in the media, could be on the left. Hardly worth discussing.

To come back to Steel and his charge that the left highjacked the Civil Rights movement and imposed "social engineering" (welfare state) as the solution to racism. This is patently ridiculous. Looking back over the last twenty-seven years, when was the left in power in the U.S.? From Nixon, to Reagan, to Bush: can one imagine more right wing regimes? Of all the leading industrial countries, the U.S. stands supreme in its lack of concern for the poor and disadvantaged. Where does the left get a look-in? It is common knowledge that a social conscience is not a priority of U.S. domestic policy. According to Mel Hurtig, "Although more than seven million U.S. children do not have health insurance, both Ronald Reagan and George Bush cut back social benefits...only 42% of the unemployed have unemployment insurance...thousands of borderline mental cases sleep on the heating grates in Manhattan because of cuts in funding that have thrown them into the street. In 1988 President Reagan, replying to a question concerning the homeless on grates near the White House, said they were there largely out of choice!" *The Betrayal of Canada*, 1991, pgs. 259/260. The idea that a leftist agenda is responsible for America's ills is the product of calculated misinformation on the part of those who benefit from the social disintegration of the society.

Each of the respondents in their discussion about "freedom" opts for superficial observations and solutions regarding U.S. ills. Since the Vietnam War a pervasive jingoistic nationalism has elevated militarism to unprecedented heights, with the first casualty being Truth. Wilson says that the U.S. enjoys "the most prosperous economy," but that money has empowered people to "reach

On Values: Freedom

for shocking things," thus undermining the "traditional value system" (of the Founding Fathers?). This Ivy League view of the economy is denied by Moynihan who points out that median family income in the country has not increased since 1973. But he does not enlarge on this revelation. Noonan conveniently ignores Moynihan's remark, and even contradicts it by repeating her favorite phrase that "in the midst of prosperity" Americans are going off the rails. Is this reputed prosperity confined to that of her panelists and viewers like them? (If readers want a critical look at the devastating sequences of Reaganomics for not-so-fortunate Americans, read *The Politics of Rich and Poor* by Kevin Phillips).

Meanwhile Moynihan, from a lofty vantage point, is busy praising "the world society which we created and which looks so good." That he is not laughed out of the room is doubtless because the general public in the U.S. is the least well informed of all the people of the industrial world. Can Moynihan be referring to East Timor, or El Salvador, or Nicaragua, or Guatemala? Is he talking about the poor people his State Department is starving through embargoes against Iraq or Cuba? He would be the last to recognize that the atrocities visited upon little brown people abroad are merely extensions of the injustices which millions of marginalized Americans experience at home. The concerns expressed in these interviews are as old as western civilization. Eighteen hundred years ago, Tertullian provided the perfect introduction to Ms. Noonan and her guests' adumbrations about the present, set against nirvana of the past, replete with hands-off moralizing and anachronistic references such as "children born out of wedlock."

> "Where is that happiness of marriage, so prospered by morals that in ....six hundred years no house registered a divorce? But nowadays among women no

> limb of the body is not heavy with gold; wine forbids the free kiss; divorce by now is prayed for as if it were the proper sequel of marriage."
>
> *Apologeticus* VI:4-9

Moynihan mentions the fact that one million Americans are in prison: more than any other country on a proportionate basis. But, apparently, his purpose is merely to shock viewers with his forthrightness. A familiar aspect of this type of approach is to cite the horrors on the ground, but to completely ignore the system that hovers above them. This gives stature to the speaker who can then scramble for a safe foothold elsewhere. Exploring why one million Americans are in prison is not for discussion here; even less is the fact that a large segment of the prison population is comprised of poor black citizens. Surely this is an important, visible manifestation of evil in the system, and it certainly touches on the panel's subject of freedom for discussion. But Noonan keeps the agenda on the straight and narrow by very quickly deflecting the issue, interjecting that it is not easy to get into jail in the U.S. The import of this observation is that everyone in jail ought to be there. Viewers need feel no guilt or responsibility for a system that incarcerates only criminals. Next!

What underlies much of the discussion between Noonan and her guests is self-praising propaganda that prosperity, freedom and human rights - the very areas of abject failure in the U.S. - are the hallmarks of U.S. culture. By contrast those countries which have actually succeeded in all three areas, notably the countries of Western Europe and Scandinavia, are mentioned disparagingly, if at all. For U.S. consumption, these countries are always put down by commentators generally as "leftist" (that word again), or gloatingly as "just about to come to their senses." Presumably, that means their adopting economic reforms to reduce or eliminate those social institutions which make them humane, civilized societies.

The Steels, Wilsons and Moynihans must own up to the reality that domestic economic inequality, endemic racism and hegemonic militarism are not definitive of "exceptionalism," but sources of incredulity - if not outright derision – on the part of Norwegians or Swedes. If our ancestors came together as communities in order to free themselves from the arbitrary laws of the jungle, is it too much to ask that those who speak to power climb the mountain and see below the deforestation they have failed to address?

From *Reflections on Our Times*, June 1995

Multilateral Agreement on Investment

The third report, by a Reform Member of Parliament, dealing with the Multilateral Agreement on Investment, speaks volumes about the blurring of party lines in Canada on economic issues. So pronounced is the situation that the Liberal Government was able to enter into secret negotiations with the Reform Opposition, thus reducing significantly this country's ability to manage its economic affairs, that is, absent needed challenges from those across the floor. The reason is not hard to find: both the Liberals and Reform are in bed with big business. If to this coupling we add culpable silence by the media, what we have is a very disturbing scenario. For this reason we can rest assured: the MAI may be shelved for now, but it will be back.

Exactly what is this agreement designed to do? Reform's weak "Opposition" answer is that international investment needs "a level playing field" and the MAI will provide it. Are they serious? They must know what big business has always been about. An international agreement guaranteeing global corporations access to resources and markets, to say nothing of cheap labour, and all these over the heads of indigenous interests and concerns, would achieve many things, but a level playing field is not one of them.

We are told that Reform's main concern is with the Federal Government failing "to clearly explain the agreement to the Canadian public." This is typical political thinking among today's ruling elites: the masses are stupid and can't deal with difficult issues; simply explain to them that you mean no harm and they will return to the hockey match. Or better: let

Presented before the Committee of the New Democratic Party of British Columbia, called to hear objections to Canada signing the *Multilateral Agreement on Investment*, November 1999

BY THE WAY...

the thirty percent of the population, who will benefit from your actions, know what's coming to them, and the other seventy won't matter in an election. Except that Canadians are getting wise to such arrogance. After all the "highly successful campaign waged against the MAI" was won in spite of our Loyal Opposition, not because of it; apart from the would-be thieves falling out over too hastily conceived designs it was real grass root individuals and organizations enjoying only the back pages of local and national media that put the planned travesty on the shelf: a very unsettling result for the ruling elite as Hill's sour grapes attest.

The propaganda of the late twentieth century is that "free markets" will one day bring forth economic salvation for all. Unfortunately, as with every other utopian vision in history, the present generation (except the minority for whom Mr. Hill speaks) must be sacrificed to a glorious, if also very indefinite, future. Neither the Federal Government, nor Reform Opposition benches, seem to have faced some very pertinent facts:

(1) For all the promises made about the North American Free Trade Agreement, Canadians as a whole have not benefitted from the increased sell-off of our businesses and resources in the last eight years. In an inherently wealthy country with an extremely low population, job shortages, child poverty, and food banks have marched in lock-step with GDP advancement. Mr. Hill himself represents a geographical area which, since "free trade" was introduced, has broken every record for the export of resources, yet consistently has suffered fifteen to twenty percent unemployment.

(2) If foreign ownership is accepted as an inevitable part of the solution to the problems of high unemployment and declining standard of living in this country, then maybe proponents of this deal can name one sovereign nation - from

Multilateral Agreement on Investment

Mexico to the southern tip of South America - where over the last forty years such a "solution" has increased the lot of the people as a whole. Surely, there must be one country where unfettered exploitation of resources by foreigners has led to prosperity for the masses.

(3) On the other hand, if it can be shown that currency devaluation and impoverishment of the poorest classes have accompanied unfettered capitalism and "freed-up" markets, let us not elect those who seek to deceive us about these matters.

(4) Are Venezuela and Brazil model economies which Canada should emulate? Jamaica "opened up" its economy in the early eighties and held the distinction of being the new star in Ronald Reagan's Caribbean pantheon. Today, Jamaica has another dubious distinction, this time, of having become the poorest English speaking country in the Western hemisphere. What exempts Canada from these realities? The say-so of Liberal and Reform hacks?

(5) Is the Canadian dollar intrinsically different from the Mexican peso? Recent history has shown that it is not. In many areas of the economy we now have to export forty percent more goods and services in order to earn the same amount of US dollars as we did twenty years ago? By what criteria is this better?

(6) In spite of their present difficulties the Asian countries grew rich in general living standards, and have become powerhouses in manufacturing capability over the last thirty years precisely because they *disavowed* "free market" pretensions. South Korea for example, if judged by Maastricht Treaty criteria right up to late 1997, had better claims to top financial management than Germany. Surpassing giants of the West in basic areas such as budget surpluses, low debt to GDP ratios, and high GDP growth, South Korea, a formerly

BY THE WAY...

peasant-based, agricultural country, became over a very short period of time a leader in the capital intensive ship-building industry, in car manufacturing, and in electronics. Yes, they took a leaf out of Japan's book and it had nothing to do with free trade and do-as-you-please foreign investment. It was the very reverse of such policies.

(7) Meanwhile, Canadians, with all the advantages of abundant resources and the supposed leverage provided by foreign investment (and more recently, free trade agreements), continue to slide towards Third World status - hewers of wood and drawers of water.

The Corporate Agenda: The ideology of the Right is so dominant in Canadian society today that there is no public examination of issues, except in the context of received wisdom. The only contrary view allowed is that ridiculed by those opposing it: hardly fair and open discussion of issues. Shrill put-downs and name-calling have become poor substitutes for debate. All this plays into the hands of corporate agenda-setters. It would be preposterous for our Reform "Opposition" to deny knowledge of this agenda, which has been driving government policy since the imposition of the Free Trade Agreement, the Goods and Services Tax legislation, and NAFTA. The MAI is merely the culmination of a decade of caving in to the present Government's agenda. Only now our weak-kneed approach is aided and abetted by some Opposition members.

In one generation the world has fallen prey to "international capital", which has no home country, is without social conscience, and which answers to no one except faceless speculators driven by greed. These capital flows now hang over the heads of nation states like proverbial vampires. No country is safe from attack. A few years ago, France lost two-thirds of its foreign reserves in three days of attempts to save

Multilateral Agreement on Investment

the Franc from the profit mongering of foreign speculators. The British pound then came under similar attack. Whole nations losing years of collective hard work overnight to predators. What sort of world do we live in that condones grand larceny?

Larceny will be the ultimate result of Canada's signing the Multilateral Agreement on Investment. Not so much among the signature countries themselves (they would disavow any such intent *inter se*), but as between those signatories representing the rich North, and those of the poor South whose resources, human and material, the former seek to control. The hidden agenda of the Agreement targets the resources of the Third World by making "investment" capital, controlled by the North, unavailable to Third World countries unless they come on board. By means of a veritable capital cartel, with not a little black-mail thrown in, twenty nine countries will relegate to themselves the power to expropriate the assets of the rest of the world.

So, if Canada will be in the driver's seat why should we be concerned? The fact is that, apart from Ontario and Quebec, Canada fits more into a Third-World mold than that of an industrial country. Indeed, Provinces like British Columbia have economies indistinguishable from many Third-World economies. Like many of these countries, not only is BC resource-dependent, the exploitation of those resources is very much in foreign hands. There are provisions in the MAI which prevent all levels of government from doing what is in the interests of Canadians. More than this, they hand over to foreigners the right to dictate economic and environmental policy, which is the ultimate betrayal of trust by our elected officials.

In July 1998 the Liberal Government came face to face with the consequences of the foregoing: faced with a "loss of

BY THE WAY...

profits" lawsuit by Ethyl Corp against a ban on the gasoline additive MMT coming into Canada, Ottawa had to back down or risk payment of $370 million to Ethyl. Not only did we beat a hasty retreat legislatively we apologized for suggesting that the product was harmful. The Ethyl challenge was under the NAFTA, which is only a shadow of the MAI in handing sovereignty to foreign corporations. Under the MAI foreign corporations could challenge the right of the BC government to fix stumpage fees in the forest industry at levels regarded as inimical to profits of foreign investors. At the least, the Agreement would be a serious intimidation to present and future provincial governments wishing to manage our forests in the public interest.

Among the worst effects of foreign ownership in any economy, is the ability of the foreign corporation to export their profits. In this writer's opinion Canada, over several generations, has not given this matter its due significance. Poor countries understand what it means to be short of foreign currency. Canada is only recently becoming aware that there is a real difference between Canadian and US dollars.

Many foreign-owned corporations operate exclusively in the local market. This means their earnings are in Canadian dollars, much the same as the rest of us. However, their owners abroad want "hard currency" when profits are remitted to them. Where does that currency come from, if not earned by the corporation itself? It comes from the earnings of others. Trees must be cut down and exported, or other resources or services must earn that hard currency before the corporation can remit its profits abroad. The facility with which Canadians traditionally have been able to buy foreign currency and to do with it as they please, has obscured the reality of the situation. The MAI replicates this not as a privilege, but as a permanent *right* given to non-Canadian

Multilateral Agreement on Investment

corporations, without regard for the sources of their earnings. This means that Canada will have surrendered her sovereign right (and responsibility) to impose exchange controls over the export of foreign currency in times of national crisis, or as part of economic policy.

At present this country is experiencing the greatest decline of its currency in history. One of the most devastating consequences of that decline very shortly will become obvious: the wholesale selling off of Canadian companies to US "investors" taking advantage of the overvalued US dollar. When the dust has settled, Canadians will have lost control of the remaining heights of their economy, so tenuously held at present. Again, the history of Third World economic servitude should bring us up short. What fit of madness prompts us to lose without so much as a murmur, what millions of our poorer relations have lost after decades of struggle? Is it sheer stupidity that blinds us to the obvious? The MAI will cement in place our inability (begun under the old Free Trade Agreement) to do anything about foreigners taking over our prized corporations. Such take-overs constitute net losses to our economy, adding no productive capacity and *not one new job*. They are predatory by nature, with no justification except the extraction of profits. Up until 1989 Canada reserved the right to reject these incursions into our economy. What has changed to make them suddenly acceptable?

But there are other, tangential problems, which have enormous consequences. One of the traditional benefits of foreign investment was the infusion of hard currency into an economy, providing the means for the host country to meet its foreign obligations. Logic, as well as economics, insisted that foreigners pay for their stake in the economy by exchanging a valuable currency for assets and rights extracted, purchased and enjoyed locally. But common sense no longer applies.

BY THE WAY...

Foreign corporations need not invest any foreign currency at all. They may simply borrow Canadian dollars from a Canadian bank to make their purchases. Having put nothing new into the economy they are free to buy foreign exchange (which others have earned) and ship out Canadian-dollar profits. Then, at the end of their sojourn in Canada, they may sell their shares for Canadian dollars if they so wish, and again ship out the proceeds *in foreign exchange* earned by other sectors of the economy. The result is a net loss in foreign exchange reserves, which if multiplied over many such arrangements, impoverish the currency and the country as a whole.

Instead of addressing directly the horrendous implications of these and other MAI provisions, the Reform Opposition has chosen to waffle and prevaricate about the Government's duty to tell us more about the negotiations, and to make excuses worthy only of foreign investors themselves - even using scare tactics concerning pension plans in order to obscure the main issues. In so doing their advocate makes plain the identity of his audience. It seems more important for Reform MPs that the Chamber of Commerce and service club members look favourably upon them, than that Reform look critically at the demands of big business. Those demands only begin, they do not end with Canadians. The underlying purpose of the MAI is to provide cartel status for investment capital to which non-MAI members will have no access. Rich nations will thus be able to stick-handle poor ones into settling for one-sided partnerships, detrimental in the long-term to local economies: veritable gifts- especially in resource sectors - to powerful corporations whose only goal is bettering their stock prices.

Reformers would have us believe that they occupy the high ground in moral rectitude. If so, then may they look beyond the narrow confines of Canadian interests and take a stand for economic justice for all nations. At least they should recognize that in seeking justice for others they will seek it for Canada, if only because our resource-based economy is not far removed from theirs.

Prince George, BC, November 1999.

Subliminal Contradictions

The recent move by the Vatican to recognize a Palestinian State may have been sudden and controversial, but it is an important step towards self-determination for the people of the West Bank and Gaza. Pope Francis has thrown down the gauntlet for non-Catholic churches to do the same. Indeed there is need for a coming together of churches throughout the world to be signatories to a formal declaration recognizing the inalienable rights of Palestinians to life and liberty. For most governments of the developed world to have stood by silent and acquiescent in the face of manifest injustices suffered by 1.8 million Gazans living in squalor and destruction, among many others in like conditions in the West Bank, is a negation of any claim to the Enlightenment by western nations.

But let us take a step back. For two millennia the Christian West blamed Jews for being "Christ-killers" and, in different degrees, questioned or opposed their societal claims. Then, out of the blue in 1962 emerged Vatican Council II, and the revolutionary idea that the Church's stereotyping of a whole people must come to an end. Of course, the new thinking did not emanate only from Rome. Jewish communities were calling for it. After all, the stigma of the accusation underlying anti-Semitism had long been a thorn in their side, and was particularly galling for the newly founded State of Israel, which Rome had refused to recognize on the grounds of deicide.

The Chief Rabbi of Rome was one of the first to officially challenge the status quo. His message sent to the opening ceremony of the Council was unequivocal: The Council must eliminate "all (derogatory) expressions…present in the liturgy" of the Catholic Church. Later, in 1961, in spite of John

BY THE WAY...

XXIII's culling of certain offensive material in the liturgy, the American Jewish Committee charged that many "Anti-Jewish passages remain within the Catholic liturgy." (See Arthur Gilbert)

Clearly, more needed to be done. Why was a prayer for the conversion of the Jews still an official part of Easter Mass in 1961? Well, because tradition demanded it, and, until Vatican II threw cold water on Catholic absoluteness, the liturgy was calling sinful Jews to account. In similar fashion, carefully selected Biblical passages, read from the pulpit at every Mass as the "Word of the Lord," direct the thoughts and actions of those in the pews.

Centuries before Vatican II (going back to 1570) there were two readings at Masses, with the Old Testament contributing some 255 verses of the Bible. However, none of such readings occurred on Sundays, according to *Missale Romanum* (The Catholic Lectionary Website). In the decades after the Council, readings were increased to three in number, and in the new regime one reading was *reserved* for the Old Testament. In total, the latter readings now covered 800-900 verses, presumably, in the wake of Catholic/Jewish rapprochement, none of which would be unfavorable to Israel. Unfortunately, this was not been without consequences. For if Jews no longer had to suffer the humiliations that for years attached to Catholic liturgical practices, suddenly their Nemesis was looking over another shoulder. Now, many liturgical readings excuse, or worse, actually celebrate Zionist positions concerning their supposed rights in Palestine, with no regard for the suffering of dispossessed Arabs under Israel's control.

As the saying goes: history begins where you start the clock. If we start the time-piece in 1917, the Jewish/Palestinian story begins with the Balfour Declaration, the

Subliminal Contradictions

famous *ex parte* "declaration of sympathy" on the part of the British Government, afforded to the Zionist Federation in November of that year. Shortly thereafter, Balfour would glibly write that he saw no purpose in consulting "the present inhabitants of the country" about the matter. This was in keeping with colonial practices of the day, wherein indigenous peoples in India, Australia, Africa, North and South America, etc., were viewed as mere pawns in the hands of empires, for which slavery had once been the norm. It would survive Wilson's so-called aversion to colonialism, in the form of temporary "Mandates" (or Protectorates) given, courtesy of the Versailles Treaty, to the Allied Powers that allowed their dominion over lesser peoples to continue unabated. In this case it was Britain's mandate over Palestine (former colony of the Ottomans) beginning in 1919.

By 1931, the residents of Palestine numbered 1,036,000, of which 175,000 were Jews. In spite of tensions brewing between Zionists and local nationalists, Palestine was a diverse society with a distinctive Arab culture, replete with modern cities and institutions. Up the ante to 1947 and UN Resolution 181, which unilaterally supported the partition of Palestine (minus Jerusalem). What a great hand that was for the Zionists, especially given flagging British interest in the Israeli/Arab dispute at that time, and, more important, the added motivation provided to the Jewish cause in the wake of increasing international awareness of Hitler's atrocities. Except that it was a bad hand for the Palestinians, who immediately up-turned the tables in righteous revolt.

Violence erupted on both sides. During 1947 and the ensuing War of Independence that ended in January 1949, the Israel Defense Force adopted a strategy of "aggressive defense" that targeted Arab cities and villages, of which some 400 were destroyed, along with as much of Palestinian culture: archives, books, and artifacts - lost, or confiscated, many destroyed, or stored in Tel Aviv beyond the reach of Palestinians. The widespread destruction of their homeland and culture, accompanied by ethnic-cleansing, came to be known by Palestinians as al-Nakba (the *Catastrophe*), wherein some 700,000 Arabs were driven out of their homes (most at gun-point), becoming refugees in the Gaza strip, the West Bank (ancient Judea and Samaria), Transjordan, Egypt, Syria and Lebanon - with no compensation or right-of-return.

For the victors, the war's end found 716,000 Jews in Palestine out of a population of 872,000. Israeli propaganda has it that the conflict was a David and Goliath affair, with Israel as the outnumbered underdog defeating marauding Arab armies. This has been shown to be a myth even by Jewish historians. At no time were the Arabs equal to the IDF in number, firepower or organization. Shortly afterwards the Knesset unilaterally made Jerusalem (effectively West Jerusalem) the capital of Israel in spite of UN resolution 303, which had declared the city a *corpus separatum*, to be administered by the UN. (In connection with the last three paragraphs, for sources and discussion, see Slaim, pgs. 28-61 & Rodinson, pgs.22-40))

Palestinians have never recovered from the tragedy they suffered in 1948. Since then they have been marginalized, to say nothing of being maligned, by the international community. Today, they are a wandering people who were forcibly deprived of their homeland by people who once were themselves wanderers, all with the blessing of the West under U. S. tutelage. Of an estimated 12 million Palestinians; 2.8 million scratch out a living as vilified residents, many under tents, in the West Bank, while 1.8 million are incarcerated in Gaza under terrible conditions. The remaining 1.5 are second-class citizens

Subliminal Contradictions

in Israel proper, and 6 million are scattered, mostly as refugees, among various Middle Eastern countries. Yes, there are a few that are well-off in Ramallah (West Bank), but everyone lives under military surveillance in the State of Emergency that has existed in Israel and the Occupied Territories for 67 years.

Even with the biased coverage provided by the Western media (usually reporting from a safe distance in Tel Aviv or Jerusalem), the IDF's indiscriminate military assaults on Gaza, under the rubric of Israel "defending itself," are well known to anyone who watches CNN or the BBC. And yet, news anchors who are quick to condemn *alleged* human rights abuses elsewhere – especially those attributed to such as the Castro government against its citizens - are loath to condemn undisputed IDF targeting of hospitals and schools in Gaza, made more reprehensible when the weapons used are supplied by the United States (in the most recent case, *during* Israeli bombardment of the Strip).

Space does not allow for even a brief overview of injustices, including land seizures, settlement expansions, water resources stolen, Palestinian homes bulldozed in the thousands, burning of farmers' olive trees in the West Bank by settlers, wages of Palestinian workers confiscated or illegally withheld, importation of basic foodstuffs restricted or forbidden - the list is open-ended. The widespread desolation left behind by assaults on Gaza remain ghost-sites, with no hope of residents' rebuilding them for lack even of cement. And all this says nothing of thousands of civilians, women and children, killed by weapons of mass destruction.

The following is one of the stories in the film *Going against the Grain*, profiling Jewish activist, Gideon Levy:

BY THE WAY...

> Fayez is Palestinian; lives in a tent in the West Bank. She is pregnant; labour is imminent. Mother-in-law asks a male family member to take them to hospital He drives them to the nearest check-point - soldiers refuse his car passage. He rushes to the next checkpoint, but again they refuse him passage. When he returns to the car he finds that Fayez has given birth in full view of soldiers. In spite of her condition, she must get the baby to the hospital; so in her parlous condition she sets off on foot. At the hospital the baby is found to be weak and is admitted, but Fayez is discharged and walks home. Next morning she is back at the hospital, where she learns the baby died.

In his story for Haaretz newspaper, Levy's rage is palpable. This is his example of Israelis *"dehumanizing Palestinians - then it becomes easy to kill them...Who the hell are...those soldiers who saw Fayez Abu Dahouk in pain as she delivered her baby in a car, [then allowed her] to wrap the infant in her clothes and walk two Kilometers to reach the hospital?"*

Is it not time Catholics asked hard questions about their Church's role in the Palestinian tragedy? Does the Church not have responsibilities that transcend guilt over past injustices to the Jewish people, responsibilities that take account of injustices to Palestinians? Advocating for a Palestinian State is not enough.

Throughout the Church's roster of Sunday liturgies First Readings often are outright gifts to Israeli Governments that have exercised colonial rule over Palestine. Passages such as:

From: *Living with Christ* Sunday Missal, for 2005-2006:

"I will appoint a place for my people Israel, and will plant them, so that they may live in their own place, and be disturbed no more…and I will give you rest from your enemies" (pg. 87 Samuel).

"Then the Lord became jealous for his land, and had pity on his people" (pg. 164 Joel).

Abraham's offspring "shall possess the gate of their enemies…" (pg. 175 Genesis).

"I will be their God and they shall be my people….I will forgive their inequity, and remember their sin no more" (pg. 206 Jeremiah).

"I will bring you back to the land of Israel; I will place you on your own land" (pgs. 210/211 Ezekiel).

From the Missal for 2006-2007:

"To your descendants I give this land, from the river of Egypt to the great river, the river Euphrates" - God's Covenant with Abram (Genesis 15).

From the Missal for 2015-2016:

"I am the Lord who brought you from Ur of the Chaldeans, to give you this land to possess." (Genesis 15).

"All this land that I have promised I will give to your descendants, and they shall inherit it forever." (Exodus 32).

Again, on the vexed question of Jerusalem, numerous readings throughout the liturgical year add to the subliminal propaganda for Israel. With no mention being made of Jerusalem in the Pentateuch, these passages are necessarily from the *later* books of the Hebrew Bible. The curious thing is that in modern times the origin of that city's iconic status was as much Christian as it was Jewish. In England and the Continent, it was in 1842 that a Christian bishopric was founded in Jerusalem. In the United States, Zionism as a movement goes back to the nineteenth century largely in

BY THE WAY...

the form of Christian (Evangelical) Zionism, which predated Jewish adoption of the cause in that country. (See Andrew Preston, for discussion.)

The story of the ambivalent attachment of Jews to the idea of the Land of Israel and their equally ambivalent attachment to Jerusalem as a *physical* location, are eminently covered by Shlomo Sand in his book *The Invention of the Land of Israel*. According to this professor of history at the University of Tel Aviv, the fact that in the late eighteenth century there were five thousand Jews living in Palestine as against 250,000 Christians and Muslims, at a time when most of the two and a half million Jews in the world lived in nearby Eastern Europe, "reflects more effectively than can any written text the nature of the Jewish religion's tie to the Holy Land up to that time" (p.117).

The Easter Vigil Mass includes carefully selected Biblical passages recalling Judeo/Christian progression over millennia. Most are from the Hebrew Scriptures, one of the most telling being the story of Moses leading the Israelites out of captivity in Egypt, and God's parting the Red Sea for them to do so. Can this story be read except as a subliminal derogation of Arabs *today*? After all, if it can be said to be history at all, it is not about some distant past wherein bad guys like Amalekites, Philistines, Ammonites, Amorites, or Gibeonites are put to the sword with God's help. No, sir. Here, Yahweh is inveighing against *Egyptians*. Moses is ordered to stretch his hand over the Red Sea "that the waters may flow back on the Egyptians and their chariots and their horsemen." This Moses does, and "the fleeing Egyptians marched right into it, and Yahweh overthrew the Egyptians in the very middle of the sea; not a single one of them was left" (Ex. 14: 26-29).

In an age when Israel and Egypt have been involved in two major wars, when deep-seated racism has defined the policies of successive Israeli governments towards Arabs, where is the "political correctness" (observed by the Church in not highlighting the many misogynistic and other human rights transgressions cited in the Hebrew Scriptures as approved by God) that should attend red-hot issues in the Middle East today? Were scriptural readings offensive to Arabs the result of blind ignorance on the part of Rome? Or were they part of Rome's "contrition" for injustices and prejudice against Jewish communities over the centuries, which the Vatican Council accepted some fifty years ago? If so, wrongs against one People were absolved by their morphing into wrongs against another.

I attend a Sunday Mass during which one of the prescribed readings is from Deuteronomy. It extolls God's favours bestowed *by any means whatsoever* on the Chosen People. The rhetorical question, emphasizing the unique character of God's intervention on behalf of the Jews, is: "…has any god ever attempted to go and take a nation for himself from the midst of another nation, by trials, by signs and wonders, by war, by a mighty hand…and by terrifying displays of power….?" (Deut. 4.34) The reason for choosing this passage escapes me, coming as it does from one of the oldest and more obscure books of the Bible; unless, of course, it is meant as *a political statement for today*. Absent that, it reeks of insensitivity on the Church's part for disseminating among the Faithful the idea that God approved what transpired in Palestine in 1947/48.

Whatever deal was cut between aggrieved Jewish communities and Rome fifty-odd years ago, when the Church was called upon to expunge her liturgy of anti-Semitism, if in 2016 Pope Francis is sincere about a Palestinian State he must revisit the Church's liturgical reforms following Vatican II. Today, they go overboard in providing succor for

BY THE WAY...

successive Israeli Governments' seizure of Palestinian land and excuses for demonizing a down-trodden people. Far from mere messages celebrating Jewish traditions and aspirations, current Biblical readings of the kind mentioned above, repeated as they are year in and year out, promote contempt for any conciliatory word for Palestinians coming from Rome. Instead, the readings are a form of brainwashing, implanting in the minds of Catholics worldwide, narrow, atavistic truisms about the Holy Land – truisms, made sacrosanct by Holy Writ, that categorize protests against an Apartheid regime as terrorism, while excusing Israeli atrocities as necessary evils in preserving God-given rights. The story has it that Israel is "defending" itself. This shame-faced lie by a nuclear power with full support from the USA, speaks volumes for Gideon Levy's position that Israel is the only occupier ever to go about claiming to be the victim.

From *Reflections on Our Times*, Prince George, November 2016

Operation Desert Storm *was launched in early 1991 when an international coalition under US auspices forced Saddam Hussein to abandon Kuwait, which he had occupied, relying on questionable US acquiescence. The "First Gulf War", as it came to be called, saw 200,000 bombing sorties reign fire and destruction on Iraqi communities and infrastructure, before Herbert W. Bush called an unexpected halt to the carnage, leaving Hussein in power after all. A hot war gave way to a silent one, in which no-fly zones were established over southern Iraq and sanctions inflicted on the entire civilian population. The excitement at an end, the Western media went home.*

War and Pieces

Forty days have passed during which the world has lived in varying degrees of apprehension and/or revulsion following the US lead coalition's mobilization against Saddam Hussein. Since January 16, 1991 the world has been inundated with propaganda justifying the killing and maiming of Iraqis. To my recollection, never before has a relatively insignificant leader been vilified and demonized to the extent that Mr. Hussein has been. But then, in order to give this "war" credence, it was necessary to have a worthy foe; if he did not exist it would have been necessary to create him. From the early days of sanctions following the Iraqi army's excursion into Kuwait last year, the US media have been parroting White House vitriol against Hussein, never being able to take an objective view even in the face of blatant coalition atrocities. Throughout the grim proceedings of these past six weeks, even Canada's supposed free and impartial media have been conspicuous for their "patriotic" bias, with seldom, if ever, a side glance at the truth staring them in the face: whether it be US control over Middle East oil resources,

Extracted from *Reflections on Our Times*, February 1991

BY THE WAY...

concern for Israeli (therefore US) hegemony in the region, or most important, concern over US arrogance in initiating the use of military force against a sovereign country.

Following the end of the Cold War, the Pentagon desperately needed an enemy to underwrite its importance as part of the US economy, indeed to justify its existence. What more could it hope for but a hot war that not only has put on hold all opposition to the military budget, but also has served as the most impressive armaments "Expo" in decades. If thirty percent of the US economy is comprised of war materiel, what could be more vital in this recession than a shot in the arm from military sales at home, augmented by sales abroad - complements of a media blitz in favour of war. Into this den of hungry beasts walked a ruthless, though naïve, Saddam Hussein. An old Jamaican saying is that "Cockroach has no business in fowl-coup." The plan from the outset was that he not escape by merely withdrawing from Kuwait. Once in that chicken-coup Saddam would not be allowed to leave before he heard the wings. Too late did he find out that sharp claws and beaks were but a swoop away.

In prosecuting this not-so-hidden agenda to humiliate him by force of arms, the coalition has carpet-bombed his troops, used Napalm against them and asphyxiated them with petrol munitions that explode above the ground sucking the air out of the most secure foxholes - to say nothing of the depleted uranium in munitions left behind in southern Iraq. In the process, countless thousands of Iraqi civilians have been killed or maimed for life – compared with next to no coalition casualties. All of which has been grist for the CNN war-mill, making for explosive coverage and high ratings. With no body-bags coming home and pervasive censorship of US atrocities in the Gulf, the result has been orchestrated hype fueled by a hate-object in Saddam Hussein, whose archetypal image blots out the blood in the sand. Every day, Newspeak proclaims it as truth that we destroy others in order to save them; kill the defenseless in order that they may live another day; wage homicidal war in order to secure lasting peace. So long as we are believers, how reassuring "truth" can be.

Ten months later...

Starvation looming: from *Reflections on Our Times,* Nov. 1991

A very brief report in the *Prince George Citizen* recently was about an imminent health crisis in Iraq. It was very instructive of the minimal interest in that country taken by western media since the Gulf War. During that tragic event both press and television coverage of our courageous efforts to bring peace, justice, and democracy to the region were dominated by accounts of atrocities carried out by Iraq against the Kurds – 5000 of whom Hussein was reported to have killed with poison gas. The media script could have been written by our war lords, so well did it fit into their purpose to blast Iraq into kingdom come.

Since our glorious victory over Iraq, and incidentally, our killing and maiming of upwards of 100,000 Iraqis - including tens of thousands shot in the back as they fled Kuwait - our hard-punching, uncensored media have taken great pains to report as little as possible about the dire situation in the country. The reason, of course, is that the latest atrocities are our own. Having destroyed the country's infrastructure, and decimated the Iraqi people, the conveniently styled "United Nations" victors are many months into draconian sanctions against war-torn people. These sanctions prevent an otherwise viable economy from functioning, by confining marketable oil resources to holes in the ground. Added to this, the sanctions deny food to the hungry and medicines to the sick. According to some

BY THE WAY...

reports, only 20% of the population (rather than the 30% mentioned in your article) have access to clean water.

Where is the western media in all of this? Except for a few cryptic reports such as the one mentioned above, there has been virtual silence since the ticker-tape parades celebrating the bloodbath. So what if 170,000 children are expected to die by the end of next month. And let us not sit back easing our consciences by blaming Iraq's "nuclear capability" and the other drummed up excuses (Hussein still at large, etc.) for this genocide.

The sad corollary is that crippling sanctions are still extant against Vietnam, against Cambodia, against Cuba – all countries which years ago defied or somehow defeated our good friends to the south – all cases where the other side has been branded totalitarian and an enemy by the Pentagon, whose post-conflict policies are designed to punish the little people and bring out the worst in the surviving regime. Indeed, now that Iraqis are at desperation point, what better news could be forthcoming than that of a repressive clamp-down by Mr. Despot himself.

Iraq's parlous situation is far beyond the "health crisis" stage suggested by your lower-case headline. Instead of relegating inconvenient truths to back pages the Canadian press should be revealing big-power vindictiveness against downtrodden countries, and urging Canada to have no part in it.

Conspiracy theory?

Saddam Hussein's recent deployment of troops on the Kuwait border has attracted attention to Iraq's plight following years

Three years later still... Published by the *Prince George Citizen*, October 1994

War and Pieces

of media silence in the wake of Desert Storm. Suddenly, the international news media are back in his country and, hopefully, cannot help but comment on the suffering wrought by the embargo. Whatever his intentions may have been, his saber-rattling has reignited interest in the country, and should be the catalyst for media action on other fronts. Three years ago a policy designed to impoverish if not starve Iraqis was put in place by the United States under a trumped up UN mandate, with the likes of Canada on board, and with full connivance of the mass media. Since 1991 the consequences of this perversion have been covered by the media only circumspectly, and then only to underline official truth: Mr. Hussein must go, and the Iraqi people will do the job for us.

Today, a year has passed since a Catholic News Service dispatch out of Baghdad by John Travis made it clear that "because food is scarce and medical supplies are practically non-existent...the young and the old are dying off in large numbers." For the most part it has been the minors such as CNS that have forced Western consciences to even admit that there is a human tragedy on the ground in Iraq. The major media players have been happy in the role of lap-dogs at White House press conferences. The recent Globe & Mail's Focus on Iraq: *Making Children Pay* was therefore long overdue. But important questions have yet to be voiced. What is this embargo really about? Does the official truth stand up to scrutiny? Why have establishment positions drowned out the John Travises for so long? From the outset, the Western media have been pre-occupied with a pervasive invective against Hussein. Righteous anger at this monster's survival in power is the order of the day. No one asks, why then was he left in power after the most crushing defeat of any country in a war since Japan after Hiroshima? This anomaly has never been addressed satisfactorily: indeed, the Canadian Government

BY THE WAY...

and our "free press," with all its trappings of probity and objectivity, have been very adept at looking the other way.

But the compelling assumption must be that Mr. Hussein would not be in power if it was not convenient that he should be. Using that as our axiom we can deduce that in 1991 the United States did not want him gone, whatever their excuses to the contrary. Then, by extending the argument one step further, the unthinkable conclusion stares us in the face: the US has been dreading the day that sanctions actually work in deposing him! Bizarre? No better place to begin our quest than among the sand dunes.

On July 25, 1990 US ambassador, April Glaspie, was invited to attend a friendly meeting with Hussein and his foreign minister, Tariq Aziz - a conference well-documented in *Before the Storm,* Bennis & Moushabeck, Eds., 1991. Glaspie was advised of Iraq's concerns over Kuwait's incursions on their common border, and, given that the world price of oil had fallen below $22 a barrel, Kuwait's alleged dumping of oil, which Iraq regarded as Iraqi property siphoned off from below the border. According to the minutes of the meeting, Glaspie's reply was unconditional: "We have no opinion on Arab-Arab conflicts, like your border disagreements with Kuwait." This was the green-light Hussein then thought he had gotten from his trusted ally, the US, to move into Kuwait if he saw fit. We know it now as the trap into which he fell headfirst.

But let us look ahead of that pivotal meeting to the situation in Iraq after Desert Storm. The country had suffered billions of dollars of damage. To pay for rebuilding the infrastructure from the bottom up, to say nothing of feeding millions of displaced people caught in an economic vacuum, a new Iraqi government would have to liquidate oil resources

War and Pieces

beginning on armistice day, if not before. Iraqi dumping would be infinitely greater than Kuwait's possibly could have been.

It is no secret that below $20 a barrel the US oil industry is in trouble. For some time the price had fallen below that price. What would it be if Iraq began inundating world markets: catastrophe at $13? Disaster at $10? Surely, the answer was not to allow this to happen. But there was no way to prevent it if Saddam was gone and "democracy had been restored", as it had been in Kuwait, of course. How could we then refuse the poor bastards anything?

There was only one "solution" to this problem. Hussein must remain in power at all costs. So long as the Monster was in Bagdad, western public opinion would be prostrate before any rationale for punishing Iraq that the US cared to provide. The war over and Kuwait oil now under US supervision, what more convenient retribution against his regime than a blanket embargo of the economy, the avowed purpose of which was to force Hussein out of power through civil unrest? A brilliant idea, except for the slight embarrassment of a few million starving people. But hold on: given media connivance few of us beyond the Arab world would know, much less care that these people existed! With the embargo in place, oil prices would stabilize; the industry would breathe easier. To keep a tight lid on things, enter the Western media; or more to the point, *exeunt*.

Prince George, October 1994

Note: In his letter of October 2, 1997 to the U.N. Security Council, as reported by *The Prairie Messenger*, Ramsey Clark - former U.S. Attorney General - charged Council members, particularly the U.S.,

BY THE WAY...

with causing through sanctions, the deaths of "750,000 human beings, perhaps twice that many, the great majority being infants, children, older people and those who have suffered serious chronic illnesses." This he said violated the Genocide Convention. Every Council member who voted to continue the sanctions would therefore be guilty of a heinous crime. Nevertheless with only minor variations, genocidal sanctions against the Iraqi population continued for another six years.

Thatcher's Enduring Legacy

Britain's parlous economic situation today began in the 1980s when the country bore the brunt of Mrs. Thatcher's innovations based largely on privatization. The process verged on criminality given that garage-sale disposals of public assets were ruinous for the society in many respects. (Of course, she had denied that the society existed.)

The main beneficiaries of privatization were top quintile taxpayers, and foreigners. To patch holes in budgets assets were sold at huge discounts. For example: Rolls Royce 73% and British Airways 70%. Similarly, sales of Jaguar and British Telecom resulted in scandalous profit-taking by insiders. In BT's case the premium was 2.5 billion pounds on the offer price in the first day of trading! Indeed the massive oversubscriptions for such plumbs – 8 times for Jaguar and 4 for BT - point inexorably to the UK government lining the pockets of insiders, through fire-sales of what belonged to the people. (Copy: dumping of public assets by Central and Eastern European countries in the 1990s - inspired by the IMF and World Bank - together with the usual open-market "solutions" to everything, that decimated their economies, to say nothing of the evisceration of Russia's economy during those years in favour of oligarchs.)

Ironically, Thatcher's neo-liberal plan for "smaller government" came to naught largely through her own "efficiencies." She had put thousands out of work in coal and other sectors, many with no bread to eat and only the *government* to provide what passed for cake. Five years later, government expenditures were at the same level as when she took power. What else but to sell more and more furniture to pay for groceries? Eventually, the railways fiasco and the moral hazard it offered "investors," would be the crowning disasters of the

BY THE WAY...

Thatcher doctrine. As for the assists that prolonged the Iron Lady's reign? One was an act of war and the other an Act of God - the Falklands and North Sea Oil. Today, the first is not over, and the second is.

Ed. Version; orig. pub. *Economia* mag. on Lady's passing, 2013

British Columbians are remembering Baroness Thatcher. Currently, thousands are marching against the Provincial Government's agenda smacking of her policies that were carefully concealed prior to the election; while, in the halls of power, the usual suspects rub their hands in anticipation of the largess they voted for. They are drooling over public assets after eight years of pandering to unions and other pariahs by "leftists."

First, the new Premier reduced taxes, then without blinking, said "BC has no money, so let the pain begin." As expected, the media are on call. We hear the message repeated time after time: Something had to be done. Sure, like massive transfers of wealth from the poor to the rich. And, oh yes, the present must be sacrificed to a Utopia that is just out of sight. So, have faith! At some indeterminable future date our man's genius and compass-sion will be revealed to all. We may be even raptured up to right-thinking Alberta. It just happens that Calgary is distinctive in being the city with the highest child-poverty rate in Canada

Back in BC the politicians who in opposition boasted of their business acumen, soon will be selling stuff to pay provincial bills. Their downsizing, garage-sale doctrine is Thatcherism writ large - "Ground-Zero Capitalism" that depends on fire-sales of productive public assets, so that "new beginnings" will rise from the ashes. By the way, it's no secret that "business friendly" governments come gunning for the North in order to enrich the South. Prince George and region will be in Victoria's cross-hairs.

From reflections on our times; Prince George, BC, March 2002

Postscript: British Columbia remained under this government for 16 years during which valuable public assets such as BC Ferries and BC Rail were sold for little, health care and education were compromised, and tax cuts made to favour the wealthy. By 2017 BC ranked first among the provinces in wealth inequality and 2nd[h] out of the 10 in poverty rating.

July 2017

CONUNDRUMS

Why I'm Not Born Again

Will we ever face the fact that religious controversy is here to stay, so long as people are on this earth? The same question obtains in the political arena, in social discourse, in economic matters. Intellectual dysfunction is endemic to progress in human understanding. For years Jamaican expatriates have been embroiled in emotional issues arising out of the great exodus from the island in the 1970s. Today, with the struggle of "coming out" on the wane, other preoccupations have surfaced among a once Catholic segment that has turned to the Bible, reflecting maybe the inevitable drift we all experience towards senility and death. After all, religion has always provided us with a refuge from the storm, and presumably will continue to do so for those who embrace fundamentalist ideology.

Looking back over many years, I have spent maybe too much of my free time in so-called academic pursuits; yet today I feel it would take another thirty years before I knew anything at all. The old saying is that the more you learn is the more you realize how little you know. This is not the case with those who turn to "religion." For such people it seems all quest for knowledge, outside of their narrow field of enquiry, ceases. Similar patterns can be discerned in the lives of political extremists and in the many cults which claim to open the doors of "knowledge" for their members. The great anomaly is that "the truth" does not set us free. As Isaiah Berlin aptly put it, "All the great liberating ideas eventually turn into suffocating straight-jackets, which in turn are liberated by new, and, at the same time, enslaving conceptions." Evangelicalism, in the form of unattached,

A commentary on *Jimmy Swaggart* articles that came to hand, February 1984

BY THE WAY...

self-appointed preachers and their followers - began around the 1520s, with men like Luther, Calvin and Zwingli. As harbingers of the Reformation, they brought new light to bear on old issues and renewed Christianity, which in the form of Catholicism at that time had become a straight-jacket. Since then, Christianity has undergone several other renewals, the latest being *The Second Vatican Council*. On the other hand, fundamentalist Evangelicalism, if that is not a tautology, has become a tired cliché, except to those who want to retreat into themselves. In saying this I have no desire to hurt anyone's feelings about the matter. At the same time it is impossible to address what are essentially emotional issues without saying some things that may hurt.

When, on a Sunday morning I have turned on the TV and seen Evangelical preachers pirouetting with Bible in hand outstretched, I have been amazed at the gullibility of so many people who seem to want simple answers to everything. As one philosopher has said, the great problem of modern man is his refusal to think. North American mass consumer society has accentuated this problem by ingesting art and culture and then spewing it into the gutter. The result is a barrage of instant replays. Mr. Swaggart is a perfect reflection of consumer religion, a variety of Bro Anansi guaranteeing instant relief in one gulp. In this make-believe bubble the good life is only a beauty product away. Just spray on 'Channel No 5' and you will be a new person with the world at your feet. The corporations that spend millions on these simplistic messages, almost insulting to our intelligence, know well what viewers want. They want their egos massaged; need to believe that eternal youth comes bottled. But does the fact that many buy the product prove that the sponsor's messages are true? Instant salvation, like instant beauty or manliness, has a powerful appeal, especially for those captivated by a

Why I'm Not Born Again

hedonistic culture that promises escape from the real world. Any high school kid will tell us that this is easily achieved by the "quick fix."

If you have read this far you may wonder why I have not tried to address Mr. Swaggart's criticisms aimed at the Catholic Church. The reason is that it would be a pointless exercise to do so: much like criticizing a TV commercial. Those committed to a product are not easily dissuaded, unless maybe by another more potent variety. In any event, how can one have an intellectual debate with ideologues who not only cherry-pick the "Word of God" to suit their argument, but also rewrite history itself? They say what adherents want to hear, otherwise they would not impress them with their vitriol. If however, you are interested in an honest, objective view of the past, don't rely on those who have a vested interest in changing it. To begin with, a good encyclopedia is all one needs. The cardinal rule in looking at history is not putting too much, if any, reliance on anyone who professes a strong ideological bias.

The past is not what it was but rather what historians say it was. The "facts" have little significance of themselves; the selection, and, most important, the interpretation of those facts are what is important. If, therefore, one wishes to seriously examine early Christianity with even a modicum of objectivity, one cannot turn to those who have axes to grind. If one is researching German history one does not rely on *Mein Kampf* as a conclusive reflection of the people unless, of course, one is of a particular persuasion.

The difficulty with fundamentalist Biblical exegesis has to do with accepting the Bible as history - in the modern sense of the word - and basing arguments on literal rather than metaphorical interpretations of passages. This practice has been exaggerated in recent years by the resurgence of "Bibliolatry" as an escape from the onerous business of thinking. In this regard, various 'proofs' of the Bible appear in bookstores detailing archeological findings concerning biblical events. What does not appear to be understood, however, is that proof of the historical existence of people and places does not make a particular account of events history. We can be fairly sure that Caesar existed; the ruins of ancient Rome are plain for any tourist to see. But this does not mean that Shakespeare's 'Julius Caesar' is definitive history. If then we imagine Martians coming to earth and accepting this work as prophetic history we can also picture ourselves answering the doorbell to green old ladies come to quote the words of Mark Anthony and the deeds of Brutus. Doubtless, we would smile and send them on their way. In high school I was versed in some of these sayings and doings and memorized long tracts for recitation at elocution contests. My "learning' would have made those Martians green with envy. Today, if I look back at my ignorance it is not that words failed me when I got up to speak or set pen to paper in an exam. Rather it is because I knew nothing of the lust for power or corruption in politics that these plays dramatized. It is because I understood with the mind of a boy and Shakespeare was not writing for children. Biblical fundamentalists live in a permanent state of adolescence, more the tragedy because they see themselves as subject to forces beyond their control.

Again, to quote Isaiah Berlin, the propensity of Western man for totalitarian structures is not a terrible aberration but a logical development of the major assumption in all the central currents of Western thought: that there is a fundamental unity underlying all phenomena, deriving from a single universal purpose which when discovered (through scientific enquiry, religious revelation or metaphorical speculation) will provide men with a final solution. This faith is rooted in traditional

Why I'm Not Born Again

morality, the yearning for absolutes, which often translates into an urge to shed responsibility for what one does by transferring it to a vast impersonal monolithic whole: nature, or history or class or 'the Word of God.'

Throughout the history of Christianity many have been slaughtered according to "The Word" by Catholic and non-Catholic alike: from the Spanish Inquisition (and before) to English puritans in Salem, Massachusetts where in 1692, as a result of accusations by some teenage girls more than 30 persons were convicted of witchcraft, some after torture. Many were executed, one by being pressed between weighted planks for his refusal to plead guilty or not guilty. Women feared worst of all in those times because of the biblical command "you shall not permit a sorceress to live" Ex. 22:18. Heretics too were condemned to death for perversions of the "truth" between the 11th and 16th centuries.

The modern variation is more subtle but no less diabolical. Fundamentalist preachers of today profess love, but consign to hellfire most of the world's peoples. Of course it is not the Jimmy Swaggarts or Tom Stokes who pass sentence. Predictably, they disclaim responsibility for Satan's fork transfixing Catholics, Muslims and Hindus to Hell's half acre. Such matters they leave to the Bible, the final authority on inscrutable truth. For as Jonathan Swift opined, "men have just enough religion to hate each other, but not enough for love."

If there are aversions that the "Saved" have above all others, the two most pervasive are intellectual pleasures, and anything that contributes to fun or "worldliness". Some are more saved than others. These are sequestered in small groups, which avoid interaction with the world and 'worldly people'. For them, morality has something to do with expectant waiting for the Spirit to descend, and bodies to ascend at the Rapture, the idea being to overcome everything impulsive and "irrational" in the meantime. These sects are exclusive communities of the elect waiting for God (their God). As true believers they are direct products of asceticism founded by, but not exclusive to, the "Reformed" wing of Reformation Europe and exported to North America by Puritans and their fellow travelers fleeing religious persecution.

One of the anomalies of human nature is that a person's ideological commitment is as weak or as strong as the things he or she has to give up are important. Sacrifice means commitment. This powerful psychology of deprivation has not been lost on the promoters of the Asian cults and the various political extremist groups that have sprung up in recent times. Since, by nature, man is pleasure loving, much energy will be harnessed for "the cause" if the baser instincts are curtailed. It is therefore important that biblical passages be found to support austerity (except the making of money) and self-restraint, and to strike fear of damnation into the hearts of those who transgress.

But be it far from me to disparage, out of hand, all who wish to withdraw from the world. Many religious take vows of poverty, chastity and obedience; the saints throughout history in one way or another denied themselves worldly pursuits. But giving up certain things for the greater glory of God is not the same as having a hang-up about normal secular life. Indeed the idea of saving oneself for God becomes a terrible delusion if one can then sit only in the front bench at church. What should be an ennobling way of life, so easily becomes a way of seeing oneself as superior to the "great unwashed" of the earth: the "Lord, I am thankful that I am not like the rest of men…" syndrome.

Following from the above it has been my observation that

Why I'm Not Born Again

the Born Again pay a lot of attention to externals, judging others by surface criteria. Because they believe that pleasure is in some respects questionable, almost anything which is associated with a 'good time' is looked down upon. This can lead to ridiculous conclusions. For example, the Puritans a century ago opposed the sport of bearbaiting, not because it gave pain to the bear, but because it gave pleasure to the spectators. But the real battle is more personal than this. A woman should not wear make-up, and must dress becoming of a matron; the eleventh command-ment is "Thou shalt not drink alcohol," the twelfth, "Thou shalt not dance." The greatest evil in the world is the evil of 'the flesh', great pains being taken to shun anything and everything dealing even vaguely with sex. This prudishness which pervades Born Again thinking (to the extent that sister leaves brother's wedding because guests are dancing) is an important aspect of the herd mentality, which characterizes fundamentalism. By promoting this behavior the leader of the flock guards against outside contamination of his proselytes and puts to work the deprivation-psychology mentioned above. One wonders what these folks would do if they saw Christ daily eating and drinking with the 'sinners' on Davie Street. Would they leave Him, as presumably they left the wedding at Cana long before the best wine was served?

I guess the point I am trying to make is that too much avoidance born of fear leads to myopia; emphasis on one or two Commandments becomes an end in itself, shutting out the big picture. It is accepted that, as bulwarks of capitalist society, Born Again Christians must interpret very narrowly the meaning of the seventh and tenth commandments. Again, there are many qualifications narrowing down the fifth commandment. However, the same cannot be said about the sixth and ninth, which apparently are more causes for concern to conservative Christians than the millions who starve to death on their television screens.

At the risk of becoming tedious, I will conclude this diatribe with hopefully only a few words on a matter which impacts too directly the discussion thus far to be omitted. This is the total preoccupation of the saved with Pauline theology. It is as if the whole Bible is to be found between the book of Acts and the letter to the Hebrews. Never a quotation from James, seldom a quotation even from the Gospels. It is not clear how this selectiveness can be justified when the Bible in its entirety is otherwise held to be the "Word of God." Paul writes as a man of his time reflecting the prejudices of his time, especially with regard to women and "the flesh." His repulsion for the world is reflected in other early teachers, and extends even to the Jewish sects of that era, as can be seen clearly in the Dead Sea Scrolls.

Accordingly, it is absurd to attempt to transplant Paul's views in total from the 1st century to the 20th. When he wrote, the earth was flat and the sun travelled around it; heaven was up in the sky and hell under the earth; death was the result of sin not the consequence of bodily degeneration. The fact is, Paul came out of a male chauvinist community natural to his fellow Jews, and reflected the eschatological beliefs of the Jewish sects of that time, who were patiently waiting for the final battle between Good and Evil. In this context he was not writing for 1984 and cannot be transplanted into our era without qualification. If the Jimmy Swaggarts of this world believe otherwise, let them ponder another fact, which is that those who accompanied Christ on his various journeys did not have Pauline theology to light their way.

Finally, when we speak of the Bible as the 'Word of God' let us not have visions of bolts from the sky or tablets from a mountain. Between the first and fourth centuries there was no

Bible as we understand it. Indeed there was much controversy in some areas as to which writings should be included in what we call the "New Testament," and which should be excluded therefrom. This was a human debate that no voice from heaven resolved. In the second century, for example, Credo, one of the prominent heretical teachers of that time who rejected most of Paul's letters (along with The Revelation of John), was excommunicated at Rome in 150 A. D. - a mere two or three generations after Paul's death.

There were many other controversies which the early Bishops had to settle before the books of the Bible were finally agreed upon in the fourth century. If Bible-Belt Christians accept the result of these deliberations as the Word of God, should they not interpret that Word in its broadest context?

Extracted from *Reflections on Our Times*, 1984.

Postscript: In this piece I did not mean to be critical *exclusively* of "Born Again" or Evangelical precepts and practices. My criticisms of Catholic fundamentalism are well documented.

Pre-Vatican II Catholicity
Introduction
Ten years ago I published a paper entitled *What Lies Beneath*, in which I discussed control exercised by the Catholic Church over its members in the 1950s, leading up to the Second Vatican Council in the early 1960s. The paper took the form of a review of a book about moral and sociological issues of those days, as seen through clerical eyes. My purpose was not to suggest that the same viewpoint persisted into the 2000s, as readers of my book *Testament of the Third Man* may have assumed from the original introduction to the paper and its title, for lots of things regarding Church practices had changed in the decades after the Council. What follows below is an attempt to put "What Lies Beneath" in its proper context.

That said, I sense there are currently factions in the North American Church that would welcome the return of old authoritarian answers to moral questions. The evidence is a revival of Catholic Evangelicalism that paradoxically seemed to accompany the anointing of Francis, in spite of the new Pope's pronouncements on issues ranging from homosexuality, to reinstating divorced Catholics; from the plight of Palestinians, to women ostracized because of a past abortion. Although these sentiments have been welcomed by liberal Catholics as wake-up calls for the Church, various strata are not impressed. Nascent conservatism now is visible at the top, while below there is a growing distance between altar and pew. Discursive group meetings, covering social justice issues and the like, have morphed into personal devotions found in ornate pamphlets; in Rosary Days and Holy Water sprinklings; in Benediction Expositions, and readings of the "Office." More and more, it seems the Faithful are treated as uncritical observers of priestly divinations.

When first published ten years ago, *What Lies Beneath* may well have been unfairly accusative of the post Vatican II Church. If so, my apologies. However, in the wake of what appears to be the new direction the Church, coupled with the backlash against Pope Francis, I trust readers will forgive my reprinting the paper.

A review of *Handbook of Moral Theology* by D. M. Prummer, 1963

BY THE WAY...

Five centuries have passed since the Lutheran Reformation in 1517. Thereafter began the proliferation of Christian churches and sects, each one anxious to attract (and hold onto) members committed to a particular version of the Truth that will set us free. Fast forward to the 1950s and the days of door-knocking by Evangelicals with Bibles in hand, Mormon youths come to sell the revelations contained in the *Book of Mormon*, or Jehovah's Witnesses those revealed in *Watch Tower Magazine*, were in full swing. But not among these missionaries would be members of a church that considered itself to be above mundane proselytizing.

That church was the Church of Rome, the one that had some two thousand years of experience in coopting, or more to the point controlling, the minds of ordinary folk. Even during the notorious Inquisition periods centuries before, when physical intimidation was the principal means of bringing heretics to right, mind control had been the end.[1] Not only did "the purifying fires of the stake" silence subversives whose ideas threatened good order, they were a terrible reminder to curious onlookers that "right thinking" was a matter of life and death. However, the enduring weapons in thought management were not confined to fear-mongering; they extended very much to proscription in the form of forbidden books. From as early as the sixteenth century until well into the twentieth, formal censorship of the written word was an obsession for those who regarded book learning as "the silent heretic?"[2] To be sure, as time went on, it had become more and more difficult for the Church to enforce censorship, and even more so to intimidate the masses with the *auto-de-fe*. The hierarchy had to find alternatives. And they did.

Pre-Vatican II Catholicity

In the wake of the 1870 Vatican Council 1, developments were aided and abetted by the convenient doctrine of papal infallibility: the ultimate claim in psychological one-up-man-ship, designed to lend divine approbation to hierarchical certitude. The following decades saw conservative prelates placing emphasis on the supposed superiority of Catholic Christianity, and, by raising threats against and demonizing suspected enemies, they exerted great effort in a fight against Modernism and other perceived challenges to Church authority. Up to the 1950s or thereabouts an important aspect of this process of intimidation was the attachment of great gobs of guilt to every conceivable sin, especially to sins "against the flesh."[3]

By playing up the "troubled conscience" of those fallen into sin pastors prescribed self-control and confession as principal remedies for the malady, but also, one suspects, as the means by which they could keep the faithful in line. More so were these remedies endemic to Catholic education wherein young people, more often than not in gender segregated schools, were daily exhorted to recount "impure thoughts and deeds" to a priest in order to avoid the tortures of hell. Looking back it is easy to see clerical arrogance underlying these encroachments on our lives. But in hindsight I believe they were a rear-guard action, born of a growing sense of desperation over a rebellious "rock and roll" era. For the church had long become an institution locked into an archaic world view of its own importance and authority. When faced with post-World War II secularism it turned increasingly to jingoism and obscurantism in dogma and ritual, and inevitably to a siege mentality in clerical circles. The old line could be defended but not advanced. John XXIII threw in the towel with Vatican II in the mid-sixties, loosening and eventually

BY THE WAY...

tearing down - in the developed countries at least, the psychological controls which the clergy had utilized to great effect for a century.

At the dawn of the new millennium only the older among us will have had a taste of super-clerical Catholicism which is euphemistically referred to (admittedly, often with negative connotation) as the "pre-Vatican II Church." The narrow imperatives implicit in the Catholic Faith of forty or fifty years ago are now outside the experience of two generations. But I believe there are lessons we can all learn from the anachronistic era that spanned some ninety years between Vatican Council I and Vatican II, and which reached its zenith in the United States in the nineteen forties and fifties amidst the prevailing political introspection and histrionics of that era. Recognizing that emotions play tricks on memory I propose to look back on those times using an aide memoir which came to hand very conveniently as I contemplated the subject of this paper.

The *Handbook of Moral Theology* is for me the epitome of the pre-Vatican II Church. The chance discovery of this little book in a discarded bin may well have led me to regard it as having more significance as a signpost to the past than it deserves. On that score I will leave final judgment in the hands of those readers who have persevered this far in our discussion. Suffice it to say that reading this Handbook took me forcibly back to a church my children would not understand.

This book is the abridged version of a larger work entitled *Manual of Moral Theology*, as cited in the Preface to the first edition (1921). It bears a *Nihil Obstat* and an *Imprimatur*. Prummer informs us that the work is meant as a "faithful companion for the young cleric" in helping him prepare for examinations, and at the same time as "a refresher course

Pre-Vatican II Catholicity

for the older priest" especially in his capacity as confessor. Therefore, it is probably not stretching the point to assume that the work reflects an insider-view of ecclesiastical authority, without any attention given to lay concerns in general, certainly not to political correctness when addressing delicate issues. For this reason I do not apologize for my lack of deference to clericalism in what follows.

As indicated above, the Handbook served primarily as a pocket-book guide for young priests and other confessors, with special emphasis on the counseling of lay penitents. In the words of the Introduction: "Moral theology is a genuine science... which directs and not merely describes human acts." Presumably, it is also deductive rather than inductive science seeing that the ultimate source of this scientific knowledge and who has the right to impart it, are both givens. The former are the "legislators" who formulate doctrine, the latter the clerical commissars who enforce it while maintaining discipline in, and promoting loyalty to, the institutional Church. Hierarchical prerogative sets the tone for all discussions which are bent on (A) celebrating clerical exclusivity in combating sin and temptation, (B) securing lay obedience to ecclesiastical law, (C) preserving liturgical rectitude, and (D) coercing unity and good order: all mixed together as mortar supporting control.

The approach includes (i), name calling and condemnation of nonbelievers (ii), a penchant for self-righteous positions and a direct-line-to-God syndrome, (iii) promotion of scrupulosity in all things Catholic and (iv), an obsession with neo-magical formulations and ritual celebrating form over substance. In order to illustrate these characteristics and provide a taste of what it meant to be a conscientious churchgoer during the decades prior to Vatican II, I have grouped the contents of the Handbook under rather arbitrary headings. Many

BY THE WAY...

of these could be combined and/or rearranged to fit other permutations with no great loss to our discussion. While the Handbook sets its own agenda and needs no elaboration for readers who grew up before 1963, I have interpolated observations where I feel these may add some light, especially for those of recent generations who find the work's general thrust somewhat removed from their idea of church. References are to section numbers in the Handbook.

Laws and Legislators: Mention of the legislator, and even the mind of the legislator, recurs throughout the Handbook which has a predisposition for atomization of precepts laid down by one or other law-giver. Extended formulations delineate laws into sub-sets, each of which again may be divided into sub-texts with technical names. For example, in expounding on the law itself the Handbook first divides the subject into two categories: divine law and human law. Human law is twofold in character - ecclesiastical and civil. Divine law on the other hand is categorized as eternal, natural, and positive law, each category followed by sub-sets totaling eleven orders, precepts, properties, and classes. There is no doubt about which category takes precedence: civil laws must conform to stated Rules of the Church before they can have validity at all (129 et sec.) In this regard everyone, even if entirely ignorant of the fact, is subject to Pope, bishop or synod, as arbiters of what is right and lawful. Doubtless for this reason, there is no need to elaborate on the term "legislator." Indeed one searches in vain for a concise definition of the word. In section 62, we learn that "the legislator is no other than he who has care of a society and this a perfect society." Exactly what that means is unclear.

The Handbook throughout its pages attributes

response-bility to various levels of the hierarchy and takes for granted that the reader will be in no doubt about who makes The Law in any given instance. In this way clerical fiat pervades the guidelines. Ecclesiastical privilege encompasses "the power of ruling, judging and coercing (emphasis added) baptized persons in matters affecting their spiritual welfare and supernatural happiness" (678). Even at the lowest level of this God-created authority, ordained priests "have the care of souls in virtue of their office" and are obliged "to provide for their subjects all that is necessary and useful for their salvation" (542).

Intimacy and Intimidation: The cardinal in Dostoevsky's *The Grand Inquisitor* prophesies:

> "They will adore us as benefactors who have taken their sins upon ourselves before God. And they will have no secrets from us. We shall allow them to live with their wives and mistresses, to have children or not have children - everything according to the measure of their obedience - and they will submit themselves to us gladly and cheerfully. The most tormented secrets of their conscience they will bring to us, and we will give them our decision for it all, and they will be glad to believe...."[4]

This old priest understands well the human dependency that derives from control over the intimate, especially where guilt intrudes;[5] for, as he points out "only he can gain possession of men's freedom who is able to set their conscience at ease."[6] The Church is master of this art, and the Handbook is replete with the rules and regulations that touch on all sources of a bad conscience. Control over the "married state" is vital to clerical control of the faithful. After all, the family is at the heart of society, and marriage traditionally has been at the heart of the family. Needless to say considerations

BY THE WAY...

such as these are irrelevant to the author of the Handbook. His work has many purposes, but elucidation of history where it contradicts church doctrine, is not one of them.

It was to be expected therefore that the birth of modern Catholicism in the Middle Ages, when papal claims to total control over the Church and the laity were first translated into action, also marked the beginning of clerical designs over the institution of marriage. The process was evolutionary over several centuries. According to Christopher Brooke the twelfth century marked the beginning of clerical formulations of the wedding vow. Up to that time marriage was regarded as largely a civil matter, governed by the vestiges of Roman Law.[7] Gradually clerical rules as to consanguinity, and what constituted the essence of a valid union (consent or consummation) increased; however, even allowing for in-roads during the intervening centuries, such as increasing clerical control over the marriage ceremony itself, it was not until the Council of Trent that marriage in *facie ecclesiae*[8], *that is,* before a priest in church (actually in the entrance thereto) became mandatory.[9]

For the Church of the 1950s, sacerdotal power over the faithful was a God-given right in the absence of which the inherently sinful laity would be doomed to perdition. The idea that you could be excluded from the fold and find yourself in the wilderness, without hope of heaven, was very real. Such dire consequences could emanate from the simple act of viewing a "condemned" movie. Indeed everything you did involved a weighty decision for or against your eternal salvation. There were few greater areas of concern, guilt, and introspection than those having to do with the opposite sex. "Marry or burn" usually meant much fire before anything else.

The Handbook leaves us in no doubt about the gravity of it all, and underlines (a) the Church's right to dictate who

Pre-Vatican II Catholicity

may be accepted for marriage and the parameters of a valid marriage, (b) the Church's right to interfere in matters of the bedroom - "the obligations of marriage", and (c) her ability to decide whether marriage unions may be dissolved, i.e. rendering the parties free to marry others. Thus we are told, "Only the Church has the right to determine and to pass judgment on everything which affects the essence of Christian marriage" (838). Particularly obnoxious are those marriages between a Catholic and a person of another (Christian) faith - euphemistically referred to as mixed marriages - "of which the Church has always expressed her disapproval and which she only tolerates with special precautions ...." (208).

The work devotes several chapters to these matters. From betrothals to annulments, every aspect of marriage comes within the Church's purview and is subject to clerical control, direct or indirect. Prior to marriage "venereal pleasure [which] arises from the movement of organs and secretions which aid the act of procreation" is strictly forbidden. This is because God "has issued a grave prohibition against any form of venereal pleasure that is directly voluntary." Such pleasure may amount to internal sins of impurity, or worse, unconsummated external sins of impurity. Occasions for such sins are inherent in those unbecoming parts of the body "which are ...usually covered by clothing, such as breast and arms"; and those parts "which are indecent, *viz*, the organs of generation and adjacent parts." Generally speaking, touching the "indecent parts of another adult" and entertaining immodest thoughts, looks, and conversation, are gravely sinful; especially so, is "fornication" between unmarried couples (507-517).

Those couples who survive the above obstacle course and the many examinations of conscience and confessions endemic to courtship must then survive the preliminary investigation which is required to start the process when

BY THE WAY...

marriage is contemplated. The parish priest questions separately each party on various issues, following which is publication of the banns to solicit information as to possible impediments affecting the proposed union. The Handbook reminds us that marriage is forbidden "most severely [and] in all countries," between a Catholic and "a member of an heretical or schismatic sect" (read non-Catholic), unless a clerical dispensation has been obtained (891).

Even with permission, the presiding priest would be forbidden to wear any "sacred vestments," perform any "sacred rites," or marry the mixed couple in a "sacred place." Once the couple is married, of course, the Catholic spouse has very definite obligations. Primary among these is that he or she must endeavor to convert his or her partner (893). But what is really kinky is the reminder that an impediment exists where a "free person", without knowledge of the other's status, seeks to marry a slave. But we need not worry as this condition "is today almost universally unknown" (899). Otherwise the ceremony itself must be before an authorized priest from the bride's locale (878), and two witnesses - for which purpose "heretics may be tolerated for a just cause" but with an important exception: they may not be both deaf and blind (877). There is no explanation why Catholics who can neither hear nor see, make better witnesses than heretics who are deaf and blind. With these and other enigmas, it is for the faithful to do or die, not reason why.

With regard to the wedding ceremony itself, a valid marriage vow is most important: "A specific formula is necessary for (the vow) to be valid, in which God is invoked" otherwise it is not a "religious" oath. Most important any "mental reservation" either in the "strict" or "wide" sense invalidates the undertaking. Once married the couple have the duties of marriage to contend with: Obligations such as

Pre-Vatican II Catholicity

mutual love, and the rendering of the marriage debt (nothing to do with visa payments) are mutual; providing for the family is the husband's obligation, while for the wife careful attention to the home and due obedience to her husband are her duties (463). In other matters we are told that "although in general woman is weaker than man in her physical and intellectual powers" some women may be capable of doing men's work. It will be reassuring for these lesser mortals to know that "capable women" may be allowed "the right to vote even in political matters." At the same time men will be relieved to learn that "God created woman as man's helper" from Adam's rib, which clearly indicates that "complete equality [was] never God's intention" (464).

In general therefore the Handbook's Theology of Women accords no parity between the sexes. Such accommodations to equality as are admitted are very soon abrogated both by tone and content. Section 464 makes definitive statements that give and take away at the same time: "So far as their souls, supernatural grace, and destiny are concerned, men and women are equal." Then comes the retraction: because woman was created from man's anatomy, and because "God has excluded her from the priesthood," all would seem to indicate clearly "that it was never God's intention for *complete* (emphasis in original) equality to exist between man and woman." She was created as man's helper and "must show due obedience to her husband (463); accordingly, she must confine her activities to the home and children; any form of emancipation which disrupts family life must be rejected." Capable women may have the right to vote as a general rule "but it is an entirely different question whether any useful purpose is served...by granting women the right to vote in any particular district (464)."

Addressing the question of the priesthood, the Handbook

is unequivocal: "Only men on earth who are delegated or consecrated are ministers of the sacraments." (Apparently this is understatement and must be emphasized by ecclesiastical *igitur* (therefore): "Therefore, neither the angels nor the souls in Purgatory have the power to administer the sacraments (537)." But woman does figure as agent provocateur, except we are told that she who "erroneously thinks that it is not grievously sinful to touch a priest immodestly could be absolved by that priest (722)." The question about absolution for the priest is not mentioned. All of which brings us to the Catholic Church's claim to universal primacy over everyone everywhere, Christian and non-Christian.

Heretics, Pagans and Jews: It will surprise the Evangelical right to learn that they, and all baptized Christians - including heretics and schematics, are subject to Roman Catholic ecclesiastical law (80). The Handbook is quite clear: "Heretics and pagans as soon as they realize the truth of the Catholic religion... are obliged to be converted immediately in their heart to the true religion …." (195). Elsewhere we read: "Protestants and all baptized non-Catholics are obliged by the law of fasting in as much as they are subject to the laws of the Church" (494). Paganism and Judaism are linked together as forms of positive infidelity, defined as "the culpable lack of faith in a person who does not want to believe." Needless to say, positive infidelity is a grave sin (199), in that it reveals "contempt for the authority of God [and] a rejection of a necessary means of salvation." Contrary to the "virtue of religion," there are vices of which we are told superstition is one. Begging the question, the Handbook cites as particularly reprehensible erroneous adoration, "such as desiring to worship God according to Jewish ritual, which supposes that Christ is yet

Pre-Vatican II Catholicity

to come. Such superstition is essentially a grave sin" (430). These precepts follow logically from the doctrine that the Catholic Church is not merely one among many churches; it is the only organization worthy of the name "church". If only for this reason, "no one can legitimately attack the Catholic faith" (200).

Accordingly, numerous difficulties attend the good Catholic in a world of the non-Catholic. For example: "Active and formal religious co-operation (such as acting as God-parent at a heretical baptism) is always forbidden" (205). Similarly, "It is never permissible [for children of a Catholic] to attend non-Catholic schools, unless it is possible to remove the proximate danger of perversion." Interesting that, in the ranking of latent "perversions," proscribed schools take second place only to mixed marriages discussed above. Not far behind educational institutions, dangers-to-the-Faith extend to reading heretical books - viewed as particularly harmful to one's religious life - and co-operation with pagans and heretics. To be exact, civil cooperation is not forbidden but discouraged because of the dangers involved; as is passive religious cooperation with heretics that is frowned on but is not as culpable as involvement with excommunicated persons, who must be avoided; and finally, active and formal religious cooperation (for example god-parenting a non-Catholic child) is always forbidden because it lends recognition to an unorthodox form of worship (206).

Cultic and Magical Practices: The Handbook is a minefield of esoteric ritual, parading under the banner of ancient orthodoxy, which would make the much maligned Pharisees of old cringe. Certainly for a non-Catholic it would be difficult squaring the many near hocus-pocus practices (and precepts)

BY THE WAY...

with any sort of rationality. Anticipating this, the Handbook self-consciously proclaims that "All modes of worshiping God approved by the Church are free from any suspicion of superstition" (430). If this is a pre-emptive strike it fails miserably.

Conditions precedent to valid administration of, and participation in, the Eucharist and Confession are cases in point. With regard to the former, which "Christ has imposed a command on the order of priests to celebrate" (618), bread that is not made from pure wheaten flour is excluded (barley, rye, oats, etc., are totally unacceptable). Milk or oil "in a noticeable quantity" also render the "matter" invalid. The hosts themselves must be *circular* (emphasis added). For its part, the wine must be from the grape and must have begun to ferment: "fresh" wine is prohibited. No additive is allowed, except that permission is given "for the addition of some wine alcohol to weak wine, to a combined total of 18% alcohol" (586). Regrettably, the theological underpinning for this admixture is not made available to us.

At the consecration the priest should "form an intention" as to the matter to be consecrated since otherwise a problem might arise as to the "extent" of the consecration. For example, lack of intention on the part of the priest could mean that hosts in a ciborium before him could be consecrated while those in the ciborium "placed inadvertently at the corner of the altar outside the corporeal [reach] might not be" (587). To be doubly sure the coverage is acceptable, the intention should be accompanied by the physical extension of celebrating arms over the intended matter. As with other value-added products quality control is important.

But the Handbook really gets off on specifics when it scans from high altar to the humble pews below. Here the laity must sit in awe of superior cult. To be worthy recipients

Pre-Vatican II Catholicity

of the Eucharist, they must wear suitable dress. What is referred to as the "immodest dress of females" is particularly forbidden, as are "dirty clothes." After all, external cleanliness is a "necessary bodily disposition [which would be] lacking in one who is dirty or suffering from visible and repulsive sores or in one who has suffered involuntary pollution (semen), or in women during their menstrual period"(594). Communicants must of course have strictly observed the Eucharistic fast, that is, abstaining from food or drink from the previous midnight. Very important is the rule that midnight be strictly "computed in accordance with solar or legal time." However, we are happy to learn that this fast "is not violated by anything received into the stomach, (a), mixed with saliva such as a few drops of water swallowed while cleaning the teeth, (b), through the action of breathing (inhaling tobacco smoke), or (c), through the injection of a nutritive substance" 595.3.

We are also assured that the Eucharist is the food of the soul and a powerful protection against the temptations of the devil. Indeed, it produces all its salutary effects even if "administered artificially through a tube inserted in the stomach." If during its administration, the host (which must be held by priest between thumb and index fingers of his right hand) should accidentally fall to the ground, the spot should be covered and later cleaned; if on the other hand it "falls on to the clothing of a woman and it cannot be recovered by the priest without scandal, the woman should be taken to the sacristy, and she herself take up the host and then wash her fingers; (then) the ablution should be poured down the *Sacrarium*" (606). As to setting the Eucharist aside for extra-liturgical adoration this is only allowed if done in a blessed tabernacle before which a flame must burn, fed with olive oil. The ciborium itself must be of "decent" material with gilded interior, must have a tightly fitting lid, and be covered with a white silk veil (608).

Cultic regulation is not confined to the administration of the Eucharist. Over fifty per cent of the Handbook is devoted directly to explicating the approach which priests should take to penitents in the confessional, depending on the nature, type, and degree of culpability of their sins. As a consequence, the work is a microcosm of the hierarchy's pre-Vatican II obsession with their own importance. Salvation comes to fallen mankind only out of obedience to God's Law - a law formulated, interpreted and administered by a divinely directed priesthood. Thus, "a Catholic who has a positive doubt concerning some article of faith is a heretic (203)," and by definition is debarred from entering heaven.

There is no alternative, but that "everything must be believed...which the Church, through her solemn or ordinary judgment and universal Magisterium, proposes for belief as a truth revealed by God" (188). The front-line officers in this tiered phalanx of authority are confessors who decide the fate of sinners. These intermediaries "enjoy the fourfold office of judge, doctor, physician, and father" - to whom perfect obedience is advocated (694/144). Disobedience (or disrespect) is an affront before God and must be forgiven if the relationship with God is to be restored. In the broad context of human culpability mortal sin "causes the death of the soul" (159), and remorse of conscience (165). This fractured relationship with God can be healed only through priestly intervention in the Sacrament of Penance, which we are told was "instituted by Christ in the form of a judgment for the remission [of sin] through sacramental absolution..." (644). Further, "the purpose of this judgment is to reconcile and free the sinner..." (646).

In order to be effective the "essential form" of the

Pre-Vatican II Catholicity

sacrament of penance must be used, both as to the prescribed Latin words (which must be spoken) and the attendant ceremonies - such as the raising of the priest's hand from the beginning of the prescribed prayer of absolution" (648-650). On the other side of the curtain the penitent must be able to hear the absolution; so, on a practical note, if a penitent leaves the confessional prior to receiving absolution, the essential words of the priest's prayer should be pronounced "before the penitent has departed more than *twenty* paces (emphasis added) from the confessional..." (651).

When the priest refuses to forgive the penitent - by "reserving" his or her sins - he does so "to preserve ecclesiastical discipline and to inflict a more effective deterrent on the penitent." Sometimes it becomes necessary to refer serious and dangerous sins to a higher authority, endowed with greater prudence and experience. In such cases, "penitents laboring under these reserved sins receive a beneficial medicinal punishment (from) more severe penance" (686). Under the heading of "ecclesiastical punishment" a penalty is defined as "a painful evil contrary to the will of the sufferer inflicted by the Church in punishment of some delinquency" (730). We are told that a penalty may be vindictive or medicinal, penal or canonical, depending on the nature of the penitent's offence (731). In many respects, therefore, the pre-Vatican II Catholic who took religion seriously, lived under the tyranny of a "tormented" conscience. For the most part the latter results from "impurity," of one kind or another, stemming from "sexual acts or thoughts" - explored in the next section.

For our present discussion the most striking example of institutional razzle-dazzle depicted by the Handbook is the traditionally sensitive matter of indulgences. These attributes of ecclesiastical authority date back to the early middle ages when crusaders were assured of heaven should they die in battle fighting for Christendom against the infidel. Over the centuries indulgencies evolved into addendums to priestly absolution, enhancing the benefits of the sacrament of penance (as it used to be called). According to Catholic doctrine, penitential absolution especially in the case of grave sin, does not leave the soul spotless enough to enter heaven when the person dies; that is, eternal punishment in hell may have been obviated by confession, but temporal punishment in purgatory may await the penitent at death. By itself therefore confession lacks a coup de grace, or otherwise is not expansive enough for the Church's divine mission. It could even be said that the prospect of purgatorial punishment, with or without confession, detracts from the Church's credibility.

An indulgence compensates for this apparent deficiency. Granted "by ecclesiastical authority from the treasury of the Church," an indulgence is "a remission in the sight of God of the temporal punishment due for sins whose guilt has been forgiven" (780). They may be granted by (a) the Pope - unlimited powers, (b) Cardinals - two hundred days maximum, (c) Archbishops - one hundred days, and so on, down the hierarchical line. But there are limitations: "Those inferior to the Roman Pontiff cannot (*inter alia*) grant indulgences applicable to the souls in Purgatory" (782).

There are two kinds of indulgence: plenary and partial, the criteria being whether they remit all or only part of the punishment. For example, un-confessed sins would blur the efficacy of an indulgence, rendering it only partial. In a rare instance of candor the Handbook admits, "it is impossible to determine with any degree of certainty how much punishment is remitted by a partial indulgence" (781). A special indulgence may be attached to a particular object such as a rosary. But what if this object is subject to "repeated minor repairs so that the object has been completely changed"? Not to worry:

Pre-Vatican II Catholicity

apparently the indulgence would cease only if the rosary were reduced to "nothing more than a handful of beads" (790). Is this is just another way of stringing us along?

What are the criteria for obtaining an indulgence? Three things: "right intention, a state of grace and perfect union with the Church, and fulfillment of a prescribed good work" (782). The latter must be performed faithfully and personally, and must be additional to any extant obligation; for example, if a church visit is prescribed the relevant indulgence will not be obtained by attending Sunday Mass - an obligation in its own right. (785). If particular prayers are prescribed any language will do. But "an addition, subtraction, or interpolation destroys the indulgence" (789).

The ultimate authority for awarding (or with-drawing) indulgences resides with the Pope. He alone can bestow on the clergy the power to grant indulgences; he alone can ennoble an object by attaching to it an indulgence; and as indicated above he alone can formulate an indulgence abrogating temporary punishment for those already in Purgatory. This is indeed a signal attribute of the man armed with the staff of Peter. Among earth's frail citizens only a pope can open the door to heaven for the unfortunate souls suffering purgatorial torments. Put another way, selected souls soiled by their former lives on earth or otherwise condemned to a slow cleansing process in the netherworld, will be happy to learn that, adequately primed, the pope can afford them a power-wash - here on terra firma. [9]

Conclusion [10]

The foregoing focuses largely on quotations from the *Handbook of Moral Theology*. I apologize if the large number of them made the process tedious for some readers, but there seemed no better way of speaking to the absurdities of the

161

BY THE WAY...

pre-Vatican II Church, than having the old-style hierarchy speak for itself. As I mentioned in the introduction, the main reason for revisiting the *Handbook* was to bring to attention what obtained fifty years ago, not to suggest that it is the face of the Church today. And yet, ten years after my earlier version of this paper, entitled *What Lies Beneath,* there are disturbing signs of a resurgence in pre-Vatican II mindsets, especially in North America, but also as far away as Africa, where in 2015 Pope Francis condemned fundamentalism as a "sickness...of those who believe they possess absolute truth" (The Christian Post). In the US, the Church is finding itself a cornerstone of a conservative upsurge and of right-wing politics. Whatever Francis might say of these developments they are not going away. Equally troubling, they are not representative of democracy but of totalitarian faithfulness born of emotionalism. According to John Halpin (back in 2011), the conservative movement in the US is "an amazing bastardization of the [Catholic faith by those] attracted to systematic thought and severely backwards gender relations..." (Washington Post). The cruel outcome of this tail-wagging-dog phenomenon in the US has been the support of a majority of Catholics (and Evangelicals} for Donald Trump in the 2016 election. The knit-picking certainties and top-down controls, eviscerated by Vatican II, are back in favour.

Postscript: Extracted from *Testament of the Third Man*, October 2007, with additional comments in 2016. For those who may be interested in democracy for the Church, the suggestions therefor, in the penultimate chapter of *Testament,* may be of interest.

Christianity From Below

Early Church studies are in vogue today, especially those centred on Jesus' ministry and the post-resurrection Apostolic Age. In the forefront have been liberal academics such as Marcus J. Borg, promoter of "Jesus at 2000" symposiums, John D. Crossan and E. P. Sanders for their work on the "Historical Jesus," and Robert Eisenman for his insights into linkages between the Dead Sea Scrolls and the Jerusalem Church. But how much "high-brow" discourses recommend themselves to the general public is an open question. It is possible the esoteric nature of such studies would tax the patience of some people, in the same way that their controversial theses would offend the orthodoxy of many.

Enter E. Glen Hinson with his early church history, and we are back in the non-threatening mould of Chadwick, Frend, Jones and others who championed that genre thirty years ago. For his *Thoughts on the Early Church* is within the realm of traditional faith-based books. At the same time its 360 pages, covering the first six centuries of Church history, have much to recommend them for objectivity and even-handedness. As a concise review of Christianity's origins, this book has something for everyone.

Hinson is Professor of Spirituality and Loftis Professor of Church History at Baptist Theological Seminary in Virginia. Except for notable, although in the overall forgivable, shortcomings, his book is exemplary for rising above many of the biases and polemics that often mar histories of the early Church, especially for books emanating from within the confines of one or other church community. Effortlessly,

A review of *Thoughts on the Early Church: Origins, to the Dawn of the Middle Ages*, by E. Glenn Hinson, Abingdon Press

BY THE WAY...

Hinson's history ranges back and forth across the invisible lines of five broad periods into which this *longue duree* is apportioned. These are first, Beginnings to 70CE: the Apostolic era; second, 70-180: growing pains; third, 175-313: persecution, apologetics and coming of age; fourth, 313-400: adjusting to new-found prominence as part of the "establishment"; and finally, 400-600: expansion and accommodation in times of schism and political upheaval.

If it is fair to assume that Christians fall into two basic church groupings – Mainline and Non-Conformist - I would guess that the latter denominations take little interest in church history (writ long or short), except that suggested by the New Testament itself; while the former take some interest, but only such as lends support to "we-were-there-first" arguments. One camp tends to jump over early church history as a whole - landing triumphantly in the sixteenth century, while the other downplays or rationalizes inconvenient parts such as the Crusades and the Inquisition. In both cases the dictum-of-irrelevance, subjectively defined, obtains.

Professor Hinson challenges both pre-determined positions, drawing us into an exciting world of real people struggling with uncertainties and making do in difficult times. Deftly he fills the gaps left by those Sunday-school orations we missed as we gazed out the window. Significant are the many vignettes of personalities and human dramas which his book delivers live and kicking for our enjoyment and edification. From rebels like Marcion - founder of the first "protestant" church in the 140sCE, to superstars like Saint Augustine; from martyrs such as Ignatius, Bishop of Antioch, who in his own words longed to be "crushed like wheat between the teeth of wild beasts," to popes such as Leo 1 who successfully stared down the Vandals; from vindictive emperors like Valerian who was determined to turn back the clock to paganism, to

Caesaropapists, like Constantine and Justinian, determined to dictate Christian theology, Hinson walks us by their homes and we see them moving about inside. Because his approach is from below, he is at pains to describe for us what Christianity meant for the "little people" of those centuries, how they were baptised, their liturgies and art, and their passion for theological debate, especially in the East.

If the work can be faulted it is in smoothing over controversial or inconvenient issues, sometimes using too modern concepts, at other times tending towards name-calling when things do not fit. For example, the Jerusalem community under James the Just is mentioned only in passing, although the implications of its authority, to say nothing of its theology, in the early days of Christianity are huge. The Jamesian/Pauline dichotomy evident in what we know of the Jerusalem Church might raise a few academic eyebrows, but is carefully shielded from view in orthodox circles. The irony is that the Book of Acts white-washes divisive walls in favour of Paul, while Paul himself applies the paint as graffiti artist.

Hinson's desire to involve the modern reader lends to his occasionally playing to the gallery, such as "conservative" Christians refusing to "attend parties in the homes of neighbours [or] send their children to public school where they would be exposed to pagan myths" (p.70), blandishments that would seem to reflect an era closer to the 1990s than that spanning the years 70 to 180AD.

Another short-coming is the author's passing reference to the *Nag Hammadi* library, some fifty-two treatises discovered by an Arab peasant who unearthed them in Upper Egypt in 1945. In dismissing the books as "Gnostic" - a derogatory term in orthodox Christian circles - the author absolves himself from further comment on these texts, except that they reveal an otherwise hidden history of early Christianity,

BY THE WAY...

ably researched by scholars such as Elaine Pagels. Certainly, the prescience of desert monks credited with saving this important collection, including the *Gospel of Thomas,* from destruction sixteen hundred years ago, deserves a line or two of explication.

Again, in discussing at some length the struggle against Arianism, Hinson prefers to dwell on the politics and bloodletting accompanying the spread of this "heresy," rather than address its theology. Adherents of this version of Christianity denied Christ's Trinitarian divinity. They included many bishops of the day, necessitating a major Ecumenical Council at Nicaea in 325CE to thwart pending, if not actual, schism. We never come to grips with legitimate questions raised by Arianism - the origins of which date back to apostolic times and groups such as the Ebionites. What of the implications of Arianism's persistence with such as the Visigoths, who planted it in Spain for two centuries? What of the Jehovah's Witnesses in our midst?

At a more fundamental level, Hinson shines little light on the development of the Christian Canon. For the most part the New Testament is a given, as if pre-existing in its present form, being referred to without much qualification throughout the book. While this may provide security for many churchgoers it will fail to satisfy those seeking informed opinion. Lastly, one must bemoan the lack of an index.

But these criticisms do not discredit the book as a whole; it is a good primer for those exploring church history for the first time. Hinson's prose is easy to read and his story moves ahead without intruding foot-notes or stressful subordinate clauses. He is never tedious when making small steps, and moves gracefully in his long strides through dark times of struggle and compromise between eastern and western Churches; between emperors and popes; and between

Christians and Barbarians. Whether discussing the primacy of the papacy, the ascendency of clergy over laity, or the reaction of the people in the street to doctrinal debates, he does so with delicacy, restraint and fairness - never belittling the debt owed by the present to the past. Whatever one's Church orientation may be, his book is exemplary of Christian goodwill: the best reason to read it.

Prince George, November, 2004

A Case Appealed (revisited)

A mock court hearing is the setting for *The Case for Christ*, wherein a "Doubting Thomas" wishes various questions, concerning Christ and the Bible, settled once and for all. The book was chosen for discussion because it presents in one volume many of the tenets which Non-Conformist Christians hold as sacrosanct (but which other Christians may question from various standpoints). The format has Strobel parading before selected Evangelical church-going scholars the doubts and reservations that his readers may have heard over time. A lawyer by profession, he invites the experts to find, if they can, evidence to the contrary. Supposed dubious readers must then, as open minded and fair jurors "subject the evidence [presented] to their common sense and logic, and, come to a verdict "based on the weight of the facts."

No doubt many of us, as jurors, will get a rise out of the tongue-in-cheek challenges Strobel presents, and welcome the refutations forthcoming from academics that decide the case. For others, including myself as a lay person reading the book from the common-sense perspective that Strobel demands, the verdict may be less than conclusive, and indeed open to appeal. In particular, readers who do not regard Bibliolatry (or Bible worship) as complementary to, or a necessary component of, Christianity, may find annoying what in my opinion are circular arguments and/or self-serving validations, which pass for "evidence" (and therefore proof) of this or that rebuttal. As they slog through one such argument after another, jurors will observe that no problem is beyond resolution in favor of some predetermined position. At the same time I must hasten to deny any intention to discredit the academic qualifications of those providing answers to questions posed by Mr. Strobel.

A review of *The Case for Christ*, by Lee Strobel, Zondervan, 1998

BY THE WAY...

Before discussing the matter further, I believe there is need for "context" in supporting, or disagreeing with, the evidence Strobel presents, especially given the confusing order in which New Testament books appear in the Bible. For this purpose, I believe we must begin with a "time-line" of the Early Church that recognizes, and as best as possible corrects this conundrum, thus enabling rational discussion. So far as possible, this time-line should be neutral in reference to partisan positions, and not egregiously objectionable in scholarly circles. For this purpose I have chosen a schema based roughly on *The Jerome Biblical Commentary*, a work noted for its Catholic scholarship, but one that is not favorable to any particular agenda, Catholic or otherwise. Question marks indicate uncertainties noted by the Commentary; the periodization and notes have been included for purposes of discussion.

Approximate timeline:

↓

Period 1 - Life of Christ – 4BC to 30CE?

Period 2 – Jerusalem Church/ Paul's letters

- 49-67 Paul's "authenticated" letters (Location: Diaspora & Rome)
- 60s Epistles of Peter and James (questionably authentic – possibly written by others towards end of first century).
- 69-70 Destruction of Jerusalem and dispersal of the Jews, and also the "Jerusalem Church," along with whatever remnant of the Apostles remained. There is little or no reliable evidence of where the latter went or what "gospel" they preached in a new location.

A Case Appealed (revisited)

Period 3 – First two Gospels
- ↓ 71   Mark's Gospel – location: Rome (?)
- 80   Matthew's Gospel – location: Antioch, Syria (?)
- 80s   Letter to the Hebrews – author(s) unknown, location: Rome (?)

Period 4
- 85   Luke's Gospel & Acts – location: southern Greece. The *Acts of the Apostles* have as their principle aim the legitimization of Paul's Gentile ministry. Whether that bias compromises the work is unclear.

Period 5
- 95   John's Gospel & Epistles – location: Ephesus (?)
- 95-100   Revelation – Author & location disputed
- 100+   Pastoral Epistles (Timothy & Titus)

Whatever else we may gather from the order New Testament books appear in traditional Bibles, it is difficult to discount an intention on the part of Churchmen to deemphasize the above timeline in the interests of a supposed continuum. One gathers that *The Case for Christ* is not unhappy with this subterfuge, as it avoids problems mentioned below. But first, the following observations are necessary for an understanding of my peeves:

(a) There is no written record of events during Period 1, Christ's lifetime;

(b) There are no definitive texts contemporary with Period 2 (Peter and James being questionably much later), except Paul's letters, which, first and foremost, are interpretations of Period 1 along with some scathing remarks about the Jerusalem Church of Period 2;

(c) In Period 3, Mark's Gospel is the first account of Period 1, and bears little resemblance to Paul's interpretations;

BY THE WAY...

(d) Period 4 has Luke's *Acts of the Apostles* as a later take on the "history" of Period 2 that smooths over various controversies alluded to by Paul. Long after the Jerusalem Church and Paul had ceased to exist, Acts would have us believe that all factions within the leadership at that time were one in purpose. This leaves:

(e) Period 5, with John's Gospel, dated late in the century, unabashedly upstaging the Gospels at 3 and 4 by lionizing Jesus as the "Superman" he had become – possibly elemental in a "parting of the ways" between the early Church and Diaspora Judaism.

Few would argue that certainty can be claimed for much of the above. However, neither can we have confidence in Strobel's courtroom charade, wherein answers to difficult questions dissolve into Sunday-School rationalizations. As author/editor he is not unaware of dissenting scholarly opinion, which he cites throughout the book; but the upshot is less in the way of cogent argument, and more in the way of refutations expounded by any means at hand. The process is one of deduction from inviolate Biblical positions, with answers neatly packaged to defang all attacks that may be made against the New Testament record. The author goes to great lengths to deny, or have his experts deny, everything that possibly could cast doubt on, or disprove his "case." The overriding purpose is clearly that of evangelical apologetics rather than academic dissertation, although notable academics do attend Strobel's court. Reading between the lines we can discern what may be termed "axioms" or "principles" driving the proceedings: precepts that are endemic to a romantic view of the early church.

Any inaccuracy or exaggeration in the NT writings would discredit that view, and maybe the whole Bible for Strobel and

A Case Appealed (revisited)

his readers. What appears to be invention or slight-of-hand comes to the rescue, if necessary. Addressing the scholarly contention that Luke's Gospel is incorrect in placing Jesus' Nativity at the time of Quirinius - whose governorship of Syria was ten years afterwards – John McRay informs readers that an archeologist has recently "found a coin" (p. 136), indicating that there were really *two* Quiriniuses: thus proving that Luke's infant Jesus was after all in Bethlehem in 4BC, the year most scholars agree was that of Christ's birth. Presumably this coin was discovered in the nick of time for Strobel's book. Again, we are treated to the dismissive assertion that archeologists have now found "a list in Aramaic" (McRay, p.137) evidencing the existence of Nazareth - a town in antiquity surprisingly without mention in the Bible outside of Luke's Gospel. Presumably, this puts to rest scholarly doubt about the matter, and, almost out-of-a-hat, proves the correctness of the Gospel story. The *obiter dictum* is: *no problema*! Generally, what is ignored or underplayed is the cross-fertilization of information among the synoptic Gospels, indeed, their inter-dependency. With these and many other difficulties one finds with Strobel's *The Case for Christ*, it is time to examine some of the principles (my own titles), which a reader may discern in the book, and which, in no particular order of importance, seem to underlie it.

The primordial principle: Quite at variance with the above introductory "time-line," very early dating of the New Testament writings is important to those who claim that Christians are the "People of the Book." By definition, a prescriptive Canon must have predated the communities it is supposed to have shaped, well almost. Craig Bloomberg is helpful in establishing this principle. While acknowledging that most Biblical scholars agree with a timeline similar to

BY THE WAY...

the above, he is at pains to construct one of much shorter duration. For example, the story of Acts, which everyone agrees was written by Luke, has Paul as a principal character but tells us nothing about Paul's death. Bloomberg postulates that this must have a bearing on the date Acts was written. By a process of deduction, he reasons that Acts "cannot be dated any later than 62 A.D." (p. 42). Then it is a hop, skip, and jump to positing that Luke's Gospel, and for that matter Mark's and Matthew's (on which Luke's is based in part) also must have been written before 62. Strobel is ecstatic at this revelation, salivating over Bloomberg's "closing the gap between the events of Jesus' life and writing of the gospels" (p. 42). Except that he provides no evidence to support such a position. Matthew's Gospel makes no mention of Jesus' Ascension into heaven. Does that mean Matthew was writing prior to 30 CE? It would seem more reasonable to postulate that Mark's omission of the Nativity stories means nothing was known about Jesus' early years, a point Bloomberg would surely dispute, especially if it followed logically that Matthew and Luke later made up these stories in order to embellish Jesus' life for later generation of Christians.

The self-defining, or stand-alone, principle: Another axiom discernible from Strobel's book is the notion that there was never any question regarding which books should be included in the Christian Canon. Conversely, even if questions did arise, they immediately resolved themselves without debate. Bruce Metzger is first to explain why the Gospel of Thomas – discovered near the Egyptian village of Nag Hammadi in 1945, and celebrated by Jesus Seminar scholars - was not included in the Canon. According to Metzger the saying attributed to Jesus in this gospel, "lift up a stone and you will find me there" constitutes "pantheism," and is "contrary to anything in the canonical Gospels" (pgs. 88/ 89). Thus is this gospel consigned to exterior darkness?

In similar fashion, Gregory Boyd claims that Thomas was not worthy of canonization, citing a passage requiring a woman to make herself male in order to be saved. According to Boyd, the passage "contradicts the attitude we know Jesus had towards women...," adding that the gospel is likely "Gnostic" (p. 165), and thereby demolishing any further argument that it could have merited canonical status. Using the same approach, would either of these experts agree that Paul's Christology, much of which is foreign to the Synoptic Gospels, makes his celebrated letters suspect also? Taken a step further, as we have discussed, misogynism is not at all foreign to the Old Testament, and, once again, is a charge that can be leveled at Paul himself. Does this invalidate the OT and much of the new?

The real question is, who decides what is meant by the many paradoxical statements attributed to the canonical Jesus? For example, we find Jesus telling his followers "If any man comes to me without hating his father, mother, wife, children...he cannot be my disciple" (Luke 14: 26 & 27). Is this proclamation "contradictory to the words of Jesus," and if not, why not?

The inerrancy principle: Evangelicals hold dear the inerrancy principle. According to this principle the Bible is "God Breathed" and therefore its words cannot err. The reason is simple: Faith is grounded in "reality" of the Word, which means that Biblical claims are absolutes. John McRay, noted archeologist, never wavers in his assurances about the value of archeological discoveries. For him they confirm the importance of the NT as a "source book." He is forthright in admitting that his profession has its limitations in proving

BY THE WAY...

the accuracy of Biblical texts, yet at the same time is quick to fall back on archeological digs in defense of any challenge to Biblical accuracy. His take on Luke is that he was a noted historian, even if there is no hard evidence, archeological or otherwise, for that. Is the claim a necessity given that Luke denies having had personal contact with Christ, and admits to have written his gospel merely as "an orderly account...of the things that have taken place" exclusively for Theophilus? Absent great historian, how else could we rely on Luke's Gospel as inerrant truth?

For his part, Bloomberg assures readers that the Christian Canon was composed by historians of the greatest integrity and objectivity. Quoting Luke's preamble to his Gospel wherein Luke confirms his good intentions in writing, Bloomberg is unequivocal about this Gospel's accuracy and fairness, citing as evidence "the way the gospels are written – in a sober and responsible fashion, with accurate incidental details, with obvious care and exactitude" (p. 50). Of the four Gospels it has long been evident that two, Matthew and Luke, are based largely on Mark and the theoretical "Q" gospel, and even have passages common only to each other. But plagiarism is clearly not an ennobling feature of the "inspired word of God," as understood by the People of the Book. At the very least, independence and originality ought to distinguish each canonical book one from the other, while admitting of no contradiction among them. Of course this ideal is very far from the reality. Not only are the Gospels obviously interdependent, there are patent theological biases inherent in each one, for example the Moses tradition in Matthew's, as opposed to the Davidic in Luke's infant narratives. Not even Strobel's experts deny these aberrations, although valiant efforts are made to explain them, or more correctly to explain them away. Bloomberg conveniently

A Case Appealed (revisited)

disputes the generally accepted view that Mark is a source for Matthew and Luke, referring to unnamed scholars in support of his position, but without providing any other evidence to back up his claim. In Strobel's court, flowery explanations, and appeals to readers to "keep the faith" should be enough for true-believers; what need have we of further evidence?

It is almost as if Strobel would have us ignore all difficulties with dating, authorship and the like, and accept that the New Testament came off the press as one publication, in pristine form, perfectly free of cultural biases and/or imperfections. On the other hand, there is no question but that the books which did not make the Christian Canon, such as the *Gospel of Thomas* mentioned above, were automatically "polluted"–by Gnosticism or some other contaminant –rendering them unworthy of inclusion in the Bible. As for the pagan environment, including the mystery religions then obtaining: we are assured there is no chance such beliefs and practices influenced the Canon; if anything, the Canon influenced these pagan religions!

The osmosis principle: Following naturally from the self-defining and inerrancy principles is the precept that no person or organization compiled the New Testament canon, or edited or authenticated any of its contents. According to Metzger, "These documents didn't derive their authority from being selected; each one was authenticated before anyone gathered them together. The early church merely listened and sensed that these were authoritative accounts" (p. 90). Therefore we must assume that their veracity leapt off the parchment, and the community fell down before the shiny new Bible and said "Amen." Of all the preposterous claims in Strobel's book, the idea of canonical authentication by some form of osmosis is the most egregious. Yet it is imperative for proponents of what amounts to canonical fictions, that some form of trickle-up theory be responsible for authenticating the New Testament as we know it. Otherwise, apologists would be hard pressed to explain how a select few writings emerged from obscurity and became sacrosanct without anyone's intervention.

Of course, the worst-case scenario for Christian fundamentalists would be evidence that the fledgling Catholic Church was responsible for producing and/or *authenticating* the Canon. Equally problematical would be the idea that the Catholic Church preserved the NT writings down the centuries, enabling their veneration today. So anxious are Strobel's experts to distant themselves from this possibility they very carefully avoid mentioning the Catholic Church by name, much less attributing to it any part in the canonical process. According to Metzger (p. 90) the Canon came about by "intuitive insight of Christian believers...." What need could there have been for further authentication?

When *The Case for Christ* cites extra-Biblical evidence in support of Biblical truth, as it does in referring to Josephus' *Antiquities* to confirm that Jesus really lived, and also in connection with James' death, care is taken to avoid mentioning other passages that the same source might refute. Accordingly Josephus is used to prove Jesus' existence and singularity as a holy-man outside of biblical attestations thereto, but ignored when the object is to prove the biblical account of a good-natured Pilate anxious to release Jesus. The idea that Pilate was a vacillating, wife-whipped procurator anxious to release Jesus but for intimidation by the "Jews" is completely foreign to Josephus, who is the most important contemporary extra-Biblical source throwing light on Pilate's character. Strobel cannot ignore completely that fact, so he raises the question in a round-about way: in effect, have "some critics" not contradicted the Biblical account? This allows his expert witness, Yamauchi, to answer the question without any reference to Josephus (pgs. 100-112). All of which makes a mockery of jurisprudence.

The "Early Creed" principle: The matters attested to in the *Nicene Creed* are accepted by most Christians, whether they recognize its authority or not. Of course, out-and-out recognition of the fourth century Council of Nicaea that gave us the Nicene Creed is not to the liking of Bible-believers. For such as Strobel's experts, the creeds came fresh out of the Jerusalem Church, and if possible, even before Period 2 above. Especially for the "absolutes" of Christianity, such as Christ's resurrection and his divinity, it is crucial that they were part of the "Faith" very early in the apostolic first century. Absent this fact and the specter of "developing theology" (or worse Catholic "Tradition") raises its ugly head. Mr. Strobel's experts are accommodating. William Craig, Gary Habermas and Craig Bloomberg are content with the view that we need not look later than Paul's ministry (Period 2 above) to find all the Christian tenets laid out and explicated. First Corinthians 15 is viewed as unequivocal evidence for much of this discussion. As Craig explains, the Christian creed therein is "Essentially...a four-line formula. The first line refers to the crucifixion, the second to the burial, the third to the resurrection and the fourth to Jesus' appearances" (p. 281). Similarly, Jesus' atoning death and his divinity are attested in First Corinthians and in Philippians—these creeds being "significant in explaining what the earliest Christians were convinced about Jesus" (Bloomberg, p. 43). Meanwhile the rest of us on the outside of these revelations may well ask: If everything was cut and dried in Period 2, why was it necessary to convene several Ecumenical Councils to settle fundamental questions, centuries later?

BY THE WAY...

Surely, this "early creed" principle is self-serving and begs several questions. First of all Paul is the only source for this early creed, which he is supposed to have preached only to Diaspora Christians. Second: there were disagreements between Paul and the Jerusalem Apostles, so serious that he alludes to them in Galatians. Again, it is very difficult to see James as a Pauline aficionado; and Peter is clearly at odds with Paul even in the sanitized context of Acts. Curiously, Strobel and his experts are oblivious to such anomalies. Third: the fact that centuries after major "creeds" were supposed to have been "settled" (such as the nature of the Trinity) there were huge differences that councils had to adjudicate, speaks volumes about the inconclusive "quick fix" apologetics dominating Strobel's book. The Arian "heresy" that Jesus was not equal with the Father, a position accepted by many highly respected Christian bishops of the day, initiated the great council of CE 325. This fact alone should put to rest the fiction that Paul's creed was a done-deal in the early church.

What we have in this book are seasoned proselytizers indulging themselves in "close readings" of material that only after many years coalesced into the New Testament Canon, followed by convenient placements of what is sacrosanct today into the hearts and minds of Christ's followers two thousand years ago. The idea that today's doctrines dominated first century Christianity is implicit in every chapter of this book. If on a Sunday (more likely Saturday), we knocked on the door of a first century Christian we would likely find a choir boy, tattered bible in hand, just about to leave for morning service. That is the book's subliminal message to welcoming readers.

In this imaginary world there are no "anomalies" such as developing doctrine, evolving moral issues, growth in liturgical practices, and the like. The reason for their forced march into antiquity is that Born-again Christians are able to

A Case Appealed (revisited)

jump over the problems of the intervening centuries and claim the high ground in Christian formation. Theirs is a foundation constructed of ancient axioms that support their philosophy without being soiled by human hands, or worse, Tradition. Either of the latter would speak to human intervention rather than God's Word. The underlying fear, even paranoia, is about admitting that the institutional church, always lurking in the background throughout the book, may have had an important part to play in formulating what they accept today. For this reason their Christology, theology, creeds, and most important - the text of the twenty seven New Testament books, were all in place during Paul's lifetime!

Such are the many egregious "defenses" at the heart of Strobel's book. Very off-putting are the many throw-away proofs used by his experts in response to "difficult" questions posed by the author. Always, somebody or something is found to support any canonical passage or position. Whether it is the dispute over the Biblical existence of Nazareth, Herod's Slaughter of the Innocents, the sudden darkness embellishing Jesus' death, Jesus' denials of his Godhead, fulfillment of prophesies, or early belief in a "creed," these are all are explained away or advocated by one or other expert witness. Nothing is left to chance, so that we are assured that ruins have been "excavated at exactly the right point along the eastern shore of the Sea of Galilee" putting to bed any doubt about where Jesus drove the demons into the swine (McRay, p. 138).

To be fair, Bloomberg admits that differences among the gospels are to be expected (p. 58), but this is complete eye-wash, given that neither he, nor any other expert questioned, allows Strobel's staged "objections" to be sustained. Where the Gospels are at variance with accepted doctrine the difference is only apparent. So for Mark 10–"Why do you call me good?

BY THE WAY...

Only my father is good": Donald Carson is quick to discount Jesus' denial of his divinity (p. 218); similarly "The Father is greater than I" (John 14:28), must be seen in context, according to Louis Lapides (p.220). What of the many other such passages that also should be read in context, but are not?

So long as a passage is supportive of received truth its literal meaning is acceptable and must not be questioned. Habermas claims that Corinthians 15:5 confirms Mark 16:7. Really? All we can say is that they agree one to the other. But such agreement adds nothing regarding Jesus' appearance to Peter, if it can be shown that Mark's Gospel was simply relying on Corinthians. Again, J. P. Moreland's statement that, "five weeks after (Jesus) is crucified, over ten thousand Jews are following him and claiming that he is the initiator of a new religion" (p. 338), is questionable in that Paul accuses the Jerusalem Church of not freeing itself from the Law.

How can documents dependent on each other attest to each other's accuracy? Lapides falls into this trap. He denies the "intentional fulfillment of prophesy" on Jesus' part by begging the question "How would (Jesus) control the fact that the Sanhedrin offered Judas thirty pieces of silver to betray him?" (p. 249) This is a strange question for an academic, seeing that the "fact" of this offering is attested to only by reference to the question itself. If Matthew (enlarging on Mark) merely lifted the incident out of the Hebrew Scriptures (Zechariah 11:12) in order to embellish with typological fiction his version of the betrayal story, there would have been be no "fact" for Jesus to "control." The same can be said for the other "prophesies" concerning soldiers dividing Jesus' clothing (Ps 22:18); and Jesus' riding into Jerusalem on a donkey and a colt (both at the same time?) to "fulfill" a dubious understanding of Zechariah 9:9. (Randal Helms' *Gospel*

A Case Appealed (revisited)

Fictions is indispensable reading for insights into OT "source-mining" throughout the Gospel stories.)

The assertion that contemporaries would have spotted inaccuracies in the Biblical stories and corrected them, simply does not hold water. Even in today's world of hourly news bulletins, the multi-media, to say nothing of instant replays, there is much that is passed off as truth that millions should question but do not. We can be sure historians favourable to "establishment" truth, or one or other political ideology, will preserve for posterity what supports their predetermined position (for example that Globalization is good for the poor), and conveniently downplay, spin or completely overlook what contradicts that position. So what does that say for first century ideologues writing generations after the events they describe? For all his posturing to the contrary, Strobel never allows real discussion. He would have readers believe he is committed to objectivity, yet he is very careful to allow only experts who agree with him to give evidence. When these experts malign the views of the Jesus Seminar Strobel calls for no rebuttals from that camp. When they dismiss the "radical fringe," no representative is invited to comment. All are convicted without a defense. Only Kangaroo courts operate in this way.

Note: Some years ago Penguin published *Early Christian Writings*, an anthology of important documents, penned by Fathers of the church, dating back to the first and second centuries. Even at this elementary level of research it is obvious that Mr. Strobel's carefully crafted updating of early Christianity is seriously flawed. To begin with among letters and sermons of such luminaries as Clement, Ignatius, and Barnabas there are precious few references to New Testament authors; and, more important, nowhere is any of the NT writings revered as Scripture. Yes, there are many references to Scripture but always they are to the Hebrew Bible. Clement, writing to the Corinthians around 96CE, makes pointed mention of Cain, Moses, Noah, Abraham, Elijah, Elisha, Daniel, Amos, and Esther. His advice includes "Read your letter from the Apostle Paul" but for him Sacred Scripture is confined to the Old Testament. According to Ignatius, the Ephesians - to whom one of his letters is addressed - should obey their bishops and clergy (not act independently of them) and celebrate the Eucharist. Again, in letters to the church at Tralles and to the Philippians, Ignatius stresses obedience to the clergy and celebration of the Eucharist. Barnabas for his part exhorts his readers to keep the traditions they have received; he makes no reference to the NT as Scripture, or the Word of God. There is no emphasis on "worshiping Jesus as God" and none of these writers refers to an indelible Creed. Quite the contrary. What seems clear is that Christian communities, at least in the "Jewish" Diaspora up to the late second century, were focused on the Old Testament as "the Scriptures" (whether OT books would have appealed to early Pagan converts to Christianity is another question). As for a first century Christian "Canon", in *Early Christian Writings* that does not arise, at least in any modern sense of word.

Strobel's attempt to square this circle is disturbing in several respects. The need, among the fundamentalist groups he represents, for certainty and transparency in matters that do not admit of either, is evidence of glitter rather than gold in his understanding of the Christian message. The convolutions necessary to assuage doubt and support the unsupportable, that is, proving what cannot be proved, speaks to a certain desperation that Biblical fundamentalists face - and here we must include Catholic fundamentalists who in essence are remarkably close to their Bible-Belt cousins. Literalism of any kind is by definition non-contextual. The Christian message is nothing if not contextual, larger than life. To reduce it to

A Case Appealed (revisited)

narrowly constructed words on a page is to destroy it. The same people who accept basic ignorance about very tangible things in which they have "faith" today – the computer in their study, the microwave in their kitchen, the airplane they fly on – must have "certainty" about nebulous events in Palestine two thousand years ago! In my opinion, Strobel's book, far from being a call to faith, is a call to abandon it. The Church Fathers of *Early Christian Writings* would throw out his case.

Extracted from *Testament of the Third Man,* October, 2007

In Deference To Mark

With due respect, the columnist from the *Prince George Citizen* is mixing science with myth and Midrash when he tries to found in astronomical fact the "Star of Bethlehem." Today, most biblical scholars regard as merely poetic Matthew's story of the Wise Men and a Star from the East. And why not? If the earliest gospel, Mark, omits the Nativity altogether, does this not mean little or nothing was known about Jesus' birth? And if Matthew and Luke penned laudatory prologues to "complete" Mark, then the star becomes a small part of a bigger conundrum. Consider that:

(1) Historians can find no Roman census at the time of Herod the Great, who died in 4B.C.

(2) Using this "revised" calendar, Luke's census - when "Quirinius was governor of Syria"- could not have been much before 6CE, when Archelaus, Herod's errant son in charge of Judea, was deposed and a Roman prefect installed. This was at least ten years after Herod's death, and therefore outside the scope of either of the Nativity stories (Crossan, p.20).

(3) A Roman census would not have necessitated Joseph's leaving Nazareth, his "home town" (Luke 2:39) situated within Herod the Great's Palestine (no part of which was then under direct Roman rule) in order to register in *Bethlehem*, another Palestinian town not under Roman jurisdiction until 6CE. There would be even less reason for Joseph to have dragged his very pregnant wife some seventy miles to do so. Luke simply tries too hard to have Jesus (a renowned Galilean) of Nazareth, born in Bethlehem of Judea - in order to promote the idea of a messiah in the Davidic line "fulfilling" Micah 5:2 (Helms, pgs. 59/60); But, even if we overlook such reservations, the core issue of "migratory" censuses is unhistorical, per Crossan (p.20) who posits that the census

story would have been "a bureaucratic nightmare" if it were not "pure fiction."

Matthew avoids these problems but invites others. He has Joseph and Mary living in Bethlehem from before Jesus' birth. Accordingly he has no need for a census or the journey occasioned thereby. Instead he has the family flee into Egypt, purportedly to escape Herod's massacre of the innocents, and thence to Nazareth-in order to make their home there (Mat. 5:27). Both the massacre, paralleling the slaughter of Hebrew boys at the birth of Moses, Ex. 1:22, and the flight into Egypt - fulfilling rather dubious "prophecy", raise serious problems for historians. Matthew is too intent on depicting Jesus as the "New Moses". Not surprisingly, there is no other record of the reported massacre: neither in the Lukan gospel nor, as scholars tell us, anywhere else. Certainly Josephus would have mentioned such a horrendous crime, if it had occurred.

There are other difficulties: reconciling Luke's accounts of the circumcision of Jesus, the temple presentation in Jerusalem, and the Holy Family's subsequent return direct to Nazareth, within the Matthean context of Herodian terror and urgent flight into Egypt, are a few. Similarly, the Davidic and Mosaic molds in which the authors place their narratives are themselves difficult to reconcile, as are other inconsistencies in the stories. For example, Jesus' genealogies in Matthew and Luke are poles apart and reflect the theology-quest peculiar to each author. Suffice it to quote distinguished professor Marcus J. Borg's point that "most mainline scholars...do not see these [birth] stories as historically factual;" they are not "history remembered;" yet, this does not mean they detract from "the central truths about Jesus's significance." (pgs. 180 et sec)

From a lay person's perspective, the positioning of

In Deference To Mark

Matthew's Gospel *before* the other three gospels in the New Testament, can lead only to the false conclusion that it was written first. The converse applies in the case of Paul's letters - that is, the ones recognized as actually written by him – which are placed *after* the Gospels, when they were written long before! Because of their positioning, it is easy to overlook that they frame, rather than follow, much of what the Gospels relate.

It is ironical therefore that "modern planetariums and computers" have located the star according to your columnist. Why bother with all the astrological manipulations and second-guessing when ancient rabbinic Midrash will do? As John Shelby Spong relates in his book, *Born of a Woman*, (p.89), where he identifies several *Midrashes* that may have contributed to the celestial wonderer in Matthew's Gospel. Not least is the *Midrash* on the *First Book of Kings*, and the star that supposedly guided the Queen of Sheba to pay homage to Solomon. If Solomon was worthy of a star, why not the Son of God? As for what actually happened? Let's defer to Mark's ignorance about it.

From: *Reflections on Our Times*
Prince George, BC - January 2000

Women Priests?

The debate about women priests in the Catholic Church has been around since time immemorial. Throughout the centuries Rome's reasons for the anomaly of a male priesthood have been drawn from actions, real or apparent, on the part of Jesus. After all, his Apostles, according to the Gospels and, by extension Church *Tradition* dating back to the Church Fathers, were exclusively male. Therefore, in paragraph #1577 of the Catechism of the Catholic Church, published in 1995, we read: "Only a baptized man (vir) validly receives sacred ordination" (Codex *Luris Canonici*). The paragraph continues, "The Lord Jesus chose men (*viri*) to form the College of the twelve apostles, and the Apostles did the same when they chose collaborators to succeed them in their ministry," (the latter position is bulwarked by references to Matthew, Luke and various epistles, including one from a Church Father, Clement of Rome - second century).

Therefore, Pope Francis merely repeats an old doctrine when he proclaims: "the ordination of women [as priests] is not possible." So, what about his alternative? Admitting women to the *diaconate* may be good news to the ears of those German theologians who voted on the "Yes" side of the argument in 2011, but that's of little comfort to women. Presumably under pressure, Francis agreed to call together a commission to study the issue. Again, of little help. Going back to the Catechism, it's clear that the diaconate is "at a lower level of the hierarchy" – a level of service to a bishop that would apply permanently for women, unlike the stepping-stone to the priesthood that it provides for men. It would leave women more or less where they have been for millennia, especially given Francis's commitment to adhere to John Paul II's earlier take on the matter, for which he cites *Ordinatio Sacerdotalis*, a 1994 letter by John Paul II that claimed the Church, based on traditional excuses, has "no authority whatsoever to ordain women to the priesthood." But, the question remains: what is the *real story* behind the roadblock?

Francis, in his commitment to stand by his predecessor, no sooner opened the door to women, than he closed it in their faces. My reasons for once more raising the question of women priests (or lack thereof) are twofold: first, I find it curious that Francis relied on *Ordinatio* to explain John Paul II's position on the matter, when the full-blown explication had been penned six years earlier under the rubric *Mulieris Dignitatem*; second, if Francis is serious about adhering to a doctrine set in stone, why choose to ignore his predecessor's main *rationale* for excluding women - a matter high on the agenda in Mulieris, but not reiterated in *Ordinatio*? Without wishing to rehash what I wrote ten years ago in *Testament of the Third Man*, I must recall my first impressions of the document that Francis seems to want left out of the current discussion.

Mulieris is very instructive of Rome's medieval world-view of women in the centuries leading up to that encyclical. For many women, especially those in North America and Europe who had protested about having no voice in the Catholic Church, and for whom the anti-feminism and prudery of the Pauline and Augustinian schools were unacceptable, this encyclical offered no hope that someday there might be a female priesthood. The tragedy resided not only in its proscription, obscured as it was by verbosity that made the verdict seem incidental to the main purpose of the document, but in the misogyny underlying the whole exercise. For those who find the last remark harsh, I beg forgiveness, but must repeat what I wrote ten years ago: "From beginning to end, some fifty five pages, [Mulieris] exudes biblical funda-mentalism and traditional taboos. In essence, woman's purpose is largely that of being man's helper and mother of his children. Aspiring to the altar of God is beyond her." Yet, at the same time (if we bend our minds sufficiently) we are supposed to accept the statement that 'both man and woman are human beings to an equal degree.' The equality here avowed is, at best an empty gesture - not unlike the notion that both slave and master are equal before God: convenient if you are the master.

It is easy to dismiss Mulieris as an anti-feminist anachronism, appropriately dressed up in Biblical authority. But should one leave the matter there? That would give credence to the core rationalization in the document, which is that women, because of their *gender*, are not qualified to be Catholic priests. In case the argument in defense of this disqualification has slipped by unnoticed, I propose that we look at it more closely.

The basic premise, not discussed until Part VII of the document, is as follows: Jesus (a male) gave himself to the Church (female) in the form of bread and wine (consecrated as His Body and Blood). He continues to do so in the Eucharist through the agency of the priest. Through a heterosexual analogy in this spiritual union between human and mystical body, it stands to rights that there be a real-life stand-in for Jesus. If the Church is depicted as a woman, the person who wears Jesus' sandals can *only do so as a man*. Deduced from the premise, this finding (which we are made to understand is much regretted by scholarly clerics), is that the Church *has no option* but to deny some six hundred million Catholics full participation in the Church.

Well, what if the premise is full of holes? Would this not make the deduction invalid, or at best questionable? When I was a schoolboy, the story of the Eucharist was founded in Christ's words and actions when he sat at table with his disciples, as described in the Synoptic Gospels – Matt. (26: 26-28), Mark 14: (22-25), and Luke 22: (17-20). Must not the very consistency of the three accounts guarantee the story's authenticity? But what if there's an elephant in the room called 1Corrintians?

It is the year 70CE. The Jewish revolt against Rome is reaching a bloody end. Josephus, in his book *The Jewish War*, finds Titus in command of Roman legions who have just about destroyed Jerusalem, pursuant to his father Vespasian's order to do so. In Rome itself there has been much unrest; the fairly large Christian community (Gentiles for the most part) is fearful of reprisals against it as a sect of fifth-columnists, especially given the fact that their leader has been crucified in Judea for sedition. One of the theories behind Mark's Gospel is that made popular by S. G. F. Brandon who, put simply, has Mark (or whoever is using that name), situated in Rome during the turmoil, as traditionally believed. There, Mark writes his account of the sayings and actions of Jesus, with the overriding purpose of distancing Christians from the rebels in Palestine. Indeed, his Gospel is designed to place the blame for Jesus' death squarely on Jewish shoulders. (And so hangs the tale which will haunt Jews for two millennia.)

Mark's presence in Rome would have put him in contact with Paul's letters, if not with Paul himself. Come the penning of the last days of Jesus' ministry, one can surmise that Mark has in front of him 1Corrinthians 11 (22-25), and transcribes Paul's account of the Last Supper (minus "Do this in memory of me").

So, fast forward to the year 80CE, or thereabouts, and we find Matthew in Antioch, Syria, or thereabouts. Times have changed since Mark wrote his Gospel. There has been no Parousia as Mark seems to have expected, so Jewish Christians need to look to the future. Because the Church has come into its own, there is need to reinforce its foundations. For example, Matthew cannot portray the Apostles as the disparaged side-show depicted by Mark. Because Matthew is writing for those with a Jewish background, he makes special use of the Hebrew Scriptures in reference to Jesus. Whatever are his other sources, he has at hand Mark's Gospel, which forms the bedrock of his Gospel; important also is a hypothetical document not known to Mark, which scholars call *Quelle* (meaning "source"). This modern academic construct is founded upon the many passages common to both Matthew and Luke's, but not found in Mark's Gospel. When it comes to describing the Last Supper that Jesus enjoys with his Disciples, Matthew cribs the institution of the Eucharist from Mark.

And finally, Luke's Gospel. Scholars posit that it was penned in the Diaspora, maybe Greece. Luke, who we are fairly sure was a companion of Paul on some of his travels, is writing sometime after Matthew, let's say 85CE. His contribution to the New Testament is enormous, given that in addition to his Gospel, he is credited with writing The Acts of the Apostles. As with Paul, he is not credited with having known Jesus. Considered to have been a scholar and historian, much more so than the other Evangelists, he directs his gospel at Gentile Christians. Accordingly, it lacks the emphasis placed by Matthew on the Hebrew Scriptures, but, like Matthew he expands Mark's Gospel "backwards and forwards" (Fredrickson). As discussed above, scholars see Luke relying on Q, in addition to Mark's Gospel. However, for his story of the Last Supper there can be no doubt that he relies on Paul's 1Corrinthians 11 (22-25). In this case, reliance is more substantive in that Luke includes the matter of agency: "Do this in memory of me," explicit in his friend's letter, but not found in Mark and Matthew,

BY THE WAY...

As we have seen, we cannot rely on the "logical" chronology of New Testament books: (1) Matthew, Mark & Luke's (Synoptic) Gospels (putting aside John's for the moment); (2) Acts of the Apostles; (3) the letters of Paul and others, in that order. This chronology is only faithful to the time-line of lived events, but is very deceptive in most other respects. The NT books were not *written* in line with events they describe, but back to front as it were, no more evident than the fact that Paul letters *predate* everything else in the Canon, but are placed after Acts. As we have seen, Luke imports Paul's dictum of the Last Supper into his Gospel that was written decades after Paul wrote. Luke cannot then be a reliable source unless Paul's account is reliable. If the latter is faulty the whole story is questionable; and if that is so, the doctrine of male exclusivity in administering the sacrament posited in Mulieris is questionable.

But I hear, Objection! Objection! It is obvious Paul could not have been the primary source of this teaching. He must have gotten the story from one of the Eleven. It would have been easy for him to admit that he had, but he does not. Bearing in mind his aversion for the Jerusalem Church, especially evident in his Epistle to the Galatians and in his claim to be preaching his own Gospel, silence about relying on an Apostle for news of what happened at the Last Supper may be expected. Then, surely, he got the story from a reliable source who heard it from one of the Apostles. Again, silence is forthcoming. Instead, without equivocation, he reveals that he received the information regarding the Last Supper direct "from the Lord" (1 Corinthians 11:23). Here we have Paul confessing that, but for the Lord giving him the heads-up, he *originated* the Eucharistic doctrine. Decades later, when neither he nor the original apostles were any longer around, that doctrine was imported partially into Mark and Matthew, and substantively complete, into Luke. But, how credible is this "evidence?" As for the importance of the Eucharist, I remember a noted professor declaring in a speech that it is the *sine qua non* of the Catholic Faith. Was this not the clergy proclaiming itself without-which-nothing of the Church?

The foregoing is a personal reflection on the certainties expressed in Mulieris Dignitatem, the pivotal document Francis does not mention in his rational for the Church's exclusion of women from the priesthood. It has not been my intention to undermine Catholic devotion to the Eucharist. Each person must decide for himself or herself whether the Sacrament is meaningful in their life. At the same time, I believe the hierarchy has undermined that devotion by using the Eucharist as a fulcrum to elevate a male clergy above not only women, but also everyone else in the Church. Must not the dignity of all supersede doctrine?

Prince George, BC - December 2016

Interview on *Love or Logic*, with Jeff Selver

JS: *For our audience, this is a special one hour interview with the author of* Testament of the Third Man *- rants from the sidelines of faith. We ran into each other in the religion/philosophy section of a local bookstore, which was neat because we got to talking about our mutual interests in Christian history - including how this religion sprung up. You showed me your book and told me a little about it, and I told you about my program* -Love or Logic.

DCS: Honored to be on your program, Jeff.

So, let's talk about your book. In reading it, and I found it a great read; you bring in many areas of history, but also tie together ancient history with religion and where it is going, which I find an intriguing approach. That's my view; tell me, what do you want readers to get out of your book?

Thank you, Jeff. *Testament* grew out of thirty years of looking closer at these issues than I had done previously. I thought that because I was growing older maybe it was time I wrote a few things down. Out of that beginning the book emerged over time – thirty years, in fact. I guess readers will get out of it whatever they do get. The sort of reaction has been "I read your book and liked it, but I don't believe in God, so it didn't help me;" or, "your book is interesting but you pulled your punches at the end of it, and I don't think that was appropriate." Well, regarding the latter, I have to point out that I did not write the book in order to debunk Christianity, or the Catholic, or any other church. So it was not an attempt to cut off the ring on what people believe, or on what Christianity has achieved over two thousand years. I saw it as a point of departure for those who wished to look at what they themselves believe, and to recognize that Christianity has had its shortcomings, its bumps in the road; to see Christianity for what it is: a great religion that gives people a lot of hope, irrespective of the problems along the way.

I believe rethinking what one has grown up with is a good thing. Whether we look at the early church, or the Reformation it's a rethinking: from Judaism to Christianity; from Catholic Christianity to Protestant, to Reform Christianity. I believe this evolution will continue over time. For Catholics, Vatican Council II was a revolution of sorts in the1960s; and I believe the Church will continue to change. I see no reason why Non-Conformist churches won't do the same. After all, everything changes over time.

So you gave the book to people, some of whom were anti-religion and wanted to debunk religion. But I believe there is power in all religions, whose job it is to organize that power. I also believe it is good that you are able to humanize Christianity, which is a bold step because once people identify with the human parts they can better find what is divine.

Yes. The Church is made up of different congregations of people with a common foundation but for whom particular dogmas or approaches are sacrosanct. But there always will be those members who have contrary views, even within a congregation. This is inevitable, especially in the developed countries. For example, in Europe there has been much falling away from the Catholic Church among educated people, whereas the Church is growing in countries where education is not as available. Catholicism's growth is a non-starter in Germany and Italy, where congregations have declined substantially - reflecting a moving away from hierarchical, top down, religion among the educated classes, but is a going-concern in South America. Catholics are supposed to accept what the Church teaches; Evangelicals what the Bible teaches.

In both cases difficulties arise. Not everyone is going to accept what is expected of him or her. Whether it's their opposition to Rome's supposed fiat, or selective interpretation on the part of non-conformists, the result is exit in one way or another.

On the Evangelical side of Christianity, Pauline theology tends to dominate. So, while they claim to believe in every word of the Bible, verse-preferences are inevitable especially among contradictory texts that allow for shopping and changing among books, depending on what one wishes to find. The Old Testament presents real difficulties for those who say the Bible is inerrant, that every word is God-breathed, given the contrary verses in Genesis, Leviticus, Exodus, etc., that militate against women, for example. One need only turn to the commandment, "Thou shalt not kill," and compare it with the Book of Samuel where God advises Saul to massacre the Amalekites – every man, woman and child! Of course, true-believers often will not see what is hiding in plain sight.

What you say is well taken. Would you give listeners your spin on Christianity's relationship with the Old Testament, which is an issue I enjoyed in your book.

My friends give me hell for it, but I believe there are problems with the Old Testament, as part of the Bible. I see these books as Jewish Scriptures, exclusively. The early church was comprised of Jews: Jesus was Jewish, and so were his apostles, so it was reasonable that the early church venerated these books, indeed for many generations they were the only writings that counted as Scriptures for the early church, wherein references to scripture - both in the New Testament and the writings of Church Fathers - were references to the OT. When it came to proselytizing beyond Jewish confines where there was no tradition in these books, however, apparently there was resistance to them, or at least failure to understand their connection to Christian mores. This is where Origen's allegorized OT scriptures, in order to marry them to Christian precepts and ideas. Some experts say that full acceptance of Old Testament books by so-called Pagan converts in the wide Diaspora did not come about before the fourth century.

Be that as it may, I can't help surmising that in those days, if I were Jewish, I would have objected to the Christian Church's usurpation of my Holy Books, in the same way that Christians would have been very upset if Muslims, who have connections with the Bible - from Abraham through Jesus and Mary - had co-opted the New Testament as their lead-up scripture to the Koran in the seventh century. But the Jews of the first century were in no position to object to *their* scriptures being stolen. The problem for Christianity is that, because of OT mores, practices antithetical to NT thinking find their way into Christian history: witch burning (Ex 22), capital punishment (Deut.), etc. The Catholic Church has condemned the latter, but that is mainly because it operates as a teaching institution able to dictate what is "doctrine", and what is not. For my own part I believe that so long as one is faithful to the precepts of love of God and love of neighbour, one is doing the right thing; it is impossible to do the wrong thing in those circumstances.

Your book is a rant against the status quo. You believe that change requires knowledge of history and why previous changes were necessary. What changes do you regard as important, both in and out of the Catholic Church?

As far as the Catholic Church is concerned, and I do regard myself as a Catholic, the most important change I would like to see, is more regard for what church-members are saying, especially young people: not only what they say, but what they don't say. Many young people, including my children and those of several of my friends, don't go to church, even though they were brought up to do so. I presume they regard the Church as irrelevant in their lives now, and incapable of change acceptable to them in the future. They want no part of the top-down relationship the Church would demand of them. Older people like myself might take the time to say what they feel should happen, but they really don't have a transforming voice amidst the administrative and theological red-tape. As people become more educated and more aware of their second-class status, they may eventually rebel, usually with their feet.

We have to remember that the Catholic Church flowered in the middle ages after the fall of the Roman Empire in the West, as part of a feudal top-down society. In the sixteenth century the Reformation, under Luther and his adherents, sought to change this. It made it plain that Christianity has a horizontal level, as well as a vertical one, and gave effect to the former. What the Catholic Church lost in the process was the opportunity to change. Instead, constrictions within the Church increased. The Council of Trent gave rise to more cloistering of women, to requirements for higher education among the clergy, and greater oversight in areas such as marriage and confession before priests. In one way or another Trent wanted and got greater control over the laity. The whole process defeated what could have been achieved through *listening* to the cry of the Reformation. There is no denying that the Reformation brought about much needed democracy outside the Catholic Church, but how democratic Protestant churches are today is a good question.

If the Catholic Church has for most of its history shut

the doors against democracy, the Second Vatican Council did open some windows. I was part of the synod movement in the 1970s that sought to bring lay people into the decision-making processes within the Church. This movement, having fallen by the wayside, needs to be revived today, especially in developed countries where educated, independent-minded people are walking away from an authoritarian structure. As for the Non-Conformist churches, and again I'm speaking for myself alone, they should espouse a broader definition of Christianity than at present. What comes across as the me-and-God, or God-in-my-back-pocket philosophy, is a passive form of Christianity wherein I am saved without having to do anything about it.

I loved that part of your book. I wrote a similar critique which I called spiritual irresponsibility, which is what your message hinges on – that it's too easy to hold that if believe, that's it - I can then go drink and do what I want. This is a kind of scapegoat, if you will.

Agreed. This is a Pauline derivation of Christianity, a misappropriation of Biblical texts to suit a certain theology. As you are aware Luther broke with Rome in the sixteenth century, disavowing allegiance to Pope and clergy, and substituting for them a Pauline doctrine, which promises salvation by faith alone. He is even said to have added the "alone" in his German translation of the Bible - published in 1634 - underlining the passivity mentioned above, that for a long time sidelined social justice issues in the Evangelical wing of Christianity.

And now?

To be fair, there have been exceptions in this area at various times: a great example being the struggle for the abolition of slavery in the nineteenth century. But I don't believe much emphasis is placed on the Book of James that Luther wanted to write out of the Bible, in spite of the fact that Jesus was deeply concerned about people and their needs. He is very much involved in "works", which non-conformist theology dismisses as not relevant to salvation.

Paul's mind-frame is just believe and that's all you need. He didn't know Jesus personally yet was the one most responsible for spreading the message: just believe, while the Gospel of Thomas ends with "if you understand these teachings, shall you be free, (as opposed to just believing), thus twisting the message towards one's responsibility to internalize it. This difference I found interesting.

On the other hand a Canonical Gospel, such as Matthew's is explicit about the necessity for works. Chapter 25 is very definitive of the work-ethic that can be seen as a foundation of Christ's teachings. Here there is no reference to a passive faith being the answer to salvation. But I don't hear non-Catholics talking about that chapter's counter to Paul. But more than this: Matthew 25 is not a "one-liner" that may cover everything and nothing, depending on predetermined points of view. On the contrary Matthew 25 includes eleven verses of cogent instruction that is unequivocal in meaning, and which eschews the "holier than thou" attitude of many Christians, be they Evangelical or Catholic. When I was young the Catholic Church was the only route to heaven. Now, the shoe is on the other foot, that of the "saved."

As indicated in *Testament* I believe all the churches should be signatories to a manifesto declaring the core principles of Christianity and the responsibilities of all who profess Christianity. It should condemn war and exploitation of people; it should call for social justice and condemn crass materialism, militarism, homelessness, capital punishment, and torture of all kinds. We are told that in Los Angeles there are a hundred thousand living on the streets. Canada is a rich country. In 1978 when I landed here it would be unheard of having to step over someone prostrate on Young Street or Hastings. Where are we today, as a country? Then there are the hands-off political issues that allow for "no comment" on the part of churches, whether it be the invasion of Iraq or merciless bombing and deprivation of people in Gaza.

Therefore, you would like to see the Churches as a worldwide voice for Christian values.

Yes, I would.

At what point would this be stepping over the line? Would the policy be confined to reaching out and saying "This is bad" or "This is good"?

The latter may be all we can expect, although this would be better than church leaders standing beside the President of the United States as that country triumphantly commences the bombing of Iraq. Where does a Christian perspective gel with this? At some point the Catholic Church did come out against these proceedings. However, the disapproval did not percolate down to parish level, where it remained as one of those political issues beyond discussion; so little if anything came of it.

Great conversation. For the next few minutes I want to understand more about you. Testament is a heavy book and, although you are still a Catholic, writing it must have meant a reforming of some of your beliefs, a new understanding of those beliefs. Did they change as a result of the book?

Difficult questions, Jeff. An old saying has it that you don't know what you believe until you write it down. In 1971 I wrote a paper for an address before a Catholic convention in Kingston, Jamaica that somehow got me thinking critically about Church matters. But it was not until ten years later that I began devoting excessive amounts of time to the study of early Christianity and medieval history, which extended over the next thirty years. Part of that time I devoted to writing, which ended up as a book I was well aware many would dislike, though I certainly did not mean to offend readers.

But you still believe in God.

Yes.

And what is your relationship to Jesus Christ?

I don't see it as a "relationship." If I did, I am not sure what that would mean. Is it necessary to view Christ as God? Many Christians use this label to upstage Muslims; we have a God-man, you only have a prophet. Such one-upmanship on the Christian side is a mistake that leads to division and discord. I prefer not to see Christ in a sentimental way, but as a pretty tough guy who says it like it is.

Of course; he disturbed those in the Temple, turned over tables, his rhetoric could be offensive.

A forceful charismatic figure, he was - not the usual weeping type we see on Christian TV. In my opinion Christians should move away from the comfortable pew that religion provides, wherein one attends church on Sundays largely to feel good about oneself.

As you say, a lot of what Christ taught was anything but comfortable,

BY THE WAY...

whether it was about giving away one's wealth or criticizing the Scribes and Pharisees.

Another concept that is questionable in my opinion is "tolerance;" this is another one-upmanship term that at best is condescending to the other side. "Acceptance" of other faiths is what is needed. Everyone has the right to his or her beliefs. Of course, it is a two-way street that the other side must accept.

That's a great place to wrap this up, Dereck. Thank you for joining us this afternoon.

My pleasure, Jeff. Thank you.

An edited transcript of an interview on *University of Northern British Columbia* Radio, January 2010

In New York, en route to England, July 1960, with mother, Gertrude

President (centre), and Council members of the Institute of Chartered Accountants of Jamaica (1976)

Delivering paper *The Auditor's Responsibility - the gathering storm,* introduced by Lancelot Reynods, FCA, at First Caribbean Conference of Accountants, 300 in attendance (April 1978)

Speaking at the banquet of the Caribbean Conference. (April 1978) On the left: Sir Florizel Glasspole, Governor General of Jamaica, and Birgitta Sale; and on right: Jasper Burnett, FCA, and Lady Glasspole

Conducting professional developing course for CAs, on behalf of Institute of Chartered Accountants of BC, at The Four Seasons Hotel, Vancouver (1982)

Touche Ross (Ja) partners' meeting, 1971

PROFESSION THAT LOST ITS WAY

The Reluctant Profession

Today marks the first official quarterly luncheon for members, an occasion that hopefully is the first of many opportunities for us to come together as a professional body. I would very much like to share with you a few thoughts on that subject, which I have been pondering for some time. There is no doubt but that we have been hiding our light for too long.. We are a disparate group each of us not knowing much about the other, each firm eyeing suspiciously the other, with no unity of purpose among us, in short, little or no communication for too long. It is therefore appropriate that we take this opportunity to look at ourselves, and take stock of where we stand as a profession in Jamaica.

I don't pretend to have special credentials for this examination, or even original ideas, but I believe it is true to say that what has been achieved in the public realm has been the work of a precious few members, including the founding of the Institute itself. Too many of us have never even attended an Annual General Meeting, much less taken an interest in the day to day operations of the Institute.

So, how have we progressed since the founding of the Jamaican Institute nine years ago, since the Public Accountancy Act gave it legal form, statutory prominence? Is the profession the vital force within the community that it should be? Having spoken to a number of members over the last few months, I am not sure it is a force at all. Should we not get together more often, exchange ideas, compare notes about where we want to go as an organization? Only then will we be able to knock the kinks out; only then will we know where our contribution, great or small, is most needed.

Presented before the *First Quarterly Luncheon* for Chartered Accountants, at Kingston, Jamaica, February 1974.

BY THE WAY...

Take education, a fundamental problem facing us. How is it that in a developing country like this there is no faculty of accountancy at our university? So far as I know we have tried to get one. Yet today the Institute, with only limited resources, is on its own in trying to maintain the high standard of learning for students who must pass British examinations. At present there are 300 active students on the roll. The practicing firms must contribute hard cash for their formal instruction. Industry and commerce are not meeting their part of the cost. Should much more training not come via the university? How else will the profession secure popular appeal and status necessary for growth and development? If such collaboration was important to the legal profession – manifested by the recently founded Norman Manley School of Law – it certainly is important to us.

So much for our students, but what about members of the Institute, what is our public rating in 1974? When I see how many other professions are represented on boards of public companies, I have to ask, are we being taken seriously? I dare say, there can be no rational explanation for this. If the Chartered Accountant is excluded, who can be included? Has our salt lost its savor, or is it the case that it has not been tasted? There are other areas where anomalies abound. As a profession we are excluded from representing clients before the Revenue Court in spite of the fact that Chartered Accountants are pre-eminent in the field of taxation in this country. How strongly have we protested these exclusions?

Yes, there are areas in which the profession has been short-changed. At the same time I cannot help but mention some of the areas where I believe we have ourselves to blame. To begin with, we have been too quick to import into this country many of the introversions (real or imagined) of our founding professional bodies abroad. It seems we have grown accustomed to and satisfied with form over substance, and a negative kind of "respectability", rather than accepting the challenges with which we are faced in this country. We have not been forthright enough on matters directly within the profession's purview. Our contribution to public debate and enlightenment on fundamental issues, such as income tax reform, has been virtually nix in recent years. Today the Government appears obsessed with tax collection to the exclusion of tax planning, no new thinking on encouraging capital inflows, no incentives for private companies to go public or for redirecting resources into labour-intensive industries. Should not tax incentives be tied to production and exports? Commenting on these matters should be our business; and those comments should come before the Government makes decisions, not afterwards.

In a slightly different vein, one of the deficiencies in the profession today is the lack of uniformity in auditing standards among practicing firms. This is cause for concern. Traditionally it is through the medium of its audit opinion that the profession's public responsibility really comes to life. We cannot afford to wait for the scandals plaguing other countries, and arising out of our negligence, to visit us here.

Again, revisiting the problem inherent in the lack of a public image, I believe this was born of distancing imported from our founding bodies. Everything operates to keep us out of the public eye. We are the proverbial back-room boys who fear the light of day. I can remember as an articled student in England in the early sixties trying unsuccessfully to fathom why a Chartered Accountant could not disclose both his name and his profession in addressing a public meeting or appearing on television. It seemed incredible that a profession, presumably wishing to have a positive effect on public opinion, could be so negative in promoting its members.

BY THE WAY...

I have no doubt that such thou-shalt-not ethics have contributed much towards conservatism among members, and indeed, to the petty jealousies and rivalries, which have done the profession no good, here or abroad. Granted, the profession in England and the US is more outgoing today than it was fifteen years ago. But are we following suit? One of the most detrimental characteristic of the local practitioner is the tendency towards isolation from fellow practitioners. This results in a "me-me" attitude among accounting firms, which is as shortsighted collective-strength wise, as it is defeatist self-image wise. This attitude is an invitation to the public to play one firm off against another, undercutting the professionalism of each and the earning power of all.

I realize I haven't painted a rosy picture or blown the trumpet for our profession today, but I felt certain things needed to be aired. I believe the Institute is home to some of the best brains in this country. My regret is that there is still a number of accountants who are eligible for membership, but who have chosen to rely on foreign qualifications instead of becoming members. These total maybe one hundred – many in the Civil Service, many in industry. Won't these come forward now? Success means all of us acting together: big firms helping small firms, members in government and industry supportive of those in practice. Reluctance is a trait we can ill afford.

Let us remember that it is not that these things have been tried and found wanting, but rather that they have been found difficult and therefore not tried.

On the State of the Profession:
Interview with *Communicator Magazine*

CM: *What in your view is the key problem facing the accounting profession?*

DCS: The key problem facing the profession today is credibility regarding its reporting function. It seems to me almost every other problem is tied directly to this one. If the profession is to be worthy of the position of judge and jury of the financial community what it will have to show is that its audit opinion adequately discharges the profession's responsibilities to the investor and the community at large.

Is it international, national, or local in scope?

The problem of reporting is one of communication. It is very international in scope.

How did the problem develop? What are its short and long term implications for the profession?

I think the age-old preoccupation of the profession with numbers contributed much to the development of a myopia regarding their meaning. I suppose in days of yore when the old accountant did not die but only lost his balance, form was more important than substance, and what was not seen was not important. Today, his sophisticated procedures and techniques allow him to see much more, but he communicates much less. Nothing has changed. So far as the public is concerned this state of suspended animation is not far removed from death. The short-term implication of this problem is public contempt

BY THE WAY...

for his hackneyed opinion. The long-term implication is its total irrelevance.

Is the profession aware of the problem?

Yes and no. By this I mean that the limitations of financial reporting have come under the microscope in recent years. Out of the soul-searching has come more meaningful financial statements. But the profession still hides behind ambiguities and generalizations in its audit opinions. In effect then, the responsibility to report has been passed completely to management, except in the case of one or two countries, e.g. Sweden, where the auditor reports on management. The other extreme obtains in the U.K., where unqualified audit reports have been reduced to two lines. How does this make sense?

And the attitude of those outside the profession to the problem?

I don't believe those outside the profession have a definite attitude to this problem. What manifests itself in so many ways is the dissatisfaction of the public with the profession. There is an awareness that something is lacking; but no amount of refinement or even re-evaluation in financial reporting *per se* is going to absolve auditors indefinitely from saying something about what is *behind* the financial statements on which they report.

Is there a solution to the problem?

The solution lies in the profession coming to grips with the auditor's responsibility to communicate. This reporting responsibility is not synonymous with that of the entity under audit. It hovers over the entity and transcends financial statements which, like the snapshot, capture only the fleeting

On the State of the Profession:

image. Each picture may be "exact" but how can "present fairly" mean the same thing in all circumstances to which it is applied?

I guess that the profession worldwide will have to de-standardize audit opinions in the years to come in order that they may fit individual circumstances. There will have to be a broadening of scope so far as content is concerned so that opinions may become more meaningful and therefore more useful. Obviously this will result in subjectivity but I think this may be more apparent than real. What we have now within the confines of stereotyped phraseology is apparent objectivity, or worse - apparent certainty.

Whose co-operation is needed to implement that solution?

First the profession must decide what its reporting function ought to embrace. This cannot be done in the splendid isolation of the proverbial "back room" but must be oriented to the needs of users. Instead self-protection has become an obsession especially in the U.S. where so much of the leadership in the profession originates. Once this myopia has been corrected the practical application will have to be worked out with the co-operation of regulatory bodies and maybe even legislation providing protection from predatory elements in the financial community. In the U.K. there has been some move towards limiting the liability of the auditor. This should be emulated internationally: the matter needs very careful study by the International Accounting Standards Committee.

Interview with *Communicator Magazine*, New York, April 1977. The author was then president of the Institute of Chartered Accountants of Jamaica.

The Auditor's Responsibilities:
The Gathering Storm

Anyone who has taken a cursory glance at the international press in recent years has discovered that many a professional auditor has changed his mode of living. His proverbial backroom now boasts iron bars and padlock. The wretched fellow huddles in darkness fearful of what will happen next, while critics hurl abuse at him. Highlighting some of his difficulties, a leading US magazine reported recently that "Never before have the activities of the conservative and secretive fraternity of Certified Public Accountants received so much attention from the public."[1] With unexpected bankruptcies, major frauds and illegal payoffs on the increase, twenty-five million stockholders were looking very askance at the reliability and diligence of auditors. One article opined:

> "The questions now being raised attest to an erosion of confidence in the accounting profession. Hundreds of lawsuits (one involving a judgment of thirty million dollars against the auditors, and another in which the settlement was forty two million), a flood of new regulations from the Securities & Exchange Commission and a barrage of criticisms from Congress, all point to the accountant's declining image."[2]

Meanwhile, across the Atlantic, an article in the *London Observer* cited one critic as saying that the two hundred and fifty million pounds, which industry spends on its auditors is money thrown away. The article, *No Accounting for Waste*, thrashed auditors for timidity, and for being mere "hired

A paper presented before *The Caribbean Conference of Accountants*, April 1978 – Published: US *Journal of Accountancy,* January 1981

BY THE WAY...

help," remarking that what was happening was just another "chapter in the story of growing public disillusion about the value of [auditors]."

Almost as if to prove that "all things that rise also converge," the difficulties of the Anglo/American profession are today quite similar in meaning. In the words of another authority on such matters the accounting profession is "blown with the wind."[3] It has no fixed purpose and no guts.

It is open to anyone here today to charge that the profession is on a firm footing in the Caribbean region, and that there is no point in citing other people's problems. Not long ago this was the view in the UK. When disturbing news came out of the US, commentators in the UK would say, "Well, those strange things could not happen here." Today, as we have seen, the situation is quite different. Our region has no reason to be complacent. We are strongly influenced by Anglo/American traditions, not only regarding professional practice, but also in our legal structure and business environment – especially the foreign element. It would be stupid to sit back and assume that we occupy a privileged place in the scheme of things.

Because my purpose here today is to trace the evolution of the storm of "public disillusion," or what may be regarded as the auditors' failure to find their place in the sun, I confess to a somewhat negative bias and do not apologize for raising issues that many will see as controversial and/or questionable. But I hope you will accept what follows as a basis for discussion, if nothing else. For the purpose of this paper, unless otherwise indicated, "profession" means public-practice firms, which in turn will be confined largely to the auditing fraternity.

Looking back, I see four "chapters" covering relatively

The Auditor's Responsibilities:

distinct phases of the storm's development. Of course, dates will not be exact given that periods inevitably overlap, but as close as I can delineate them they are as follows:

1850 (and before) to 1930	- Early Warning
1931 to 1948	- The Doldrums
1949 to 1965	- An Ominous Calm
1966 to the Present	- The Storm Breaks

Early Warning (1850 to 1930)

As the Scottish commissioned work by Richard Brown shows, the audit function in one form or another reaches back into antiquity.[4] Recognized as important in each advance of western civilization beginning probably with Egyptians, it was adopted by the Greeks and the Romans in their time, each according to the extent to which public property was entrusted to individuals. The book traces this development, regarding the importance of auditing, through medieval Italy (where modern bookkeeping was invented in 1494 and, incidentally, where, in Milan, the first private "institute" of accountants was formed in 1739;[5] and finally to Britain where there were audits of Exchequer officials, and of accounts kept by Sheriffs, in order to ensure that Crown revenues were duly accounted for.[6] Even before that, the accounts of "The Worshipful Company of Pewterers of the City of London" were audited by craft members – who, interestingly, refused to certify accounts for the fiscal year 1465-1466, and who qualified their report on a number of occasions.[7]

There is a familiar ring to the story that by the time William Pitt became Chancellor of the Exchequer in the eighteenth century, the whole system of auditing the national accounts "had become a farce." The two *Auditors of Imprest* were drawing sixteen thousand pounds annually, but had

BY THE WAY...

"delegated their work to clerks" who made no attempt at a real investigation, allowing every kind of fraud and collusion to grow up, and overlooking fees, perquisites and gratuities to be given to persons in official situations.[8] The result: Pitt abolished the position of *Auditors of Imprest* and appointed a special board with wide powers to do their work.

Maybe the most important lesson we can learn from the distant past is that the financial auditor represented the community. We are told that as far back as 1310, the records of the City of London reveal "six good men of the City were elected in the presence of the whole community" to audit the accounts of the Chamberlain. Presumably, they also reported to the whole community, thus putting-paid to the idea that the profession's broad responsibility is a twentieth century development.

Although recognizable in earlier times, however, the audit function does not assume its modern role until after 1850. In England, the Joint Stock Companies Act of 1844 provided for mandatory audits of companies registered under the Act. In 1855 the Limited Liability Act conferred the privilege of limited liability to companies, on condition that (inter alia) they had auditors approved by the Board of Trade.[9] Although these requirements were short-lived in England, at least for the moment, in Scotland the Companies Act of 1862 contained provisions for the appointment of auditors and became known as the "the accountants' friend." It is rather anomalous, therefore, that we find the first modern institutes in Scotland granted Royal Charters by Queen Victoria in 1844/45 without any mention made of auditing in the originating petitions.

In this way, auditing was recognized in law before it was adopted officially by a fledgling accounting profession. I find this fascinating - can't help but feel that an explanation for the anomaly would help us understand better this early period of modern auditing. My own theory, if you will allow me, is that the young profession at first was somewhat embarrassed by a rather mundane function, which was not confined to accountants. Striving to establish themselves as respectable, accountants preferred to see themselves as appendages of the legal profession, out of which they had sprung. Whatever the explanation for initial skepticism, up-turned noses were already smelling the roses.

For the modern audit function was a late child of the Industrial Revolution, conceived when industrial expansion became impossible without the marriage of management and external capital. At first it was unwanted, left out in the cold at times, farmed out to various foster homes - finally ending up in the arms of a young profession which had better things to do, until it recognized its true calling. By the end of the nineteenth century we find that if auditing were excluded from his roster the chartered accountant in the UK "would be deprived of the most regular and the most remunerative portion [of his business]."[10] A typical case of stone rejected becoming the corner-stone. The same thing is happening in the USA about this time. We see auditing given a little more prominence as a function of the profession. There is also favourable reference to auditing by speakers at the Golden Jubilee of the Scottish Institute in 1904.

But already in the latter part of the nineteenth century there had been a number of cases involving auditors brought before UK courts. In today's context, the auditor received the court's blessing in many of these cases - being referred to in very tame, condescending language, such as his being a watchdog not a bloodhound; his having to use only "reasonable care and skill" and "not bound to approach his work with suspicion." Commenting on these turn-of-the- century apologies for auditors, Gower makes the point

BY THE WAY...

that they are unlikely to be of much assistance today. When one studies the accounting profession of that time, one sees through a glass darkly the beginning of the storm that is very threatening in our day.[11].

It was during the first three decades of the twentieth century that the modern accounting profession lost its innocence, causing the first stones to be thrown with bad intention. As the extensive research of J. I. Edwards shows, UK auditors rationalized their responsibilities during that period, remaining silent in the face of financial information that was often "designed to mislead rather than educate."[12]. In this regard, the evidence cited by leading members of the profession, and that on behalf of various Institutes coming before the Green Committee on Company Law in 1925, showed not only the scant regard being paid to ethical standards in financial reporting, but also the profession's contentment with the status quo. For these reasons it is not surprising that auditors considered it quite sufficient to take a legalistic view of their responsibilities. Indeed, according to a prominent professional body, it was "unreasonable to expect the auditors to progress beyond the minimum requirements laid down by law."[13] The result of this head-in-the-sand approach was that the auditor's report was no guarantee that financial statements showed "a true and correct view." The reason for this failure was adduced by Justice Wright in the famous Royal Mail case, which marked the end of the UK profession's gestation period of willful blindness in the face of misleading financial reports: "Possibly it may be said [the auditor] was too pliant with the wishes of those in authority."

Turning to the situation in the United States at this time, we find a similar evolution of the audit function. Prior to 1890 most audits were of owner-managed enterprises. By the last decade of the century, however, the separation of ownership from management as businesses grew in size gave rise to demands for protection of investors and the public at large. Then, around 1900, a shift in this view found less emphasis being placed on accountability, and more on auditors regarding themselves as advisors to the business community. Encouraged to foster co-operation among businessmen, the auditor now came to be seen as providing a service to management.[14] It is noteworthy that in 1912, one authority was prescient in asserting that auditors were expected to exercise their judgment "to ascertain the actual financial condition and earnings of an enterprise."[15] However, given that it was the overarching view that financial statements were largely matters of opinion, we are left in doubt of the effectiveness of this assertion. Be that as it may, it seems reasonable to assume that standards were higher in the U.S. than in Europe. After all, the American Institute issued a statement on auditing procedures as early as 1917!

By whatever guideline chosen, leading institutes were little more than gentlemen's clubs whose main purpose was to gain respectability and establish professional status for self-conscious accountants too eager to make friends with those who only sought to use them for their own ends. This period ends with the Great Crash of 1929, which shook the US profession to its roots, and in the UK with the moment of truth brought about by the Royal Mail case, for more on which see below.

The Doldrums, 1931 – 1948

During the next phase of its development, which I place between 1931 and 1948, the audit function in the UK does not progress beyond the stage of immaturity. But eyes have been opened to the need for change when the sensational Royal Mail case of 1931 exposed the profession's soft

231

underbelly. Following the financial collapse of this shipping giant, it was revealed that for seven years the company's financial statements had not disclosed whether the business was making a profit or a loss, because of the manipulation of secret reserves. At that time secret reserves were regarded as "one of the corner stones of modern company finances,"[16] allowing companies large and small to do as they pleased in "managing" their profits (or in the Mail case, their losses). Although the auditor and co-defendant in the case apparently had done what his profession, as well as legal precedent, expected of him (i.e. nothing), in the words of Justice Wright, one could assume "that he ought to have taken some drastic step....in order to bring to the minds of the shareholders the true position of the company's affairs."[17]

There is no doubt this case set the stage for a rethinking of auditors' responsibilities between 1931 and 1948, but one hunts in vain to find an official statement on auditing standards during this period. In the absence of comprehensive company legislation in the UK the malaise of the earlier period persisted. While internal upgrades in the quality of work may have obtained for many firms, there was still the temptation for others to remain behind a barbed-wire fence of imaginary constraints. These were waiting for a Companies Act that would set them free. As one commentator proclaimed in 1942: "Attempts to persuade the accounting profession to take a wider view of its public responsibilities have so far met with little success. There is little or no evidence during the last twenty or twenty-five years to show that the professional accountant ...has produced a single idea of value to industry or the state. He has merely ticked and cast (added) and trusted in God."[18]

The Situation was somewhat different in the United States. After the Stock Market Crash of 1929, the American public woke up to the importance of financial reporting. For this disaster became the catalyst for a great leap forward in accounting and auditing standards, and with them the rapid advance of the profession generally. By the turn of the decade nearly fifty years ago George O. May, who was to become chairman of a special committee on accounting principles, made the prophetic statement, "the time has come when auditors must assume larger responsibilities, and their position [should] be more clearly defined."[19] In 1934, Congress obliged by passing the Securities and Exchange Act, providing for the establishment of the SEC, which was given wide powers over auditors of listed companies, including the ability to expel them from practicing before the Commission.

Things were moving fast. In 1936 the American Institute of Certified Public Accountants issued its pivotal bulletin, *Examination of Financial Statements by Independent Public Accountants*, which contained the principal steps considered necessary for an auditor to perform in the examination of a typical manufacturing enterprise before he would be justified in expressing an opinion on those statements. The need for improvements in auditing standards became obvious almost immediately. In 1936 the McKesson & Robbins fraud was discovered in which $19m of inventories and receivables out of total assets of $87m were found to be fictitious. A wave of publicity ensued in which auditing procedures were widely criticized. Largely because of this case, especially given that the SEC was threatening to take over the auditing standard-setting function, the American Institute of CPAs took the initiative in 1939 to create the Special Committee on Auditing Procedures.[20] In October of that year its publication "Extensions of Auditing Procedures" recommended the observation of inventory-taking and direct confirmation of receivables by the auditor, as essential prerequisites in formulating an audit opinion.

The Committee also began work on the development of "generally accepted auditing standards," but took until 1947 to issue its report setting out nine basic rules - with a tenth to follow a year later. The now historic bulletin, Statement No. 23, recommended that in any audit report to which his name was attached in conjunction with financial statements, the auditor should either (a), express an opinion as to fairness, with or without qualification; or (b), if his examination was insufficient, or if for other reasons he ought to withhold an opinion, he should state clearly that he was unable to express an opinion and give the reasons why.

This bulletin was debated for two years before being accepted by the members in the General Meeting of 1949. During this period, therefore, we see the professional auditor, having been buffeted somewhat, coming to recognize that there is need for higher standards and/or more recognition in law, depending on which side of the Atlantic he finds himself. What he gets in the form of *Generally Accepted Auditing Standards* in the US, or a new Companies Act in the UK, is significant, but not enough.

An Ominous Calm, 1949 to 1965

Marching briskly into the 1950s and 60s, the profession was confident in the mild prestige it had won during the previous generation which had been almost devoid of financial scandals and devastating lawsuits. At last it could feel secure that the auditor performed an important function, and occupied a pivotal place in the business community. Especially in the US, this was the time of the great industrial boom, when the profession convinced expansionist businessmen that audits were vital to their credibility. Practicing firms were enjoying unprecedented growth, aided and abetted by the demand for auditing services.

Mergers abounded during this period as firms (especially the large ones) took advantage of the bonanza in big-business clients. As evidence of this, in 1952 the 620 largest corporations in the US were audited by ninety-two different firms; by 1965 some 600 of them were audited by a mere sixteen.[21] In the 1950s alone, seven accounting firms had opened 134 offices throughout the US, and seventy new ones overseas.[22] Much of the same was happening in the UK during this period.[23]

However, on both sides of the Atlantic, the trouble was that the practicing profession was not being challenged intellectually. In this regard the Cohen Commission suggested that the lack of focus in the US, during much of this period, resulted from a protracted falling out between the profession and the universities whereby advancement of the profession was stalled, and "only a few professors were openly critical of those accounting and reporting abuses which gave rise to much of the present criticisms of the profession."[24]

In the UK, bearing in mind that the 1948 Companies Act had given overriding importance to financial statements showing a "true and fair view" of the affairs of the corporation, leaving auditors to guard that sacred trust, one is dumbfounded to find popular textbooks published in the 1950s defining an audit as "detection of fraud, the detection of technical errors and [those] of principle." The 1950 edition of one major work, containing 950 pages of fine print, devotes 750 pages to transcripts of court cases and statutes, as well as discussions of accounting principles. Only 150 relate to auditing procedures – with no mention of audit philosophy. Further, the required attributes of auditors at this time were supposed to comprise a thorough knowledge of accounting, a thorough grasp of the law, and an understanding of business.

Given the above it is not surprising that out of twenty-nine major presentations before nine years of Oxford summer courses relative to the accounting profession during the period 1951 to 1962, only three were devoted to auditing. Of the three only one presentation attempted to look below the surface of accepted practice. Indeed, the similarity in outlook is remarkably similar at the beginning and end of the 1950s. Considering that practitioners had earned 85% of their high incomes from auditing since the turn of the century, it is curious that little had been done to meet the intellectual challenges that lay beneath their work. Between 1854 and 1965 only five statements on auditing had been issued (compared with thirty in the US - five being issued there in the 1950s alone). The official explanation for this dearth in publications by the premier UK institute was that it had been reluctant "to issue views on technical subjects lest they should be resented by members, and lest standards should come to be set which might, on occasion, be embarrassing to members."[25]

All in all, the ominous calm between 1949 and 1965 was a period during which, on both sides of the Atlantic, the profession flexed its muscles and convinced itself that it looked good, not realizing that looks count for very little in the long run.

The reporting function: Financial auditing in the broadest context is a reporting function, at the core of which is the auditor's opinion. If a financial audit does not result in an opinion – positive, negative, or in between - about the financial statements under audit the work of the auditor would be incomplete. As with all good reporters the auditor is first and foremost an investigator, who must ask not only what, but how and why. After weeks of detective work, sometimes spanning the globe, after maybe millions of dollars in fees are billed, his work culminates in a report addressed, if not specifically then surreptitiously, to the corporate world and its adherents. The report may be the manifesto on which the auditor's reputation (and that of the financial system) stands, and yet throughout the history of the accounting profession it has received little public accreditation, or attention - except when things go wrong, of course.

The crucial question is whether the auditing fraternity fully appreciates the depth and breadth of its public responsibilities. Recent research shows that the practitioner "once accepted as a qualified member of a professional group, conforms by subscribing to group norms, and accepting the implied obligations to colleagues, clients and the public."[26] In a sense this finding can be turned on its head to find the public, and especially the financial press, equally accepting of the passive role they attribute to the auditor. Textbooks and academic courses, up to very recently, tended to emphasize procedural tests as appropriate in the carrying out of audits. Only when these laborious tasks were completed, did students, rather casually, turn to a report that articulates an opinion, the rigid form of which was usually enshrined in some law or convention denoting "clear and unambiguous." Given this situation, the lack of public attention is understandable. In the early days, financial audits were carried out primarily to detect fraud and error; now auditors, more often than not, are meant to report whether financial statements show a "true and fair view." But what does this mean?

A dictionary definition of True may be "in accordance with fact or reality." But what determines fact or reality? Certainly not historical cost, which is almost meaningless, and in current inflationary times is a dead weight around the profession's neck. On the other hand, "fairness" may mean "characterized honest and just" or "just and equitable." Again, how does the auditor make a judgment about this? As one commentator puts it, fairness suggests conflicting interests. But one is led to ask, fair to whom?[27] Transfers of materials between subsidiary and parent companies are seldom at arm's length prices; absent disclosure, do the financial statements show a fair view of the results? They may be true, but that is about all: certainly not clear or unambiguous. A recent call in the UN to have transnationals disclose the basis of transfer prices between developing and developed countries is a case of the profession not recognizing it had the responsibility to call attention to this matter all along. And let us not confuse the issue by asserting that the subsidiary in the developing country is a separate legal entity. And that the financial statements agree with the books. But the question is, "Are they fair?"

Traditionally, in the UK especially, auditing standards have been matters of "judgment," which meant simply that there were no official pronouncements regarding what was expected of auditors. Today, practicing firms make up for deficiencies at institute levels by setting their own standards. In this regard US accounting firms, and their affiliates abroad, are more focused on having to dance to the same tune, in that they must abide by official precepts. The alternative approach is a poor one. We cannot be satisfied with a legalistic straight-jacket such as the UK Companies Act, which at best lays down minimum standards, rendering the standard audit report more obfuscating than revealing. The US Cohen Commission is scathing in its finding that, inter alia, the current stereotyped report in many cases compresses "tens of thousands of working hours, involving scores of educated people, into a pitiful few words."[28]

Conceptual Role: One of the underlying problems of the auditing profession (part and parcel of the larger accounting profession) throughout its history has been the lack of a conceptual framework for the auditor's role in society. I presume the physician sees his or her role as that of preserving or improving patients' lives, and very important, that concept is undoubtedly shared by the public at large. Similarly, the conceptual role of the lawyer is that of defender and preserver of the law, advocate for justice (according to the law), and what goes with those responsibilities. Again, one presumes that society accepts these ideals. Unfortunately for the accounting profession the importance of, and the benefits derived from, the audit function go unsung. Instead, misconceptions prevail.

Currently, the view gaining ground in the US is that the audits insure investors against financial loss. In Australia, a research study done between 1970 and 1973 showed that a very large majority of users of financial statements regarded a "positive" auditors' opinion as assurance of the honesty of management and workers.[29] Yet another view is that an unqualified auditors' report means that the business is financially sound.[30] However off the mark these opinions are, the profession can no longer dismiss them out of hand. One thing is certain: there is a growing call for the auditor to be more aggressive in protecting the interests of shareholders, investors, creditors, workers, and everyone else who relies on financial information in making decisions. Accordingly, the profession must act to belie these misunderstandings, must admit what cannot, and going forward must have confidence in what can be done: must have a vision, no less.

The Storm Breaks – 1966 to the present

Since the mid-sixties a generation of accountants raised on introversion has been faced with an increasingly hostile public,

BY THE WAY...

a public that was supposed to see them as financial saviors but now was asking "Auditor, where is thy sting?" In the US the auditor is on the brink of losing professional status before the courts. On both sides of the Atlantic government takeover of one kind or another is but a jump away for the profession. In order to counteract these incursions the major institutes have brought up their big guns both in the way of new "independence" rules and also by undertaking large research projects designed to improve and expand auditing and accounting standards. But, with what effect?

A 1972 survey of client/auditor relationships in the US showed that when judging audit firms, top company executives regarded "accessibility of partners" as an important factor: executives most in agreement with this regarded the auditor as an advisor to, and friend of, management.[31] Indeed, the horrendous Equity Funding case in the US found that audit partners were "so close" with management that they came to be regarded by company staff as fellow employees.[32] Yet, the second general standard of the American Institute requires that the auditor "must be without bias with respect to his client under audit" because if he is not, his findings will not be dependable – irrespective of his proficiency. This is undoubtedly true, but how many of us in this room observe that rule? According to one newspaper report some accounting firms encourage their audit staff to gain entry to the playgrounds of corporate executives, by joining the right civic groups, the most prestigious country clubs, and even the churches to which prospective clients belong. One firm went so far as keeping tabs on the schools attended by children of executives whose businesses it sought.[33]

Is this preoccupation with expanding one's audit base at all costs, confined to the developed countries? Not likely, more a worldwide phenomenon of large firms trying to serve two masters: on the one hand, serving the corporate community in which they move and identify themselves, and on the other, a vague commitment to serving the public good. Towards these ends, auditors have been aided and abetted by home-grown rules that can be interpreted to suit ambivalence.

By pushing financial statements into the forefront of corporate information and relegating audit reports to stereotypical formats, the result is a public ignorant of what lies behind those financial statements and the congenial smiles at general meetings, at which both auditors and board members are re-elected. What lies behind is covered by "confidentiality" rules. The problem for the profession is that the public is more sophisticated today and cannot be fobbed off as easily as it was fifty years ago.

If as Emerson said, "the use of history is to give light to the present hour and its duty," what has the profession's history illuminated? If you can bear with me a few minutes more, I believe we have seen that the modern auditor began in service to the community, in so far as he was an important linkman in the protection of private capital. Somewhat reluctantly at first he embodies the fledgling accounting profession during the last two decades of the nineteenth century. But, the early decades of the twentieth, the auditor misunderstands his vocation, and loses his innocence by observing the letter of the law and genuflecting to the business community. His development as a flawed professional stems in part from the paucity of official standards and leadership at the top; partly from little thought being given to exploring and redefining the reporting function in tune with changing needs and expectations; and, at back of these denouements, the lack of an overriding philosophy. Finally, we see how the auditor, exemplified by the big firms, comes

BY THE WAY...

to be made in the and likeness of large corporations, with size (profit) as his motivating force. It is in these contexts that impassioned outbursts, like the Metcalf Report must be seen.[34] The cries seem to point in one direction, and ask the same question I must put to you: Can big capital protect big capital?

When the traditional London press accuses the profession by saying "the once feared watchdog is now management's poodle," that "auditors...have been relegated to the status of a sheik's eunuch," what this means is that the whole reason for the profession's existence in being questioned. Like the *Auditors of Imprest* nearly two hundred years ago, we are being called upon to account for our failure to put duty before profit. In essence, this is what the storm of public disillusion has always been about.

With capitalist countries worldwide needing assurance regarding corporate stewardship; with stock exchanges, investors, creditors, labour unions, even tax authorities, relying on our audit opinions; the profession's day of reckoning has arrived. What is required of us is the *energy* to change our way of thinking. If this energy can't be found within the profession itself, "the forces outside stand ready to provide it."[35] The storm has broken; and in Bob Dylan's words, I think it means *A Hard Rain's A-Gonna Fall.*

Kingston, Jamaica, April 1978

Note: This paper considered issues having to do exclusively with audits of financial statements. Such audits, usually performed annually, are in the "macro" category dealing with overall fairness of financial reports issued by corporations listed on stock exchanges throughout the world. Often involving weeks of painstaking examination of evidence at locations in different countries, such audits require high levels of investigative skill, and involve weighty responsibilities to investors and the public. The micro categories, such as forensic audits, may be more media friendly, but they do not have the broad scope and public accountability attached to them that financial audits do. They are not covered by this paper, a section of which has been redacted because of its technical content

Falling on Our Swords

Some thirty years have passed since, with much enthusiasm, I joined the Canadian Institute of Chartered Accountants. Having been a partner in a Big 8 firm and president of a national institute abroad (where I promoted the CICA as a model for regional cooperation), I was excited about seeing the Canadian profession up close.

The whirlwind romance: leading professional development courses as early as 1978, teaching at the BC School of Chartered Accountancy, was indeed short-lived. By 1987 I saw what I regarded as a weak-kneed Canadian Institute cow-towing to big-firm interests, ignoring the plight of small practitioners, and failing to protect the profession against the migration of traditional practice areas. But it took two critical articles, in *The Bottom Line* magazine that year, to get things off my chest to those who strutted the halls of power back east. Disillusionment was not new to me. Although I had served as a partner in an international firm for eleven years, and had had partners committed to freedom of expression and fully supportive of my youthful endeavors, I early began to look askance at the profession as a whole, becoming critical of the oligarchical dominance of flagship firms that had metamorphosed into Big-Business - the very same sector of the economy they were supposed to oversee as auditors.

The Canadian profession is not a victim of history; that outcome is self-imposed. In my opinion, the rot began thirty-years ago when most practitioners today were still in short pants. CICA's embraced "formal specialization" in the early 1980s, a move that was a genuflection to the overlords and their quest for greater "market share": greed that would lead to tragedy twenty years later. Back then, the official line was that

BY THE WAY...

a *formalized* "diversity" in services would be a great benefit to the public.

But, instead of broadening its training requirements to meet perceived needs of the public, it was easier for CICA to ring-fence firms providing these services, by playing into their hands. Not only did flagship firms already have specialist departments, they now were able to more or less control *access* to specialties. After all, aspirants from the wider profession would have to run big-firm gauntlets in order to obtain the practical experience mandated for specialist privileges - a win-win situation for those firms that were more equal than others.

Looking back, the process that cut off the ring for small firms and sole-practitioners was not free of anomalies. After many years of the new regime, the most obvious one remains the absence of an "income tax specialist." (This point is not meant as support for more of the same; it merely questions CICA's autonomy in bringing about changes that affect core financial interests of the big firms, especially any of them answering to New York or Chicago.) Neither do I dispute that accountants specialize, and that the profession should protect their interests and those of the public. What must be criticized, however, is an over-the-top "solution" that formally internalized what was, and continues to be, an *external* fragmentation of the profession.

Traditionally, income tax was the CA's perceived area of expertise: one that for generations provided an important academic component, or something of the "mystique" vital to any profession's public standing. Today, except within the narrow confines of business groups, our "tax" advantage, at least in the broader public realm, is fast eroding. At the level of public visibility, exclusive of the heavy stuff comprising complex tax issues, the Chartered Accountant has been ignored by the media in favour of splinter groups (financial planners, etc.) unheard of outside the profession thirty years ago. Now, from news reports to commissions of enquiry, "forensic accountants" have risen above the fray, almost detached from any accounting body, making pronouncements about matters outside their prescript. CAs as a whole ignore these developments at their peril.

So dismissive have the media become that during Enron when guns were pointed at accountants, they did not allow us a fox hole. For the better part of two years of television and newspaper attacks on the profession, I do not remember one instance where members were invited to take part in major public forums discussing the issues. The scorn that accountants elicit from business-media folk, who theoretically should be our friends, is instructive. According to Eric Reguly, "When you think about accounting firms, images of lumpy white men in blue suits poring over financial statements come to mind. If you join an accounting firm, you check your personality at the door and enter a life of number-crunching servitude. The career is suitable to anyone with the emotional range of drywall...." Further on, Mr Reguly finds it "hard to imagine a more diverse industry than the so-called accounting profession." (Globe & Mail– March 9, 2002) This from someone who is a member of the most questionable "profession" in the world?

Well, look across the pond, where Jon Boone cites the joke about "accountancy attracting people who lack the charisma to become undertakers," quoting a public relations worker complaining about occasionally being seated next to accountants at dinner parties only "to ask to be moved before they actually managed to bore me to death." (Financial Times – April 30, 2006) These stereotypes are constantly being brought to life in popular films, where "He is just a

BY THE WAY...

glorified accountant" abounds. Such denouements are set against accolades placed at the feet of lawyers, doctors, economists, architects, MBAs - expressions of "extremely intelligent," "genius," "professorial," "brilliant." Should our leaders not be asking: What are the other professionals doing, that accountants are not?

Instead of combating the many negatives the profession faces, our leaders lock themselves in a closet and venture to open the door only to such as surveys designed to make silk out of a sow's ear. Mirror-gazing was very common in the 1980s and 1990s, when much ink was being applied in comparing the earnings of practicing CAs with those of lawyers and doctors, or the Angus Reid finding in 1998 that inexplicably found members supportive of CICA to the tune of 90-99%.

The last BC survey to crow over the (self) image of CAs was that done in 2004. As expected, it was long on supposed pluses, and short everywhere else. By targeting those least likely to offend us – for example, members' clients - by asking them the right questions, welcomed-responses were almost guaranteed: press the right buttons and the "correct" answers appear. So we learn that CAs "dominate CFO, auditing, and treasury positions;" that they are "viewed as experts who are intelligent, skilled ....[and having a] high level of expertise in accounting and finance." We expected soft answers and we got them - the hard ones would have come from the public at large, so why go there?

But soft answers do not count for much in the real-world. In his detailed article exploring the mysteries of company balance sheets for the benefit of investors, Mr. Dave Ebner (Globe – March 23, 2002) begins by deferring to the views of a university professor, then looks to one supposed authority followed by another, to flesh out his article. Again, Bob

Carrick (Globe May 15, 2003) taking readers through annual reports, with much discussion centering around financial statements, defers to an authority who "knows what to look for because he has an MBA and a Chartered *Financial Analyst* designation;" and another doyen who is a member of the Canadian Management Centre. Not one mention of a Chartered Accountant in these pieces. Strange, that. Apparently the Business Section of the Globe is completely unaware of the celebrated CA profession and its band of experts, who, we tell ourselves, bestride the financial world.

A glance at job postings might shed more light: like the huge advertisement for a provincial auditor-general some years ago that omitted any reference to an accountant, much less a CA; or the one by the African Development Bank for [internal] auditors, calling exclusively for MBAs to fill the positions. Could it be these organizations are unaware that CAs "dominate" the practice of auditing? On a different tack, an advertisement by a certain University for a chartered accountant requested that the candidate also have an "academic" degree such as an MBA. What is distinctively academic about the latter, given that an aspiring CA must *already* have a university degree in order to enter the CA study program? Is it imaginable that an advertisement for a lawyer would all but insult applicants by suggesting that their qualification was not *academic*?

And yet, the fault is not in polls and pollsters but in ourselves, that we are underlings. Canadian CAs have squandered their heritage. Taking for granted what was but fleeting "pre-eminence" in the financial world, relying on mantras about their superior status, they looked on as pirate-organizations stormed over the gunnels of their beleaguered craft, and made off with now this, now that, box of treasure. Unlike any other profession, CAs have lost by attrition much

BY THE WAY...

of what was traditionally within their profession's purview. In the 1950s, my father, an accountant for sixty years before he passed away, loved to say of "business" that he "brought them into the world, and buried them." Today CAs do neither. Now, so laughable is the CA's plight that he or she no longer can claim to be a "financial planner." What does that say about our supposed "high level of expertise in accounting and finance" if we have to tip-toe around a traditional practice area? How low have the mighty fallen. It is equivalent to doctors losing to midwives the ability to deliver babies! If our leaders do not find this absurdly funny, they should not have gone to university.

And this is not to denigrate the services of financial planners, especially in the area of investment planning. It is a criticism aimed at our leaders for their abysmal lack of vision. If indeed there was a need for a new approach to traditional financial planning services, CICA should have made provision for it and not allowed outsiders to poach a core area of professional practice. Much the same neglect accompanied the hiving off of "business valuation" services, a traditional part of public practice in the days when the auditor was the recognized specialist in that field. Back in the 1970s that privilege was deftly purloined by, and made the preserve of, a few enterprising members. How long will we have to wait for yet more defections?

Even if we discount further leakage, the accounting profession is far from robust, surrounded as it is by hurry-come-up organizations vying for kudos and "market share." Part of their game is to claim that CAs are "well placed" to challenge their exams (thereby moving up a notch). The question is: Why are we encouraging this one-up-man-ship in "special editions" of the CA Magazine? Are we masochists, as well as misfits?

In recent years CICA has been busy "branding" the CA designation. Thus, with a minimum of effort (but at no little cost), we are bound and determined to become yet another acronymic body. What was CICA thinking? We had a name that meant something for over one hundred years. Why should the elliptical "CA" brand suddenly supersede the Chartered Accountant? What could be more satisfying to the hurry-come-ups than to see their mentor Institute selling its soul for a mess of potage? The now media-made "forensic" variety says it all. The tail is wagging the bull - branded or not.

Is there an official viewpoint on these issues? Last February (2008), in answer to questions I had raised, I was surprised to receive a letter from a CICA executive who admonished me for my ignorance about such matters as Institute websites, publications, the *CICA/RBC Business Monitor*, and telling press releases underpinning significant outreach programs. He insisted that "our profession is ...widely respected," citing, in regard to the current economic crisis, "our bias toward taking meaningful action, rather than simply posturing to garner recognition in the press." Yet, the facts are the international profession stands accused of *not taking meaningful action* to warn of the present financial meltdown, culminating in lawsuits pending or in process against some auditors. On the matter of CICA press releases published in the media, I fail to see why these should excite public interest, positive or otherwise. Even as someone interested in these issues, I completely missed the Globe & Mail publications that he cited. As for the *Business Monitor*, I do not remember mention of this publication's prognostications, much less any discussion thereof, in the business press. In any case, if the accounting profession is serious about its "independence" why is CICA sucking up to a major chartered bank? Can we not come to our own conclusions about the

BY THE WAY...

economy, and take responsibility for our own findings, without hanging on to the coattails of big business? Should not CICA where necessary laisse with economists in its endeavors, and have the confidence to stand by its findings and opinions? The current edition of the *Monitor* appears to hide behind percentages of this, and trends of that. There is no "academic" treatment of the issues. The magazine is the epitome of a "safe" publication, in which the findings of the faceless and nameless are regurgitated in dull, numeric bites.

A profession is not built around statistics, but around living, breathing individuals speaking and writing out of their worldly experiences and their grasp of, and perspicacity in, matters of public interest or concerns. It is the ability to garner public recognition of their integrity, even-handedness, and "superior knowledge" that makes them professionals. There are two or three professions whose names roll off the tongue in all of these categories. Unfortunately, Chartered Accountants prefer their proverbial back-rooms. Instead of strutting their stuff in the halls of academia and political power, accountants are known for crouching behind shoeboxes of receipts, with calculators at the ready. Not a book in sight. Indeed, they flaunt their crass utilitarianism: look no further than its "branding" images on the television.

A serious disconnect exists between what is entailed in building public respect, and the profession's simplistic overtures to "stakeholders" in the business community. There is a pathetic irony in the latter, of course: for all the talk and posturing about "independence" in the wake of Enron, the profession maintains a dualistic, if mainly sycophantic, relationship with business, never looking beyond that rarefied sector. This is the Faustian bargain compromising our claim to be a profession. For without universality, a profession exists in name only. (The legal profession deftly side-steps a

Falling on Our Swords

not dissimilar problem, by having *individuals* in the spotlight defending the "little person" against the world.) By contrast the accounting profession is faceless and silent, except for the occasional libertarian mantra about lower taxes. No one can imagine the headline, circa 2001: "CICA executives deplore deregulation of banking industry." That would be unheard of. But doesn't a profession have the responsibility to speak to power, to say without fear or favour what needs to be said?

Not how the accounting profession works, of course. Years ago the Institute adopted a distinctly Big-Firm structure, replete with CEO in the chair, rather than the traditional "president." More and more power accumulated at the top (until various "regulatory" bodies stepped in, that is). Democracy all but disappeared, replaced by polls whose respondents were predominantly…well, need one spell it out? With authority ceded to big-firm interests, there was precious little left for general meetings to decide. Even the annual get-togethers became events of the distant past, replaced by "goodwill" executive tours. And all of this was accompanied by flagship firms turning their backs on the CA designation. If the story is true that some of these firms actively discourage the addition of "CA" after employees' names on business cards, we have problems that go far beyond mere image-destruction.

But I have digressed. No profession can hope to make an indelible mark on the public at large by in-house publications, press releases, and paid advertisements. At the same time, there is no limit to what can be done at a more personal level if some of the obstacles mentioned above were overcome. Nothing prevents CICA (and provincial institutes) from hosting "public policy" conferences in which members, *billed and introduced first and foremost as chartered accountants*, address issues of public interest. These conferences would

BY THE WAY...

be organized to include students, academics, government representatives, as well as executives of large and small businesses. Programs would highlight the profession's expertise in a broad range of topics, with attention given to public policy and changes therein that presenters consider necessary. They would be broadcast over public television, CPAC, etc., like the teachers do, like the nurses, architects, economists, environmentalists, chambers of commerce do; and need we mention doctors and lawyers? Is it expecting too much that accountants demand their day in the sun?

This memorandum has focused on the profession from the viewpoint of the accountant in public practice. Yes, I believe the big firms should have come to the defense of their compatriot, Arthur Andersen when its very existence was threatened. How exactly? I am not sure. Unfortunately, after Sarbanes-Oxley the US profession lay down and promptly sank into a coma, which it is not likely to survive. In the UK the profession became a shadow of its former self; while in Canada our decline mirrored that of the US: everyone paranoid about government interference in the profession's carefully guarded "self-regulatory" status. Jumping to attention, our leaders made that interference self-inflicted. Is this incontrovertible evidence that fear of the outsider begets tyranny within? Small practitioners may well think so. At the same time the profession writ large is floundering. Unless members wake up and do something about it, their children will not follow them in this calling.

Prince George, BC, August 1, 2009

Accountant, Where is Your Soul?

A few months ago, the magazine of the BC Institute of Chartered Accountants, *Beyond Numbers*, featured the article: "Adding Tools to the Toolbox," and included a plea for "lifelong learning" among members. It reminded me that Chartered Accountants had long laid claim to being members of a "learned" profession. At least that was the perception in my days in England where the profession looked back with pride to the mid-1800s when its founding fathers declared independence from a divided legal profession and moved into their own home.

Sometime later the profession set up shop in Canada, but had to step more gingerly around lawyers when it sought a room at the top. Unfortunately, as the years went by, it failed to protect against roommates breaking into the larder and running off with various "specialties" they were able to call their own. The resulting losses left the Canadian profession with only a few core areas under its control in comparison with other senior Commonwealth institutes.

Auditing, semi-assurance services, and taxation are a far cry from the robust range of "high-brow" service areas traditionally enjoyed by our Commonwealth cousins. (Research is needed here. For my brief survey, now out of date, see *The Bottom Line*, July/August 1987.) The point is that the Canadian profession must strengthen and grow its intellectual base if it is to maintain credibility. Most important, it must stop the dilution of the CA currency that acronymic *internal* specialization has wrought.

Why should we care? Surely, the penthouse is superfluous if we can earn a good living in the basement. The question is for how long? An organization without honor and respect in the public realm ceases to be a profession. Standards fall, recruiting dries up, rivals encroach on core areas, and governance is compromised. Yes, accountants are among the high-earners in Canada, but money cannot become our *raison d'être'*. This was the aberration which, in the run-up to Enron, was the subtext in our own "vision" literature that celebrated the idea of "market forces" instead of warning against them.

The greatest challenge facing accountants today is not utilitarian skill-sets if we are to cross the post-Enron divide. What is lacking is a broad-based credibility, founded in ethics and integrity and underpinned by that vague attribute called "learning." Vague, because paradoxical. The mythos of learning, especially when applied to the professions, extends beyond so-called education. It is almost beyond definition; but that has not prevented professions such as Law and Medicine from promoting their versions of it.

So, what are Chartered Accountants missing? In 1960, I went to London and became a student of the English Institute at about the same time that a good friend had arrived to study for the Bar. I completed my studies at the end of 1965, by which time my friend, having spent a mere three years at the Inns of Court (not university), had been a barrister for over two years. In the public arena his apparent education-deficit mattered not at all. I imagine his contemporaries today preside over the Supreme Court, or have become members of the Privy Council. What is going on here? Three-piece suits? Bowler hats?

Today a Chartered Accountant must first acquire a university degree; then he or she spends thirty months in "articles" to a practicing firm - with a heavy course load to match - in order to satisfy the experience requirement. Certainly, after six or seven years the new member has no less "education" than the lawyer next door. Once qualified, the new member may specialize - requiring more education and more experience. Finally, whether serving in or out

Accountant, Where is Your Soul?

of public practice, the CA provides services sought after by businesses, the public at large, and other professionals, notably lawyers, who often depend on CAs in income tax matters. Yet their academics, business experience, responsibilities have not endeared members to the media or general public. Intangibles, intangibles! For too long professional accountants have invited a negative public response by snuggling up to the big and powerful, whose boardrooms they frequent. Their governing bodies are not far behind, partnering with the likes of financial institutions and preaching corporatist slogans such as "lower taxes." Right-wing economic positions type-cast these organizations as rooted in the status quo, with nothing to contribute in serious discussion: intellectual lightweights who cringe off camera, as happened throughout the Enron scandal.

If our challenge is to build a profession that inspires the best and the brightest, that is, one not on the brink of destruction every time it screws up (our lot is to be judged for failings rather than successes), we will have to be more proactive. This means reexamining why we exist, whom we represent, and what we "profess." Must we always be spokespersons for corporate Canada, or conservative think-tanks like the Fraser and C. D. Howe Institutes? Can we not re-evaluate our free-market conservatism; condemn fire sales of public assets; criticize corporate waste: all without looking over our shoulders at Bay Street? Make no mistake about it, Enron condemned us to a clerical Hades from which we are unable to see the heavens. Redemption once resided in the soul which we lost; we must seek to replace it with a more human version.

The original piece, here expanded, was published by *The Bottom Line* Magazine, August 2004

The Small Practitioner: Virtual Casualty?

Mandatory rules and regulations governing public practice are expanding at such a rate they soon will negate our claim to be a profession. For small firms they are, even now, completely counter-productive.

Official directives regarding public practice have grown progressively more invasive over the past twenty-five years. From the acceptance of a client, to the field work, to file preparation, to file review, to reports and letters: minutiae at every level are now grist for the "Standards" mill. Institute "recommendations" are out, institute micro-management is in. In the same way that professional development courses ceased being recommended, and became mandatory events; that minimum public liability insurance became mandatory; that "practice review" by institute staff became mandatory, top-down policy-making is now the all-encompassing rubric. In the wake of the Enron debacle quality control became control, period.

In the absence of unusual circumstances it is the "monitoring" standards that are most offensive for small practitioners. Sneaked in a few years ago were mandatory peer reviews of working papers, office policies, and procedures – in addition to existing practice reviews. Now, as if two levels of visitation were not enough, there is a third tier: that of mandatory peer reviews of *assurance engagement* files! Presumably, the rule means (a) multiple visitations depending on the number of assurance engagements, and (b) file reviews-regardless of their size or the complexity of the job, and without reference to the results of previous reviews.

Particularly for the majority of sole practitioners whose offices are without qualified staff, peer reviews will be done

Published by *The Bottom Line* magazine, August 2010

BY THE WAY...

by members from other firms. More to the point, certain assurance reviews will be required *before* files are completed, meaning they will not be detective, but prescriptive by nature. In one foul swoop many practitioners will have lost the autonomy that is inherent in, if not synonymous with, their professional standing. (It is instructive that neither the medical nor legal profession presumes to micro manage practitioners. They would not stand for it anyway.)

Everyone agrees that quality control is necessary. And it is certainly within the purview of professional bodies not only to hold members accountable for their failings, on an exception basis, but to protect the public through a modicum of general mandates, which may or may not be supported by specific recommendations promoting "best-practice." However, regulators cannot usurp practitioners' rights in carrying out their duties, without jeopardizing their status as professionals. As a former professional standards review partner responsible for signing off on listed-company and international-referral audits in a Big 8 firm, I believe I have some knowledge of the issues involved, and hope I will not be accused of being averse to quality work.

What we must be averse to is overkill: essentially Big-Brother ensconced in our offices causing, inter alia, the following problems:

(1) At a guess, there are 10,000 or more sole-practitioners, bending beneath the weight of externally imposed red-tape rolled out under the mantra "protecting the public interest." Some of it is productive, much is purely defensive, and the rest is motherhood stuff that implies practitioners are by nature irresponsible and illiterate. Suffice it to say that policy makers should be careful what they wish for: the Handbook is already a veritable gift to the courts in cases against practitioners.

The Small Practitioner: Virtual Casualty?

(2) Those sole-practitioners and small firms that lack qualified "quality control" staff, but are determined to hold on to assurance engagements, will be obliged to tell clients that someone from another firm will be brought in to vet their work – at a cost, of course. What clients will think of this confession is anyone's guess.

(3) If for no other reason than avoiding hassle, many small firms are already busy convincing clients to move from review engagements to compilation engagements. Auditing will become a thing of the past for these firms.

(4)The irony is that by downgrading practice offerings, practitioners will dumb-down not only the profession in general, but the CA brand itself.

How did we get into this mess, and how does it protect the public interest? In 2002 the Enron scandal almost destroyed the profession. Feared was government takeover of what Time Magazine dismissively called "the whole bean-counting industry." Running scared, accountancy bodies worldwide felt hard-pressed to purge public practice of a mysterious "conflict" pandemic traceable to Arthur Anderson and other high-ups. Except that little effort was made to quarantine the source. By increasing contagion they conveniently obscured culpability.

Independence, like liberty, truth, or justice, is a relative, not an absolute concept. For over one hundred years small practices dealing with small business clients have had to wear several hats simultaneously. The users of financial information have always known about, and accepted, the symbiotic relationship between sole practitioner and client. To attempt an absolutist reversal of this tradition is delusionary at best, destructive at worst.

Is it not true that threatened and embattled groups turn

BY THE WAY...

inwards and become obsessed with "right" thinking and "pure" utility, even if that means cutting off heads? Small practitioners had nothing to do with the profession's fall from grace; nevertheless, today they stand shackled in the carts.

Postscript: This paper attracted many responses from practitioners across Canada who, among other issues, were angry about growing micro-management of practitioners by governing bodies.

Requiem for a Profession

I first became aware of our profession's defrocking when reference to the accounting "industry" surfaced in a newspaper editorial at the outbreak of the Enron scandal. Only a jaundiced notion about our esteemed calling by the general media? Maybe. I quickly put the matter behind me. But then the dreaded word turned up again - in lead articles written by business editors, no less. One was disingenuous enough to refer to us as a "so called" profession. Again, what could we expect from the ill-informed and bigoted business media? Not so fast. The newly minted classification is now everywhere, and being penned by the most unlikely people. In the mid-October issue of the "independent voice" of accountants an FCA stabs us with the proverbial, not once but five times, including a pointed juxtaposition of accounting *industry* and legal *profession*!

Guess I overlooked a demotion obvious to everyone else. Yet, on reflection, I cannot deny I had a certain foreboding two decades ago when multinational firms began emulating their multinational clients. It was curious how soon the accounting designation was expunged from firm names. In the eighties various pretenses at professional restraint also fell by the wayside, aided and abetted by official relaxation of advertising and solicitation rules. Very soon, officially blessed "specialization" became part of the obsession to maximize market share. In the nineties CICA literature began substituting the term "customer" for the traditional "client".

More recently, our "corporatism" culminated in touting the CA designation as a "brand." Well, so what? Surely, it is mere semantics which name - practicing profession or accounting industry - is more appropriate for the work we do.

Published by *The Bottom Line* magazine, December 2002

BY THE WAY...

After all, accountants will always be an important part of the broad shoulders on which rests the future of capitalism. I must get back to my ticking and vouching. But at what price?

Fertile ground for conspiracy theorists? Is our new status a neurotic death wish by the profession at large? Or is it part of a destabilizing agenda of the usual suspects in the vicinity of Bay Street? Might it be that some years ago our erstwhile position in the world, at least the public practice side of it, bartered our soul for a business philosophy that put profit and empire-building before ethics? What exactly is behind the hype surrounding "market forces" and "globalization" in recent times? Apparently overlooked by the business plan, was the inevitable reduction in policing that would accompany large firms' abandoning their ties to governing bodies. Indeed, according to the new paradigm, these firms would eschew linkage to the accounting profession itself. Needless to say, that divorce was good news for big capital. Weary of traditional meddling by auditors, the business giants would have been ecstatic when their erstwhile monitors were reborn as one of them! Even at the student level, we now have what is glibly referred to as "competency based" training, sounding rather like an old, clerical model; or to put it less subtly, the do-or-die rather than reason-why variety of auditing. Shades of roll top desks and quill pens! Absent "intellectual property" what have we got? The accounting *industry*, stupid.

Remember the days when insurance marketing revolved around "life agents" who boasted the CLU acronym? Remember bank tellers aspiring to some prestigious Chartered Bankers' designation? Maybe they still do, but no insurance company or bank identifies itself by reference to a professional body. Today the so-called "practitioners" in those corporations must dance to the tune of their industry, which for all intents and purposes is by nature devoid of any but

Requiem for a Profession

a corporate personality. When we think of the Savings and Loans scandal the last image we conjure up is that of warm-blooded *professionals*. Rather, we see an amorphous mass of lifeless institutions that put profit before responsibility and ended up speaking through ubiquitous lawyers. Designations, per se, counted for nothing in the *post-mortem* analysis. Is it not instructive that, likewise, accountants have been faceless and speechless since Enron imploded? Given the culpability laid at our door over the past year, why have we been conspicuous for our absence on business news-spots, in interviews with the press, as participants in the plethora of talk-shows that discuss auditing and accounting issues? Surely it would be quite impossible for scandal to threaten the legal or medical professions without lawyers and doctors- publicly recognized as such - speaking volumes in their own behalf. In our case the media shamelessly muzzled the accounting profession while cutting its throat. Worse still, we have seemed quite happy going as sheep to the slaughter.

According to a young public-practice CA with whom I spoke recently, he views himself as "a sort of professional." A profession worthy of respect by opinion makers and the public at large cannot grow out of that response. Great professions speak to the issues affecting people's lives and wellbeing; they have a social voice. They do not simply pat themselves on the back or rely on opinion polls for self-worth; nor do they hide from criticism in some back room. Unfortunately, very early in the game, accountants decided that their incestuous relationship with business would define them. It has. They began as watchdogs over big capital and ended up cuddled in the laps of the rich.

Unless we are passionate about our status as a profession, including everything that status entails, the public will dismiss us as number crunching peons. There is

BY THE WAY...

no middle ground. What's in a word? Our future depends on it.

•

December 2002

Note: The unsolicited claim recently made by a noted lawyer that it is more difficult to qualify as a Chartered Accountant than it is to qualify as a lawyer, is but cold comfort for the CA.

Dubious Resurrection

Canadian accounting bodies have merged. Amidst the official hoopla that has accompanied the enactment of provincial legislation recognizing the merger, members who had reservations about this turn of events find themselves on the wrong side of history. The CA is no more; neither is the CGA or CMA. In their place is an imported CPA designation - except that tolerable "Public" has become tautological "Professional," making "Chartered Professional Accountant": Canadian CPAs had to be the same as US CPAs, only different.

Chartered accountants, who remembered the fortune spent on "branding" the CA qualification not too long ago, had to endure tasteless television advertisements for the new one, including buckets of water emptied on seemingly unsuspecting heads. Yet, there is much more to this merger than acronyms thrown out with the dishwater. Significant is the fact that the "Organization" (as the national governing body is now called) is legally exclusive, a privilege practitioners long dreamed of. Unfortunately, it may be a pyrrhic victory seeing that the enlarged membership of 210,000 is top-heavy in *non-practitioners*, who traditionally comprise a passive segment of the profession. With the journey ahead in great need of a high road of objectivity and corporate oversight, Canada appears to have taken the entrepreneurial low road.

We have seen something of the foundation of the accounting profession in Britain and the Commonwealth. Significant is the fact that the earliest UK charter for accountants (1854) was handed down a mere 25 years after that for solicitors (1831), and 54 years after the charter for surgeons (1800). The "English" institute's charter spoke to its "elevation of the profession of *public* accountants," citing their

BY THE WAY...

work as auditors of public companies. But equally important in the early days (and far beyond that) were members' roles as liquidators of corporations, as well as their acting as receivers, and trustees in bankruptcy. How far have the mighty fallen?

In the 1950s and 60s investment (and speculative) capital began tightening its grip on corporations across the globe. Transnational corporations and their financial backers began calling for rules covering reports of capital flows. The profession was forced on to its back-foot, no sector more so than public practice, which lacked unified reporting standards. By the 1970s, national accounting bodies, both in First and Third-World countries (or most of them), had acquiesced in the need for such rules. Thus began the outsourcing of standard-setting by national institutes, beginning with accounting standards - minimal at first, but soon to include auditing standards. More to the point, as the incidence of audit scandals increased, accounting bodies found themselves handing over various prerogatives to home-grown "oversight" boards of one kind and another.

In Canada, independent policing of the profession includes the country's *Canadian Public Accountability Board*, and abroad the *International Forum of Independent Audit Regulators*, among others. In the UK the *Financial Reporting Council*, operating under government mandate, promulgates accounting and assurance standards independently of accounting bodies and can discipline their members, ex parte. Across the Channel the EU's *Accounting Directives* hold sway over national institutes. In the US, the *Public Companies Accounting Oversight Board* (under the *Sarbanes-Oxley Act* of 2002) wields a big stick over the profession, both in its regulatory and policing functions. Again on the world stage, the *International Federation of Accountants* and affiliates must be factored into the mix of oversight prerogatives that have left national accounting

Dubious Resurrection

bodies mere members' clubs responsible mostly for training and certification. In many cases, non-accountants occupy front-row seats in these organizations, which, since the 1990s have become juggernauts in defense of their mantra to "protect the public interest," an undertaking they believe cannot be gainsaid. And yet, how was the public interest protected in the run-up to the 2007/8 financial disaster? That said, where does empire-building stop once complete autonomy reigns?

Given the above scenario, it is no wonder that as a career path, public practice is less attractive than it used to be. As we have seen, even small practitioners are under the heels of scrutinizers. Tip-toeing around "specialisms" they must avoid work they are not licensed or insured to do. At the same time, tiered gradations of firms make a mockery of professional expertise.

Presumably, restrictions are necessary because of too little time and supervision devoted to broad based study and training. Whose fault is that? Yes, it ends with students graduating to do *something*. In so far as separate accreditations are available for what used to be attributes endemic to a stand-alone qualification, the current obfuscations are regressive. The most anomalous example is the restrictions often placed on certain members performing assurance engagements. One has to ask, if the general qualification is not comprehensive enough for general public practice, of what value is it except for a bookkeeping job elsewhere?

With national accounting bodies reduced to onlooker status and public practice suffering from regulation overkill, a vacuum in professional confidence followed. Given that the Enron disaster was a major contributor, it is curious that it could have been the catalyst for what has transpired over the last fifteen years to resuscitate a fading profession. Whatever

BY THE WAY...

the explanation may be, seductive overtures to the corporate sector became the new normal. Formerly the ugly ducklings of the profession, corporations began getting top billings among national institutes. More than ever before, accountancy journals were featuring cover stories on CEOs (especially those who were members of the profession) and their business achievements. Suddenly there was much to be written about turning water into wine.

Currently, this seismic shift away from public practice is evident in vision statements of institutes around the world. For example, in promoting student training, ICAEW is short on citing public practice, which used to be the *sine qua non* for aspiring chartered accountants. Across the ocean, we find the vision statement for US CPAs speaking to "Powering the success of global business"; while in the blue beyond, Australian & New Zealand CAs are "leaders in business and finance"; and finally, CPA Canada's aim is to be a "globally respected business and accounting designation."

Complementing this "diversion" have been moves to promote growth in memberships. National institutes seem to be rolling out red carpets for new members - even those pinched from sister organizations, as well as for aspiring students. Routes to qualification have increased: through the easing of entry requirements, to increasing the number and variety of training sources, to the narrowing of study programs, shortening of qualification time-lines, and of course, layering certificates and "subprime" certificates in order to satisfy employment objectives. Peculiar to Britain was the call that the ACA qualification be made more accessible to the under-privileged than it has been in the past.

If exponential growth and identification with the business sector mean anything, hope for the way forward in this new dispensation must reside with CPA Canada. Now a unified body, CPA Canada is the product of a unique merger that not only holds the numbers-prize, but also the distinction of having put public practice in its place. The goal was business, even if it meant tens of thousands of accountants coming together with little commonality in training or experience across the aisles. Intentionally or otherwise, these developments may be in line with global trends as the profession wrestles with interlopers, but is it the long-term answer to our problems? Of the many questions facing Canadian regulators, this is the one they must address before long.

Thirty years ago, rather prematurely as it turned out, I suggested that small firms in Canada were operating in an intellectual wasteland. Today that wasteland has become a desert. In the brave new world of British Columbia, licenses are already being granted for practicing firms that specialize in, yes, *Notice to Reader* engagements–traditionally a large part of a book-keeper's clerical livelihood. No one denies that practitioners provide NTR services, but specific licenses to do so?

If we are to remain a profession, the public at large will have to respect accountants for being professionals, not technicians, professionals with broad shoulders, able to speak to and report on corporate power without fear or favour; advise moneyed interests without being a visceral part thereof; and provide a host of other services that have nothing to do with shoeboxes of receipts. Towards these ends, should we cast our bread upon the waters so to reel in future members from among "the best and the brightest," we will have to bait our hooks with better than the spoils of clerical plunder. A Nobel Prize, anyone?

Prince George, October 2016

Books Read, Enjoyed & Recommended

What follows is a book-list of many of the non-fiction books (academic, for want of a better word) that I have been fortunate to be able to read and enjoy over the last thirty six years. Books always have been a source of great pleasure for me, but I only began listing them in 1980. What follows represents those I believe may be of general interest Titles are delineated within rough categories, which I hope will be helpful to bookworms interested enough to burrow into particular subject-areas.

For those who may be interested, acronyms in the Note section of each publication mean:

p.	number of pages
R	year book was read
PG	Prince George Library
CNC	College library
UNBC	University library
DL	Collection

Biography :

TOLSTOY * Troyat, Henri (Trans. by Nancy Amphoux)
Publisher: Doubleday (NY-1967)   Note: 775p; R80; DL

A PASSION FOR TRUTH - BIOG. OF HANS KUNG * Nowell, R.
Publisher: (Collins-1981)   Note:365p; R81; CNC

KARL MARX, HIS LIFE AND ENVIRONMENT * Berlin, Isaiah.
Publisher: Oxford U.P. (Lon-1939)   Note: 230p; R83; DL

GEORGE ORWELL * Atkins, J.
Publisher: John Calder- 1954   Note: 350p; R83

BY THE WAY...

GEORGE ORWELL * Hopkinson, Tom
Publisher: Longmans, Green -1953　　　　　　　　　　Note: 35p; R83, CNC

PERSONAL IMPRESSIONS * Berlin, Isaiah
Publisher: Oxford UP (Lon-1980)　　　　　　　　　　Note: 232p; R84; DL

PORTRAITS FROM MEMORY & OTHER ESSAYS * Russel, B.
Publisher: G. Allen & Unwin (Lon-1956)　　　　　　　Note: 220p; R87; DL

GIBBON * Burrow, J.W.
Publisher: Oxford U.P. (Oxford-1985)　　　　　　　　Note: 112p; R88

MEETINGS WITH PASTERNAK : A MEMOIR * A. Gladkov; Haywood, Ed
Publisher: Harcourt & Brace (NY-1973)　　　　　　　Note: 220p; R91; DL

BERTRAND RUSSELL: A POLITICAL LIFE * Ryan, Alan
Publisher: Penguin (Lon-1988)　　　　　　　　　　　Note: 220p; R92; DL

MEMOIRS 1925-1950 * Kennan, George F.
Publisher: Little Brown (Boston-1967)　　　　　　　　Note: 570p; R93; DL

JOHN PAUL 11 * Walsh, Michael
Publisher:HarperCollins(Lon-1994　　　　　　　　　Note:320p;R96;S123;DL

BERTRAND RUSSELL: PHILOSOPHER AND HUMANIST*Lewis, John
Publisher: Lawrence & Wischart (Lon-1968)　　　　　Note: 96p; R96; DL

THE INKLINGS * Carpenter, Humphrey
Publisher: Harper Collins (Lon-1978)　　　　　　　　Note: 280p; R98; DL

LUTHER * Friedenthal, Richard
Publisher: Weidenfield & Nicholson (Lon-1967)　　　　Note:566p;R98;S163;DL

ISAIAH BERLIN: A LIFE * Ignetief, Michael
Publisher: Penguin (Tor-1998)　　　　　　　　　　　Note: 356p; R00;DL

A MAN WITHOUT A COUNTRY * Vonnegut, Kurt - D. Simon Ed.
Publisher: Seven Stories Press (NY-2005)　　　　　　Note: 146p; R06; DL

ERRATA: AN EXAMINED LIFE * Steiner, George
Publisher: Phoenix (Lon-1997)　　　　　　　　　　　Note: 806p;; R11; DL

MARGIN RELEASED * Priestly, J.B.
Publisher: Reprint Soc (Lon-1961)　　　　　　　　　Note: 231p; R11,DL

Books Read, Enjoyed & Recommended

EXAMINED LIVES: SOCRATES TO NIETZSCHE * Miller, James
Publisher:Farrar Stairs & Giroux, NY-2011   Note: 422p;R12;;DL

SALINGER: A BIOGRAPHY * Alexander, Paul
Publisher: St. Martin's (NY-1999)   Note:351p;R13;DL

MARTIN LUTHER: A LIFE * Marty, Marty
Publisher: Penguin (NY-2004)   Note: 204p; R13; DL

INNOCENT III * Powell, James M.,Ed.
Publisher: Cath U of A (Wash-1994)   Note: 197p;R13;;DL

MACHIAVELLI * Skinner, Quentin
Publisher: Sterling (NY-2010)   Note: 260p;R13;DL

HERMAN MELVILLE * Hardwick, Elizabeth
Publisher: Viking Pr (NY-2000)   Note: 161p;R14;DL

WHO WAS JACQUES DERRIDA? * Mikeis, David
Publisher: Yale UP (NY-2009)   Note: 273p;R14;DL

HITCH 22 * Hitchins, Christopher
Publisher: Twelve (NY-2010)   Note: 424p; R14; DL

THE SUMMING UP * Maugham, W. Summerset
Publisher: Pan Bks (Lon-1938)   Note:203p;R15;;DL

A SORT OF LIFE * Greene, Graham
Publisher: Simon& Schuster (NY-1971   Note: 220p; R2015;DL

Economics

THE NATURE OF MASS POVERTY * Galbraith, J.K.
Publisher: Harvard U.P. (Camb.-1979)   Note: 150 p; R80; DL

THE GREAT ASCENT * Heilbroner, R.
Publisher: Harper & Row (-)   Note: 160p; R80; CNC

THE AGE OF UNCERTAINTY * Galbraith J.K.
Publisher: Haughton Mifflin (Boston-1977)   Note: R80; DL

THE WORLD IN DEPRESSION 1929 - 1939 * Kindleberger,C.P.
Publisher: U of Cal. Press (Berkeley-1973)   Note: 320p; R83; DL

BY THE WAY...

AFTERTHOUGHTS ON MATERIAL CIVILIZATION
and CAPITALISM * Braudel, F. (Trans P.M.Ranum)
Publisher: John Hopkins (Balt.-1977) Note:120p; R83;DL.

PROTESTANT ETHIC & SPIRIT CAPATALISM * Weber, Max
Publisher: Scribners (NY-1920) Note: 300p;;R85;DL

THE ANATOMY OF POWER * Galbraith, John K. H.
Publisher: Haughton Mifflen (Boston-1985) Note: 192p; R86;DL

THE END OF THE THIRD WORLD * Harris, Nigel
Publisher: Penguin (Lon-1986) Note: 220p;R88;DL

GALBRAITH AND THE LOWER ECONOMICS * Sharpe, MyronE.
Publisher: Intl Arts @ Scs Press (NY-1974) Note: 5p;R88;CNC

THE FUTURE OF CAPITALISM * Thurow, Lester C.
Publisher: Wllm. Morrow & Co (-) Note: 384p; R98; DL

THE GREAT CRASH 1929 * Galbraith, John Kenneth
Publisher: Penguin (Lon-1975) Note: 220p; R91; DL

DEBT: FIRST 5000 YEARS * Graeber, David
Publisher: Melville House (NY – 2014) Note: 542p; R16; S373; DL

ECONOMICS IN PERSPECTIVE * Galbraith, John K.
Publisher: Houghton Miffin (Boston-1987) Note: 324p;R93;S98;DL

DICTIONARY OF MODERN ECONOMICS * Pearce, David W. Ed
Publisher: ELBS/Macmillan (Lon-1986) Note: 450p;S111;R94;DL

LOSING GROUND * Murray, Charles
Publisher: Basic Books (NY-1984) Note: 300p; R95; DL

THE POLITICS OF RICH & POOR * Phillips, Kevin
Publisher: Harper (NY-1990) Note: 250p; R95; DL

ODIOUS DEBTS * Adams, Patricia
Publisher: Earthscan Pub (Lon-1991) Note:238p;R96; DL

FAITH & CREDIT: THE WORLD BANK'S
SECULAR EMPIRE * George, S & Sabilli, F.
Publisher: Penguin (Lon-1994) Note: 275p;R97;UNBC

ECONOMICS AND THE PUBLIC PURPOSE * Galbraith, John K.
Publisher: Houghton Miffin (Boston-1973) Note: 334p; R98; DL

Books Read, Enjoyed & Recommended

BENHAM'S ECONOMICS * Paish, F.W.
Publisher: Pitman (Lon-1973)   Note: 560p;R98;;DL

THE SECRET WORLD OF MONEY * Gause, Andrew
Publisher: Hawthorne Pr (Hawthorn-1996)   Note: 138;R99;DL

THE JUDAS ECONOMY * Wolman & Colomosco
Publisher: Addison Wesley (NY-1997)   Note: 230p; R00; DL

MILLENNIAL DREAMS * Smith, Paul
Publisher: Verso (Lon-1997)   Note: 270p;R00; DL

HAMILTON'S BLESSING * Gordon, J.S.
Publisher: Penguin (NY-1998)   Note: 217p; R00;DL

THE UK ECONOMY TODAY * Holden,Matthews,Thompson
Publisher: ManUP (Man.-1995)   Note: 166p; R01; DL

THE RISE & FALL OF ECONOMIC JUSTICE * Macpherson, C.B.
Publisher: Oxford UP (NY-1985)   Note: 154p; R01; DL

THE CRISIS OF VISION IN MODERN
ECONOMIC THOUGHT * Heilbroner & Milberg
Publisher: Camb UP (NY-1995)   Note: 130p; R02; UNBC

GETTING IT RIGHT: MARKETS & CHOICES IN A FREE SOCIETY. *
    Barro, Robert J.
Publisher: MIT Press (Camb.-1996)   Note: 190p; R02; UNBC

ECONOMIC ISSUES TODAY * Carson,Thomas,Hecht
Publisher: ME Sharpe (NY-1999)   Note: 360p; R02; S202; UNBC

THE DEATH OF ECONOMICS * Ormerod, Paul
Publisher: Faber & Faber (Lon-1994)   Note: 230p;R02; UNBC

THE TROUBLE WITH CAPITALISM * Shutt, Harry
Publisher: Zed Bks (Lon-1998)   Note: 238p; R02; UNBC

GLOBALIZATION & DECLINE OF SOCIAL REFORM * Tuple, G.
Publisher: GaramondPr (Tor-1995)   Note: 190p;R02; UNBC

THE ECONOMICS OF PRIVATIZATION * McFetridge, D.G.
Publisher: CD Howe (Lon-1998)   Note: 69p; R02; UNBC

THE RETURN OF DEPRESSION ECONOMICS * Krugman, Paul
Publisher: WNorton (NY-1999)   Note: 175p; R02; UNBC

BY THE WAY...

DEBT AND DELUSION * Warburton, Peter
Publisher: Penguin (Lon-2000)　　　　　　　　　　Note: 332p; R02; DL

WORLD,CLASS,BRITAIN * Calum, Paton
Publisher: MacMillan (Lon-2000)　　　　　　　　Note: 237p; R02; UNBC

THE GLOBAL POLITICAL ECONOMY * DeBoer, Elizabeth
Publisher: Macmillan (Lon-2000)　　　　　　　　Note: 203p; R02; UNBC

SHRINKING THE STATE * Feigenbaum, Henig,Hammett
Publisher: CambUP (Camb.-1998)　　　　　　　　Note: 182p; R02; UNBC

LIBERALISM IN THE DEVELOPING WORLD*Fernandez & Momsen, Eds.
Publisher: Routledge (Lon-1996)　　　　　　　　Note: 320p; R02; UNBC

THE PRIVATIZATION PUTSCH * Hardin, Herschel
Publisher: Inst for Research (Hal.-'89)　　　　　Note: 224p; R02; UNBC

GLOBAL FORTUNE * Vasquez, Ian
Publisher: Cato Inst (Wash.-2000)　　　　　　　Note: 295p; R02; UNBC

GLOBALIZATION & ITS DISCONTENTS * Stiglitz, Joseph E.
Publisher: WWNorton (NY-2003)　　　　　　　　Note: 290p; R03; DL

ECONOMICS * Stein, Slavin
Publisher: John Wiley & Son (NY-1999)　　　　　Note: 248p;R05; UNBC

AMERICAN THEOCRACY * Phillips, Kevin
Publisher: Penguin (NY-2006)　　　　　　　　　Note: 464p;R2008; DL

FREEFALL * Stiglitz
Publisher: Norton (NY-2010)　　　　　　　　　　Note: 443p; R2011; DL

GLOBAL SLUMP * McNally, David
Publisher: PM Pr (Oakland-2011)　　　　　　　　Note: 230p;R11;DL

THE PRICE OF INEQUALITY * Stiglitz, Joseph
Publisher: WW Norton (NY-2012)　　　　　　　　Note: 414p;R12; DL

THE BIG SHORT * Lewis, Michael
Publisher: WW Norton (NY-2010)　　　　　　　　Note: 266p;R13; DL

CAPITALISM'S LAST STAND * Bello, Walden
Publisher: Zed Bks (Lon-2013)　　　　　　　　　Note: 282;R14;DL

Books Read, Enjoyed & Recommended

TOO BIG TO KNOW * Weinberger, David
Publisher: Basic Bks (NY-2011)   Note: 231p;R14;DL

Essays & Miscellaneous

IN PRAISE OF IDLENESS * Russell Bertram
Publisher: Allen & Unwin (Lon-1935)   Note: 175p; R80; DL

NOBEL PRIZE ACCEPTANCE SPEECH * Solzenitsyn, Aleksandr
Publisher: Harper (-)   Note: 30p; R80

RECOLLECTIONS AND ESSAYS * Tolstoy, Leo
Publisher: (-)   Note: 300p; R81; PG

FACT AND FICTION * Russell,B.
Publisher: Unwin (-)   Note: 250; R81; PG

POINTS OF VIEW * Maugham, Somerset W.
Publisher: Penguin (-)   Note: 245p; R81; CNC

COLLECTED ESSAYS * Lichtheim, G.
Publisher: Viking Press (NY-1973)   Note: 492p; R82; CNC

ESSAYS * Montaigne, M. (tran J M Cohen)
Publisher: Penguin (Harms.-1958)   Note: 406p; R84; DL

GEORGE STEINER-A READER * Steiner, George
Publisher: Penguin (Harms.-1984)   Note: 447p; R84; DL.

ON DIFFICULTY AND OTHER ESSAYS * Steiner, G.]
Publisher: Oxford U.P. (Oxford-1978)   Note: 205p; R86; DL

A FREE MAN'S WORSHIP * Russell,B.
Publisher: Allen-Unwin (Lon-1917)   Note: 220p; R88;DL

TRAVELS IN HYPER REALITY * Eco, Umberto
Publisher: Harcourt Brace (SanDiego-1986)   Note: 306p; R91; DL

THE MORONIC INFERNO * Amis, Martin
Publisher: Penguin (Harms-1986)   Note: 208p; R93; DL

REPRESENTATIONS OF THE INTELLECTUAL * Said, Edward W.
Publisher: Vintage Books (NY-1994)   Note: 121p;R98;DL

BY THE WAY...

VIEWS FROM A WINDOW: CONVERSATIONS WITH GORE VIDAL *
  Stenton & Vidal, Eds
Publisher: LyleStuart (NJ-1980)   Note: 319; R2000; DL

MATTERS OF FACT & FICTION * Vidal, Gore
Publisher: Random Hse (NY-1977)   Note: 284p; R2000; DL

THE AGE OF THE WARRIOR * Fisk, Robert
Publisher: Fourth Estate (Lon-2008)   Note: 522p; R09;DL

THE VISIONARY EYE: ESSAYS * Bronowsky J.
Publisher: MIT Pr (Camb Mass-1978)   Note: 185p; R11; DL

JAMES T. FARRELL: SELECTED ESSAYS * Wolf, Luna, Ed.
Publisher: McGraw Hill (NY-1964)   Note: 198p; R13; DL

THE SECOND OLDEST PROFESSION * Knightley, Phillip
Publisher: PanBooks (Lon-1986)   Note: 400p; R88; DL

THE ROMANCE OF SAIL * Leitch, Michael
Publisher: Hamlyn (Lon-1975)   Note: 125p;R03;DL

THE ELSEWHERE COMMUNITY * Kenner, Hugh
Publisher: AnansiPr (Concord-1998)   Note: 112p;R03;DL

COMMA SENSE * Liderer, R. & Shore, J.
Publisher: St Martins Pr (NY-2005)   Note: 160p;R09;DL

ARCHITECTURE * Ballantyne, Andrew
Publisher: Sterling (NY-2002)   Note: 184p;R2014;DL

DEPRESSION AND THE BODY * Lowen, A.
Publisher: Penguin (harms-1972)   Note: 314p; R81; DL

A GUIDE FOR THE PERPLEXED * Shumacher, E. F.
Publisher: Harper & Row (NY-1977)   Note: 146p; R91; DL

THE MAKING OF INTELLIGENCE * Richardson, Ken
Publisher: Weidenfeld & Nick. (Lon-1999)   Note: 218p;R04;DL

THE INTELLECTUAL * Fuller, Steve
Publisher: Icon Books (Camb.,Mass.-2005)   Note: 184p;R05;DL

Books Read, Enjoyed & Recommended

History: Ancient

ANTIQUITY * Cantor, Norman F.
Publisher: Perennial (NY-2003)　　　　　　　　Note: 240p; R2005; DL

THE ROMANS * Barrow, R.H.
Publisher: Penguin (Harms-1949)　　　　　　　Note: 220p; R82; DL

THE ORIGINS OF HISTORY * Butterfield, H.; A Watson Ed
Publisher: Methuen (Lon-1981)　　　　　　　　Note: 230p; R84; DL

NEW TESTAMENT HISTORY * Bruce,F.F.
Publisher: Doubleday (Lon-1969)　　　　　　　Note: 430p; R85; PG

THE EARLY CHURCH * Trend, W.H.C.
Publisher: Fortress Press (Phil.-1982)　　　　　Note: 250p; R86; DL

MAN, STATE AND DEITY - ESSAYS IN ANCIENT HISTORY
　* Ehrenberg, Victor
Publisher: Methuen & Co (Lon-1974)　　　　　Note: 183p; R86;CNC

THE PATRIARCHS OF ISRAEL * Holt, John M. Prof.
Publisher: Vandblt U.P. (Nash.-1964)　　　　　Note: 235p; R87; PG

THE DEAD SEA COMMUNITY: IT'S ORIGIN AND TEACHING
　* Schubert, Hurt ; Dober, trans.
Publisher: Greenwood (Westport-1959)　　　　Note: 165p; R87; "PG

THE LAW OF THE ANCIENT ROMANS * Watson, Alan
Publisher: Southern Method. U.P. (Dallas-1970)　Note: 105p; R88; CNC

ASPECTS OF ANTIQUITY: DISCOVERIES & CONTROVERSIES * Finley, M.I.
Publisher: Pelican (Dallas-1977)　　　　　　　Note: 200p; R88; DL

PASSAGES FROM ANTIQUITY TO FEUDALISM * Anderson, Perry
Publisher: Verso (Lon-1974)　　　　　　　　　Note: 300p; R88; DL

SOCIAL CONFLICTS IN THE ROMAN REPUBLIC * Brunt, P.A.
Publisher: W.W. Norton (NY-1971)　　　　　　Note: 160p; R88; DL

THE ROMANS AND THEIR GODS * Ogilvie, R.M.
Publisher: Chatto & Winders (Lon-1974)　　　　Note: 130p; R88; DL

BY THE WAY...

THE BARBARIAN WEST, A.D. 400-1000, THE EARLY MIDDLE AGES. *
Wallace-Hadrill, J.M.
Publisher: Harper (NY-1962)　　　　　　　　　　　Note: 150p; R89; Dl

PAGAN ROME AND THE EARLY CHRISTIANS * Benko, S.
Publisher: Indiana U.P. (Bloomington-1984)　　　　Note: 180p; R89; DL

ANCIENT HISTORY: 4,000 BC-400 AD* Cantor & Worthman (Eds.)
Publisher: Crowell (NY-1972)　　　　　　　　　　Note: 280pp. R89; DL

JESUS AND THE POLITICS OF HIS DAY * Bammel, E.-Ed
Publisher: Camb. U Press (Camb.-1984)　　　　　　Note: 510p; R90; DL

BYZANTIUM-THE EMPIRE OF THE NEW ROME * Mango, Cyril
Publisher: Weidenfield & Nicholson (Lon-1980)　　　Note: 330p; R90; DL

THE USE AND ABUSE OF HISTORY * Finley, M. I.
Publisher: Hogarth Press (Lon-1975)　　　　　　　Note: 246p; R90; DL

EARLY GREECE: THE BRONZE & ARCHAIC AGES * Finley, M. I.
Publisher: Norton, W. W. (NY-1981)　　　　　　　Note: 150p; R91; DL

THE RELIGIONS OF THE ROMAN EMPIRE * Ferguson, John
Publisher: Cornell U P (NY-1970)　　　　　　　　Note: 295p; R91; DL

THE FORMATION OF CHRISTENDOM * Herrin, Judith
Publisher: Princeton U P (NJ-1987)　　　　　　　　Note: 530p; R91; DL

CHRISTIANS & THE ROMAN EMPIRE* Sordi, M., Tr. A. Bedini
Publisher: Croom Helm (Lon-1983)　　　　　　　　Note: 205p;R92; DL

THE MAKING OF LATE ANTIQUITY * Brown, Pet
Publisher: Harvard U.P. (Camb.-1978)　　　　　　Note: 129p; R92; DL

NERO : THE END OF A DYNASTY * Griffin, Miriam T.
Publisher: Yale U.P. (NewH-1985)　　　　　　　　Note: 303p; R92; DL

CONSTANTINE * McMullen, Ramsay
Publisher: Harper Torch Bks (NY-1969)　　　　　　Note: 250p; R93; DL

POWER & PERSUASION IN LATE ANTIQUITY * Brown, Peter
Publisher: U of Wisconsin Pr (Wisc.-1992)　　　　　Note:182p;R94;DL

THE CULT OF THE SAINTS * Brown, Peter
Publisher: U of Chicago Press (Chic-1981)　　　　　Note: 175p; R94; DL

Books Read, Enjoyed & Recommended

THE HISTORY OF ANCIENT ISRAEL * Grant, Michael
Publisher: Chs Scribners (NY-1984)   Note: 317p; R96; DL

THE EARLY CHURCH * Hinson, E. Glenn
Publisher: Abingdon Press (Nash.-1996)   Note: 360p; R99; DL

THE LATER ROMAN EMPIRE * Cameron, Avril
Publisher: Fontana (Lon-1993)   Note: 238p; R00; DL

THE JEWS IN THE ROMAN EMPIRE * Grant, Michael
Publisher: Dorset Pr (NY-1973)   Note: 347p; R01; DL

THE END OF THE PAST: ANCIENT ROME & THE MEDIEVAL WEST *
   Schiavom, Aldo Tr M. J. Schnider
Publisher: Harv. UP (Camb.-2000)   Note: 278p; R01; DL

THE ROMAN EMPIRE 27BC-476AD * Starr, Chester G.
Publisher: OxfordUP (NY-1982)   Note: 205p; R02;DL

AN INTELLIGENTPERSON'S GUIDE TO CLASSICS * Jones, Peter
Publisher: Widenfield & Nicholson (Lon-1998)   Note: 176p; R04; DL

THE DAY OF THE BARBARIANS * Barbero, Alesandro;J Cullen Tr
Publisher: Walker & Co (NY-2005)   Note: 179p; R13; DL

History of Ideas

RUSSIAN THINKERS * Berlin, Isaiah
Publisher: Penguin (Harms-1978)   Note: 340p; R82; DL.

ESSAYS ON RUSSIAN INTELLECTUAL HISTORY * Blair, L., Ed.
Publisher: U of Texas (-1971)   Note: 120p; R82; PG.

RENAISSANCE THOUGHT AND THE ARTS – COLLECTED ESSAYS *
   Kristeller, P.
Publisher: Princeton UP (-1965)   Note: 235p; R83; PG

AN OUTLINE OF EUROPEAN INTELLECTUAL HISTORY * Foster, H. J
Publisher: Penguin (Harms-1969)   Note: 178; R84;PG

AGAINST THE CURRENT: ESSAYS IN THE HISTORY OF IDEAS *
   Berlin, I.
Publisher: Oxford UP (Lon-1979)   Note: 425p; R85 DL.

BY THE WAY...

THE ENLIGHTENMENT * Hampson, Norman
Publisher: Penquin (Lon-1968) Note: 290p; R86; DL

EUROPE: THE EMERGENCE OF AN IDEA * Hay, Denis
Publisher: Edinb. U.P. (Edinb.-1968) Note: 160p; R86; CNC

THE AWAKENING OF EUROPE – A HISTORY OF EUROPEAN
 THOUGHT * Wolff, Philippe,
Publisher: Penguin (Lon-1968) Note: 300p; R86; CNC

THE ROMAN MIND: STUDIES IN THE HISTORY OF THOUGHT -
 CICERO TO AURELEUS * Clarke, M.L. Prof.
Publisher: Penguin (NY-1968) Note: 155p; R87; DL

THE SECULARIZATION OF THE EUROPEAN MIND IN THE 19TH
 CENTURY * Chadwick, Owen
Publisher: Cambridge U. P. (Camb.-1975) Note: 270p; R87; CNC

THE EVOLUTION OF MEDIEVAL THOUGHT * Knowles, David
Publisher: Helicon (Balt.-1962) Note: 340p; R87; DL

THE MEDIEVAL MIND- VOL 2 * Taylor, Henry O
Publisher: Harvard U Press (Camb.-1966) Note: 500p;R90;CNC

THE VISION OF THE ANOINTED * Sowell, Thomas
Publisher: Basic Bks (NY-1995) Note: 260; R2000; DL

IDEAS THAT MATTER * Grayling, A.C.
Publisher: Phoenix (Lon-2009) Note: 610p; R2011; DL

A SHORT HISTORY OF PROGRESS * Wright, Ronald
Publisher: Anansi Pr. (Tor-2004) Note: 211p; R2013; DL

History, Modern

SHADOW OF THE WINTER PALACE * Crankshaw, Eward Ed.
Publisher: Viking Press (NY-1976) Note: 425p; R80;DL

THE TWENTY YEARS CRISES (1919-1939) * Carr,E.H.
Publisher: MacMillan (Lon-1954) Note: 245p; R80; DL

IN THE LIGHT OF HISTORY * Plumb, J.H.
Publisher: Delta (NY-1972) Note: 265p; R80; DL

Books Read, Enjoyed & Recommended

HISTORICAL ESSAYS * Trevor-Roper, H
Publisher: Penguin   Note: 325p; R81; CNC

MAIN TRENDS IN HISTORY * Barraclough, Geoffrey
Publisher: Penguin)   Note: 215p; R81; CNC

ESSAYS ON MODERN EUROPEAN REVOLUTIONARY HISTORY, Lakner
   & Philip, Eds.
Publisher: Webb Memorial Lecture 1977   Note: 130p; R82; CNC

EUROPE: GRANDEUR AND DECLINE * Taylor, A. P.
Publisher: Penguin (Harms-1967)   Note: 375p; R82; DL

HISTORIANS & EIGHTEENTH CENTURY EUROP1715-1789 * Anderson, M.S.
Publisher: Oxford UP (Lon-)   Note: 250p; R82, CNC.

THE SHAPE OF EUROPEAN HISTORY * McNeil, W.H.
Publisher: Oxford UP, 1974   Note: 180p; R82, CNC

THE COMING OF THE FRENCH REVOLUTION * Lefebvre, G
Publisher: Princeton UP (NJ-1947)   Note: 240p; R82; CNC.

PRELUDE TO MODERN EUROPE 1815-1914 * Woodward, L.
Publisher: Methuen (Lon-1972)   Note: 280p; R82;PG

REFORMATION EUROPE 1517-1559 * Elton, G.R.
Publisher: Fontana (Lon-1963)   Note: 330p; R83;DL

THE CHALLENGE OF THE AMERICAN REVOLUTION * Morgan, E.S.
Publisher: William Norton (NY-1976)   Note: 225p; R83;PG

ISRAEL AND THE ARABS * Rodinson, M.
Publisher: Penguin (Harms-1968)   Note: 250p; R83; DL

RISE TO GLOBALISM, AMERICAN FOREIGN POLICY 1938-1980 * Ambrose, S.C.
Publisher: Penguin (NY-1980)   Note: 404; R83; DL

EUROPE:JOURNEY TO AN UNKNOWN DESTINATION * Shonfield, Andrew
Publisher: Penguin (Harms-)   Note: 96p; R83;DL

THE OCTOBER REVOLUTION: BEFORE AND AFTER * Carr, E.H
Publisher: A.A. Knopf (-1969)   Note: 180p; R84; PG

DOCUMENTARY HISTORY OF WESTERN CIVILIZATION
   * Hillerbrand, H. Ed
Publisher: Penguin (-)   Note: 310p; R84; PG

BY THE WAY...

ASPECTS OF EUROPEAN HISTORY: 1494-1789 * Lee, S. J.
Publisher: Methuen (Lon-1984)   Note: 300p; R84; DL

ESSAYS ON AMERICAN REVOLUTION * Kurtz & Hutson, Eds.
Publisher: UNC Pr. Enduring Edition (1973)   Note: 310p; R84;PG.

A HISTORY OF MODERN JAPAN * Storey, R.
Publisher: Penguin (Lon-1982)   Note: 300p; R85; DL

THE PELICAN HISTORY OF CANADA * McNaught, K
Publisher: Penguin (Lon-1975)   Note: 307p; R85; DL

RUSSIA AND THE WEST UNDER LENIN AND STALIN * Kennan, George
Publisher: Little Brown (Boston-1960)   Note: 403p; R85; DL

A HISTORY OF THE MODERN WORLD - 1917 TO 1980s * Johnson, Paul
Publisher: Weidenfeld & Nicholson (Lon-'83)   Note: 800p; R86;CNC

THE HARD AND BITTER PEACE- WORLD POLITICS
    SINCE 1945 * Hudson, G.F.
Publisher: Burns & MacEakern (Tor-1967)   Note: 300p; R86; DL

MEDIEVAL ASPECTS OF RENAISSANCE LEARNING,
    Kristeller,P;Mahoney,Eds
Publisher: Duke U.P. (-1974)   Note: 125p; R87; CNC

THE OLD EUROPEAN ORDER, 1660-1800 * Doyle, W.
Publisher: Oxford UP (Oxford-1978)   Note: 175p; R87; CNC

VANISHED SUPREMACIES: ESSAYS ON EUROPEAN HISTORY.
    1812-1918. * Namier, L. –
Publisher: Harper (NY-1963)   Note: 180p; R88; DL

LENIN: REVOLUTION A & POWER-A HISTORY OF THE SOVIET UNION
    1917-1953, V. Ionescu * D'Encausse, H,Tr.
Publisher: Longmans (NY-1982)   Note: 240p; R89; CNC

TRANSITION & REVOLUTION – PROBLEMS OF EUROPEAN
    RENAISSANCE & REFORMTN HISTORY * Kingdom, R.M.Ed
Publisher: Burgess Pub. (NY-1977)   Note: 274p;R90;CNC

HIDDEN HISTORY * Boorstin, Daniel
Publisher: Vantage Books (NY-1987)   Note: 330p;R90;DL

THE RENAISSANCE-SIX ESSAYS * Ferguson, WK et al
Publisher: Harper & Row (NY-1962)   Note: 184p; R90; DL

Books Read, Enjoyed & Recommended

THE RENAISSANCE & THE REFORMATION IN
GERMANY, Hoffmeister, G.-Ed
Publisher: Frederick Ungar Pub (NY-1977)   Note: 230p;R90; CNC

PATH BETWEEN THE SEAS: CREATION OF THE PANAMA CANAL 1870-
1914 * McCullough, David
Publisher: Simon & Shuster (NY-1977)   Note: 652p;R90; DL

A CYCLE OF OUTRAGE: A REACTION TO JUVENILE DELINQUENCY IN
THE 1950s * Gilbert, James
Publisher: Oxford U P (NY-1986)   Note:230p;R91; DL

THE PAST & THE PRESENT * Stone, Lawrence
Publisher: Routlege & Keegan (Boston-1981)   Note:260p;R91; CNC

ROLE OF RELIGION IN MODERN EUROPEAN * S. Burrell, Ed
Publisher: Macmillian (NY-1964)   Note: 149p; R92; DL

RENAISSANCE EUROPE:THE INDIVIDUAL & SOCIETY 1480-1520 * Hale, J. R.
Publisher: Harper & Row (NY-1971)   Note: 340p; R94; DL

THE CHURCH & THE AGE OF REASON:1648-1789 * Cragg, Gerald R.
Publisher: Penguin (Harms.-1960)   Note: 290p; R94;DL

THE NEXT CENTURY * Haberstam, David
Publisher: William Morrow (NY-1991)   Note: 126p; R94; DL

THE REFORMATION * Chadwick, Owen
Publisher: Penguin (Lon-1972)   Note: 450p; R94; DL

STRATEGY & DIPLOMACY 1870-1945 * Kennedy, Paul
Publisher: Verso (Lon-1984)   Note: 245p;R00;DL

ISRAEL AND THE ARABS * Rodinson, Maxime
Publisher: Pelican (Harms.-1970)   Note: 250p; R2000;DL

THE STRUGGLE FOR STABILITY IN EARLY MODERN EUROPE *
Rabb, T.K.
Publisher: Oxford UP (NY-1975)   Note: 170p; R01;DL

THE ROLE OF RELIGION IN MODERN EUROPEAN
HISTORY * Burrell, S.A.Ed.
Publisher: Macmillan (N.Y.-1966)   Note: 147p; R2004;DL

A HISTORY OF THE ARAB PEOPLE * Hourani, Albert
Publisher: Faber & Faber (Lon-2002)   Note: 566p;R2006;DL

BY THE WAY...

POLITICS WITHOUT DEMOCRACY: 1815-1914 * Bently, Michael
Publisher: Fontana (Lon-1989)   Note: 446p;R2006;DL

REFORMATION EUROPE'S HOUSE DIVIDED
1490-1700, McCulloch, Diarmaid
Publisher: Penguin (Lon-2003)   Note: 831p;R2007; DL

THE RISE & FALL OF THE BRITISH EMPIRE * James, Lawrence
Publisher: Little Brown (Lon-1994)   Note: 714p;R2007; DL

AFTER TAMBERLANE: RISE & FALL OF GLOBAL EMPIRES * Darwin, John
Publisher: Bloomsbury (Lon-2008)   Note: 575p; R11;DL

PARIS 1919 * Macmillan, Margaret
Publisher: Random House (NY-2003)   Note: 570p; R12; DL

THINKING THE TWENTIETH CENTURY * Judt, Tony (with T. Snyder)
Publisher: Penguin (NY-2012)   Note: 434p;R2012;;DL

PAKISTAN ON THE BRINK * Rashid, Ahmed
Publisher: Viking Pr. (NY-2012)   Note: 234p;R2012;DL

REAPPRAISALS: REFLECTIONS ON THE FORGOTTEN
20TH CENTURY. * Judt,Tony
Publisher: Penguin (NY-2008)   Note: 448p;R12;10;DL

POSTWAR: A HISTORY OF EUROPE SINCE 1945 * Judt, Tony
Publisher: Penguin (NY-2005)   Note: 933p;R12; DL

WATERLOO: JUNE 18,1815 * Roberts, Andrew
Publisher: Harper (NY-2005)   Note: 143p; R12; DL

THE UNTOLD HISTORY OF THE U. S. * Stone & Kuznick
Publisher: Gallery Bks (NY-2012)   Note: 749p; R2014; DL

MODERN HISTORIANS ON BRITISH HISTORY * Elton, G.R.
Publisher: Cornell UP (NY-1970)   Note: 239p; R2015; DL

History, Medieval

THE HOLY WAR * Murphy, T., Ed.
Publisher: Ohio State UP (Clev.-1976)   Note: 200p; R82; CNC.

Books Read, Enjoyed & Recommended

THE MEDIEVAL CENTURIES * Hay, D.
Publisher: Methuen (Lon-1964)   Note: 170p; R82;PG

THE ITALIAN RENAISSANCE IN ITS HISTORICAL
    BACKGROUND * Hay, Denys
Publisher: Cambridge U.P. (Camb.-1977)   Note: 220p; R82; PG

ESSAYS ON MEDIEVAL CIVILIZATION - (W.P.WEBB MEMORIAL
    LECTURES) * Lechner & Philip, Eds.
Publisher: (-1978)   Note: 190p; R82; CNC

MEDIEVAL HISTORY: THE LIFE & DEATH OF A CIVILIZATION
    * Cantor, Norman F.
Publisher: Macmillan (Lon-1969)   Note: 575p; R84;DL

ESSAYS ON THE RECONSTRUCTION OF MEDIEVAL HISTORY
    * Mudroch & Course, Eds.
Publisher: McGill U P (Mont.-1974)   Note: 173p;R84;CNC

THE PERSUIT OF THE MILLENNIUM * Cohn, Norman.
Publisher: Paladin (Lon-1970)   Note: 400p; R84; DL.

WESTERN SOCIETY AND THE CHURCH IN THE
    MIDDLE AGES * Southern, R.W.
Publisher: Penguin (Lon-1970)   Note: 360p; R85; DL.

ESSAYS ON MEDIEVAL CIVILIZATION (EXTRACTS) * Herlihy &Cheyeth
Publisher: U of Texas (-1978)   Note: 80p; R85;CNC

12TH CENTURY EUROPE: INTERPRETIVE ESSAY * Packard, S.R
Published 1973   Note: 350p; R85; CNC

MIDDLE AGES,V READINGS IN MED. HISTORY * Tierney, B.
Publisher: Prentice Hall (-1974)   Note: 192p; R85; CNC

ORIGINS OF THE MEDIEVAL WORLD * Bark, W
Publisher: Anchor (-1960)   Note: 210p; R85; CNC

THE MEANING OF THE MIDDLE AGES * Cantor, Norman F.
Publisher: Allyn Bacon (NY-1973)   Note: 310p; R85;CNC

THE MEDIEVAL EXPERIENCE: FOUNDATIONS OF WESTN CULTURAL
    SINGULARITY * Oakley, F.
Publisher: (-1974)   Note: 220p; R85; CNC

BY THE WAY...

THE GROWTH OF PAPAL GOVERNMENT IN THE
  MIDDLE AGES * Ullman, W.
Publisher: Methuen (Lon-1970)   Note: 500p;R85;CNC

EUROPE : HIERARCHY AND REVOLT * Holmes, George
Publisher: Penguin (Lon-1975)   Note: 300p; R85; CNC

ONE THOUSAND YEARS, WESTERN EUROPE IN THE MIDDLE AGES *
  Herliky,Nicholas & Queller
Publisher: Houghton Miffin (Bost-'74)   Note: 150p;R85;CNC

THE MAKING OF THE MIDDLE AGES * Southern, R.W.
Publisher: Yale UP. (Lon-1953)   Note: 260p; R86; CNC

THE VISION OF POLITICS ON THE EVE OF THE REFORMATION *
  Hexter, J.H.
Publisher: Basic Books (NY-1973)   Note: 230p;R86;DL

CONTEMPORARY REFLECTIONS ON THE MEDIEVEL CHRISTIAN
  TRADITION * Shriver, C.H. Ed
Publisher: Duke U.P. (-1974)   Note: 260p; R86; CNC

ONE THOUSAND YEARS, WESTERN EUROPE IN THE MIDDLE AGES *
  Lerner,R;Russel,J:Contributr
Publisher: Hougthon Miffin (Boston-1974)   Note: 140p; R86; CNC

DISSENT AND REFORM IN THE EARLY MIDDLE AGES * Russell, J.B.
Publisher: U. of Calif. Pr. (LA-1965)   Note: 250p;R88;CNC

THE INQUISITION * O'Brien, John
Publisher: Macmillan (NY-1973)   Note: 214p; R89; CNC

SPEAKING OF THE MIDDLE AGES * Zumthor, P. trans. White, S.
Publisher: Univ. of Nebraska (Lincoln-1986) Note: 100p; R89;CNC

THE MEDIEVAL PAPACY * Barraclough, G.
Publisher: Thames & Hudson (Lon-1968)   Note: 209p; R89; DL

PENGUIN ATLAS OF MEDIEVAL HISTORY * McEvedy, Colin
Publisher: Penguin (Harms.-1986)   Note: 96p; R90; DL

A WORLD MADE BY MAN- COGNITION & SOCIETY 400-1200AD *
  Radding, Charles M
Publisher:U. of N. Carol. Pr (CHill-1985)   Note: 280p;R90;CNC

Books Read, Enjoyed & Recommended

MEDIEVAL FEUDALISM * Stevenson, Carl
Publisher: Cornell U Press (Itacha-1973)　　　　Note: 111p; R90; DL

THE CRISIS OF CHURCH & STATE- 1050-1300 * Tierney, Brian
Publisher: Prentice Hall (NJ, 1964)　　　　Note: 210p;R91;DL

MEDIEVAL FOUNDATIONS OF RENAISSANCE HUMANISM * Ullman, W.
Publisher: Cornel U.P. (NY-1977)　　　　Note: 202p; R92; CNC

THE MEDIEVAL IDEA OF MARRIAGE * Brooke, Christopher
Publisher: Oxford U.P. (Oxford-1989)　　　　Note: 300p; R92; DL

POLITICAL THOUGHT IN MEDIEVAL TIMES * Morrall, John B.
Publisher: Harper & Row (NY-1962)　　　　Note: 146p; R92; DL

INVENTING THE MIDDLE AGES * Cantor, Norman F.
Publisher: Quill William Morrow (NY-1991)　　　　Note: 448p;R94;DL

EUROPE'S INNER DEMONS * Cohn, Norman
Publisher: Pimlico (Lon-1993)　　　　Note: 270p;R94;DL

THE WANING OF THE MIDDLE AGES * Huizinga, J.
Publisher: St Martin's Press (NY-1924)　　　　Note: 300p;R94;DL

THE INVESTITURE CONTROVERSY: CHURCH STATE - 9TH TO 12TH
　　CENTURY * Blumenthall, Ute Renate
Publisher: U of Pensilvania Prs (Phil-1988)　　　　Note: 190p;R94;UNBC

INQUISITION * Peters, Edward
Publisher: The Free Press (NY-1988)　　　　Note: 347p; R94;UNBC

THE JUST WAR IN THE MIDDLE AGES * Russell, Frederick H.
Publisher: Cambridge UP (Camb.-1977)　　　　Note: 300p;R94;DL

THE CHURCH IN WESTERN EUROPE FROM 10TH TO EARLY 12TH
　　CENTURIES * Tellenbach, Gerd
Publisher: Cambridge UP (Camb-1993)　　　　Note: 402p; R96; DL

THE FORMATION OF A PERSECUTING SOCIETY * Moore, R.I.
Publisher: B Blackwell (Oxford-1987)　　　　Note: 170P; R99; DL

THE EUROPEAN WITCH CRAZE OF THE 16TH & 17TH CENTURIES *
　　Trevor-Roper,H.R.
Publisher: Penguin (Lon-1967)　　　　Note: 140p; R99;DL

BY THE WAY...

CHRISTENDOM & CHRISTIANITY IN THE MIDDLE AGES *
    Bredero, Adriann
Publisher: Wm.B.Erdmann (Mich-1994)   Note: 401p; R01; DL

THE ELIZABETHAN WORLD PICTURE * Tillgard, E.M.W.
Publisher: Vintage Bks (NY-)   Note: 116p;R05; DL

THE LAST VOYAGE OF COLUMBUS * Dugard, Martin
Publisher: Little Brown (NY-2005)   Note: 294p;R06;DL

History, Philosophy of

THE PHILOSOPHY OF HISTORY * Hegel
Publisher: Great Books (NY-1952)   Note: 450p; R80; DL

REAPPRAISALS IN HISTORY * Hexter, J.H.
Publisher: Basic Books (NY-1979)   Note: 250p; R80; PG

DECLINE OF THE WEST II * Spengler, Oswald; Atkinson Tr.
Publisher: Knopf (-1928)   Note: 400p;R80;PG

THE NATURE OF HISTORICAL INQUIRY * Marsak L., Ed.
Publisher: (-)   Note: 250p;R81;PG

A PATTERN FOR HISTORY * Lowen, Arthur R.M.
Publisher: (-)   Note: 350p; R81; CNC

ON HISTORIANS * Hexter, J.H.
Publisher: Norton (1979)   Note: 300p; R81; PG

DOING HISTORY * Hexter, J.H.
Publisher: Indiana UP (1972)   Note: 180p; R81; CNC

NEW DIRECTIONS IN EUROPEAN HISTORIOGRAPHY * Iggers, G.C.
Publisher: Weslayen UP (1975)   Note: 180p; R82; PG

BETWEEN PHILOSOPHY AND HISTORY * Fain, H.
Publisher: Princeton UP (NJ-1970)   Note: 300p; R82;PG.

HISTORY THE BETRAYER - A STUDY IN BIAS * Dance, E.H.
Publisher: Hutchinson (Lon-1964)   Note: 150p; R82; DL.

Books Read, Enjoyed & Recommended

TURNING POINTS IN WORLD HISTORY * Barraclough, G.
Publisher: Thames Hudson] (NY-1977) Note: 90p; R82;PG

HISTORY: CHOICE AND COMMITMENT * Gilbert, F.
Publisher: Bilknys Press (-1977) Note: 450p;R84;CNC

THE HISTORIAN AND HISTORY * Smith, Page
Publisher: A.Knopf (NY-1964) Note: 250p; R85; DL

EARLY CHRISTIAN INTERPRETATIONS OF HISTORY * Milburn,R.L.P.
Publisher: Adam Black (-1954) Note: 215p;R85;CNC.

CHRISTIANITY & THE STATE IN THE LIGHT OF HISTORY * Parker, T. M.
Publisher: Oxford U P (Oxford-1955) Note: 172p;R85; CNC.

HISTORY: REMEMBERED, RECOVERED, INVENTED * Lewis, Bernard
Publisher: (1975) Note: 100p; R85; CNC.

ON HISTORY * Braudel, F.
Publisher: Weidenfield (Lon-1969) Note: 218p; R85; DL

MAN ON HIS PAST: THE STUDY OF THE HISTORY OF HISTORICAL
   SCHOLARSHIP * Butterfield, H.
Publisher: Beacon (Lon-1955) Note: 245p; R85; DL

WESTERN CIVILIZATION, RECENT INTERPRETATIONS *
   Morse,Sauer,Lasch, et al
Publisher: Thomas Y. Crowell (NY-1973) Note: 120p; R86;CNC

THE WHIG INTERPRETATION OF HISTORY * Butterfield, H.
Publisher: C. Bell & Sons (Lon-1931) Note: 134p; R86; DL

HISTORY, GUILT AND HABIT (Lectures) * Barfield Owen
Publisher: Harcourt Brace (Con-1979) Note: 110p; R86;CNC

HISTORY AND HISTORICAL UNDERSTANDING * McIntire,C.T.& Wells,
   R.A. Eds;CNC
Publisher: Erdmans (Mich.-1984) Note: 140p; R88;CNC

FREUD FOR HISTORIANS * Gay, Peter
Publisher: Oxford U.P. (NY-1985) Note: 218p;R88;DL

ESSAYS IN MODERN EUROPEAN HISTORIOGRAPHY * Halperin S. W. Ed
Publisher: U of Chicago Press (Chic.-1970) Note: 383p; R88; DL

BY THE WAY...

MAN AND HIS PAST: THE NATURE AND ROLE OF HISTORIOGRAPHY
 * Gagnon, S. Tr. M.Heap
Publisher: Harvest House (Harv-1982) Note: 70p; R89;DL

HISTORY AND SYSTEMS:HEGEL'S PHILOSOPHY OF HISTORY
 * Perkins, Robert L, Ed
Publisher: N.Y State Univ. (NY-1984) Note: 250p;R89;DL

THE USES OF HISTORY- ESSAYS IN INTELLECTUAL & SOCIAL
 HISTORY * White, H. W., Ed.
Publisher: Wayne State U P (Lon-1975) Note: 270P; R90; DL

MAN AND HIS PAST * Gagnon, Serge
Publisher: Penguin (Mont.-1982) Note: 79p;R08;DL

A HISTORY OF HISTORIES * Burrow, John
Publisher: Penguin (Lon-2007) Note: 553p;R09;DL

THEORIES AND NARRATIVES: REFLECTIONS ON PHIL.OF HISTORY. *
 Callicos, A.
Publisher: Duke UP (NC-1995) Note: 252p;R10;DL

THE USES AND ABUSES OF HISTORY * MacMillan, Margaret
Publisher: Penguin (Tor-2008) Note: 194p;R11;DL

HISTORY * Arnold, John A.
Publisher: Sterling (NY-2000) Note: 182p;R13;DL

THE INVENTION OF THE LAND OF ISRAEL * Sand, Shlomo
Publisher: Veroo (Lon-2012) Note: 295p;R13;DL

History of Christianity

HISTORY OF CATHOLIC TRADITION. 100 TO 600 A.D. (CHRISTIAN
 TRAD. VOL 1) * Pelikan, Jaroslav
Publisher: U of Chic (Chic-1970) Note: 375p; R83;PG

SPIRIT OF EASTERN CHRISTENDOM 600-1700 (CHRISTIAN
 TRADITION. VOL 2) * Pelikan, J.
Publisher: Yale U.P. (-) Note: 302p; R84; PG.

THE MYTH OF CHRISTIAN BEGINNINGS - * Wilken, R.L.
Publisher: (1971) Note: 208p; R84; CN

Books Read, Enjoyed & Recommended

GROWTH OF MEDIEVAL THEOLOGY 600-1300 (CHRISTIAN TRAD. VOL 3) * Pelikan, J.
Publisher: Yale UP (NY-1978)　　　　　　　　　　Note: 310p; R84; PG

WRITINGS ON CHRISTIANITY & HISTORY * Butterfield, H.
Publisher: Eyre Methuen (1977)　　　　　　　　　Note: 320p; R84;CNC

REFORMATION OF CHURCH & DOGMA, 1300-1700 (CHRISTIAN TRAD. VOL 4) * Pelikan, J.
Publisher: U of Chic. Pr (1984)　　　　　　　　　Note: 400p; R83; PG

OUR COMMON HISTORY AS CHRISTIANS *Dischner et al, Eds.
Publisher: Oxford UP (NY-1975)　　　　　　　　　Note: 290p; R85; PG

HOW IT ALL BEGAN-ORIGINS OF THE CHRISTIAN CHURCH * Edwards, D.C.
Publisher: Seabury (NY-1973)　　　　　　　　　　Note: 145p;R86;PG

THE COUNTER-REFORMATION: CATHOLIC EUROPE & THE NON-CHRISTIAN WORLD * Wright, A.D.
Publisher: St. Martin Press (NY-1982)　　　　　　Note:310p;R87;CNC

CHURCH AND PEOPLE.1450-1660. TRIUMPH OF THE LAITY IN ENGLISH CHURCH * Cross, C.
Publisher: Humington Press (1976)　　　　　　　 Note: 250p;R87;CNC

PAPAL POWER - A STUDY OF VATICAN CONTROL OVER LAY ELITES * Vaillancourt, J.
Publisher: Berkely U.P. (Berkley-1980)　　　　　　ote: 325p; R87;CNC

THE TRIUMPH OF THE HOLY SEE-HISTORY OF THE PAPACY INTHE 19THCENTURY * Holms, J.D.
Publisher: (1978)　　　　　　　　　　　　　　　Note: 200p;R87;CNC

JESUS THROUGH THE CENTURIES: HIS PLACE IN HISTORY OF CULTURE * Pelikan, J.
Publisher: Yale U.P. (NHarm-1985)　　　　　　　 Note: 260p; R87; PG

RELIGION AND SEXISM: * Ruether, Rosemary,Ed
Publisher: Simon & Schuster (NY-1974)　　　　　 Note: 340p;R87; CNC

THE CAMBRIDGE HISTORY OF THE BIBLE, VOL 1, FROM THE BEGINNING TO JEROME * Lampe, G.W.H. Ed
Publisher: Cambridge U.P. (Camb.-1970)　　　　　Note: 606p;R88;PG

CHRISTIANITY THROUGH THE THIRTEENTH CENTURY * Baldwin, M.W. Ed
Publisher: Walker & Co (NY-1970)　　　　　　　　Note: 373p;R88;PG

BY THE WAY...

THE EARLY CHURCH * Chadwick, Henry
Publisher: Penguin (Lon-1967)　　　　　　　　　　　Note: 300p;R89;DL

CAMBRIDGE.HISTORY OF THE BIBLE:VOL 2 WESTERN FATHERS TO
　THE REFORMTN * Lampe, G.W.H. Ed
Publisher: Camb. U.P. (Camb.-1969)　　　　　　　　Note:540p; R89; P.G.

JESUS AND THE ZEALOTS : STUDY OF POLITCAL FACT IN PRIMITIVE
　CHRISTNITY * Brandon, S.G.F.
Publisher: Univ. of Manchester (Man.-1967)　　　　　Note: 412p; R89; DL

THE ORIGINS OF THE NEW TESTAMENT * Loisy, Alfred (Trans P Jacks)
Publisher: Allen & Unwin (Lon-1950)　　　　　　　　Note: 330p; R90; DL

THE MAKING OF THE OLD TESTAMENT * Millor, Enid B. Ed
Publisher: Camb. U P (Camb.-1972)　　　　　　　　Note: 210p; R90; DL

APOSTOLIC & POST-APOSTOLIC TIMES * Gopelt, Leonard
Publisher: Harper & Row (NY-1970)　　　　　　　　Note: 230p;R94;DL

THE JESUS PARTY * Schonfield, Hugh J.
Publisher: Macmillan Publishing (NY-1974)　　　　　Note: 320p; R95; DL

CHRONICLE OF THE LAST PAGANS * Chuvin, P. Tr B Archer
Publisher: Harvard UP (Camb-1990)　　　　　　　　Note: 180p;R96; UNBC

THE POPE'S DIVISIONS: THE RC CHURCH TODAY * Nichols, Peter
Publisher: Holt Rinehart (NY-1981)　　　　　　　　Note: 382p; R96; DL

CATHOLICISM IN AMERICA * Walsh, Timothy
Publisher: Rob. E Krieger (malabar-1989)　　　　　　Note: 112p;R96;UNBC

THE END OF ANCIENT CHRISTIANITY * Markus, Robert
Publisher: Camb. UP (Camb-1990)　　　　　　　　Note: 250p;R96;DL

THE RISE OF WESTERN CHRISTENDOM * Brown, Peter
Publisher: Blackwell Pub. (Oxford-1996)　　　　　　Note: 350p;R97;DL

INQUISITION & SOCIETY IN EARLY MODERN EUROPE * Halizer, S. Ed.& Tr.
Publisher: Barnes & Noble (Totowan-1987)　　　　　Note: 196;R97;UNBC

THE PAPAL PRINCE * Prodi, Paolo; Tr. S. Haskins
Publisher: Camb. UP (Camb-1982)　　　　　　　　Note: 250p;R97; UNBC

Books Read, Enjoyed & Recommended

THE SPIRIT OF THE COUNTER-REFORMATION* Evennett, H.
Outram,Ed.J.Bossy
Publisher: U of Notre Dame Pr (Camb-1970)   Note: 153p;R97;UNBC

THE ORIGINS OF EUROPEAN DISSENT * Moore, R.I.
Publisher: U of Toronto Press (Tor-1977)   Note: 300p; R97; UNBC

HISTORY THROUGH THE EYES OF FAITH * Wells, Ronald A.
Publisher: Harper (SanFran-1989)   Note: 250p; R97;DL

CATHOLICISM: AN HISTORICAL SURVEY * Nolan, John P.
Publisher: Barron (NY-1968)   Note: 250p; R97; DL

JESUS, THE SERVANT MESSIAH * De Jong, Marinus
Publisher: Yale Up (NewHaven-1991)   Note: 115p; R97; UNBC

THE JESUS LEGEND * Wells, G.A.
Publisher: Open Court Pub. (Chic.-1996)   Note: 287p;R97;UNBC

PAGANS AND CHRISTIANS * Fox, Robin Lane
Publisher: Penguin (Lon-1986)   Note: 795p;R98;DL

JESUS: THE EVIDENCE * Wilson, Ian
Publisher: Pan Books (Lon-1984)   Note: 180p;R98;DL

WHO KILLED JESUS? * Crossan, John Dominic
Publisher: Harper (SanFran-1995)   Note: 238p;R98; DL

THE HISTORICAL FIGURE OF JESUS * Sanders, E. P.
Publisher: Penguin (Lon-1993)   Note: 336p;R98;DL

THE BIRTH OF CHRISTIANITY * Crossan, John Dominic
Publisher: Harper (SanFran-1998)   Note: 645p;R98;DL

JESUS, A REVOLUTIONARY BIOGRAPHY * Crossan, J. Dominic
Publisher: Harper (SanFran-1994)   Note: 209p; R99; DL

JAMES THE BROTHER OF JESUS * Eisenman, Robert
Publisher: Penguin (NY-1997)   Note: 1035p; R99;DL

THE CHURCH IN AN AGE OF REVOLUTION * Vidler, Alec R.
Publisher: Penguin (Lon-1961)   Note: 302p;R99;UNBC

WHO REALLY WROTE THE BOOK
OF MORMON? * Cowdrey, Davis & Scales
Publisher: Vision Press (St.Ant.-1977)   Note: 256p; R99

BY THE WAY...

THE SEARCH FOR JESUS * Shanks,Patterson,Borg,Crossan
Publisher: Bib.Arch. Soc. (Wash-1994)					Note: 152P;R99;DL

JESUS OF NAZARETH,KING OF THE JEWS * Fredricksen, P.
Publisher: Vintage (NY-1999)					Note: 325p;R01;DL

THE BIBLE IN HISTORY * Thompson, Thomas
Publisher: RandHse (Lon-1999)					Note: 410p;R01;DL

HISTORICAL FUNDAMENTALS &
THE STUDY OF RELIGIONS * Rudolph, K.
Publisher: MacMilln (Lon-1985)					Note: 120p; R02; UNBC

THE LOST HISTORY OF CHRISTIANITY * Jenkins, Philip
Publisher: Harper (NY-2008)					Note: 315p; R2009; DL

CHRISTIANITY: THE FIRST 3000 YEARS * MacCulloch,D.
Publisher: Viking (NY-2009)					Note: 1161p; R2010: DL

Literary Criticism
THE GREAT CODE-THE BIBLE & LITERATURE * Frye, Northrop
Publisher: Academic Press (Tor-1982)					Note: 270p; R80;DL

WORLD LITERATURE * Trawick, B.R.
Publisher: Barnes & Noble (NY-1953)					Note: 250p; R80; DL

CONCEPTIONS OF SHAKESPEARE * Harbage, A.
Publisher: Schocken Books (NY-1968)					Note: 160p; R80; DL

NORMAN MAILER - COLLECTION OF CRITICAL ESSAYS * Braudy, Leo Ed.
Publisher: Prentice H (Englewood Clfs-1972)					Note: 250p; R80; DL

THE HISTORICAL NOVEL * Lucas, Georg (Tr H&S Mitchell)
Publisher: Penguin Books (Harms.-1962)					Note: 250 p; R80; DL

THE NOVEL TODAY * Bradbury, M. Ed.
Publisher: Fontana (Lon-1977)					Note: 250p; R80; DL

LIFE MADE REAL: CHARACTERIZATION IN THE NOVEL SINCE
    PROUST & JOYCE * Petruso, Thomas F.
Publisher: U of Mich. Pr (Ann Arbor-1991)					Note: 214p; R2007 ;DL

TWENTIETH CENTURY INTERPRETATIONS OF 1984 *
Publisher: (-)					Note: 200p; R81,PG

Books Read, Enjoyed & Recommended

GEORGE ORWELL AND THE ORIGINS OF 1984 * Loff, W.S.
Publisher: (-)   Note: 222p; R81,PG

SOLZENITSYN: A COLLECTION OF CRITICAL ESSAYS * Feuer, Kathryn., Ed
Publisher: Prentice Hall (Englewood-1976)   Note: 175p; R81; DL

THE EPIC OF RUSSIAN LITERATURE * Slonim, Marc
Publisher: Oxford U.P. (Lon-1964)   Note: 369p; R83; DL

NECESSARY RUSSELL – INTRO. BERTRAM RUSSELL*Ready, W.
Publisher: Copp Clark (1969)   Note: 118p; R83;DL

TOLSTOY - A COLLECTION OF CRITICAL ESSAYS * Matlaw, R.Ed
Publisher: Princeton Hall (-1967)   Note: 178p; R83; DL

BOOKS AND PORTRAITS * Wolf, Virginia - Mary Lyon Ed
Publisher: Triad (Frogmore-1979)   Note: 200p; R83; DL

ROMAN LITERATURE AND SOCIETY * Ogilvie, R.M.
Publisher: Penguin (Lon-1980)   Note: 280p; R86;DL

PROUST-A COLLECTION OF CRITICAL ESSAYS * Girard R. Ed
Publisher: Prentice Hall (NJ-1962)   Note: 180p; R86; DL

THE BEOWULF POET- COLLECTION OF CRITICAL ESSAYS * Fry, D. Ed
Publisher: Prentice Hall (NJ-1968)   Note: 170p; R87,CNC

THE KING JAMES VERSION OF THE ENGLISH BIBLE * Daiches, David
Publisher: Archon Press (Chic-1941)   Note: 210p; R87; CNC

THE MODERN AMERICAN NOVEL * Bradbury, M.
Publisher: Oxford Univ. Press (Oxford-1983)   Note: 200p; R88; DL

IN DEFENSE OF HISTORICAL LITERATURE * Levin, D.
Publisher: Hill & Wang (NY-1967)   Note: 143p; R89; DL

TOLSTOY AND THE RUSSIANS * Fodor, Alexander
Publisher: Ann Arbor (Lon-1984)   Note: 170p; R91; DL

THE FICTION EDITOR * McCormack, Thomas
Publisher: St Martins Pr (NY-1988)   Note: 200p; R99; UNBC

THE HEDGEHOG & THE FOX * Berlin, Isaiah
Publisher: Ivan R Du (Chicago-1953)   Note: 85p; R99; DL

BY THE WAY...

JACK LONDON, HEMINGWAY AND THE CONSTITUTION * Doctorow, E.L.
Publisher: Harper (NY-1993)　　　　　　　　　　Note: 203p; R00; DL

TOLSTOY * Citati, Pietro: Tr. Rosenthal
Publisher: Schochen Bks (NY-1986)　　　　　　　Note: 265p; R2000; DL

NORTHTHROP FRY IN CONVERSATION * Cayley, David
Publisher: Anansi (Concord-1992)　　　　　　　　Note: 228p; R07; DL

LITERATURE AND THE SIXTH SENSE * Rahv, Philip
Publisher: Houghton Mifflin (Bos-1969)　　　　　Note: 445p; R2008;DL

FIGURES OF DISSENT * Eagleton, Terry
Publisher: Verso (Lon-2003)　　　　　　　　　　Note: 272p; R09; DL

DOSTOEVSKY'S CRITIQUE OF THE WEST * Ward, Bruce K.
Publisher: Willfred Laurier (Waterloo-'86)　　　　Note: 202p;R2009;DL

PHANTOMS OF THE BOOKSHELVES * Bonnet, J.; B.Reynolds Tr.
Publisher: Over60K Pr. (NY-2010)　　　　　　　Note: 133p; R2012; DL

CHARLES DICKENS:
A CRITICAL ANTHOLOGY * Wall, S., Ed.
Publisher: Penguin (Harms.-1970)　　　　　　　　Note: 551p; R2012; DL

THE CRISIS OF CRITICISM * Berger, Maurice, Ed.
Publisher: The New Press (NY-1998)　　　　　　Note: 172p; R12; DL

THE CLASSICS * Beard, Mary & Henderson S.
Publisher: Sterling (NY-2010)　　　　　　　　　Note: 181p; R13; DL

RUSSIAN LITERATURE * Kelly, Catriona
Publisher: Sterling (NY-2010)　　　　　　　　　Note: 204p; R2013; S328; DL

TEN NOVELS AND THEIR AUTHORS * Maugham, W. Sumerset
Publisher: Penguin (Harms-1954)　　　　　　　　Note: 301p; R15; DL

CONTEMPORARY AMERICAN NOVELISTS * Moore, Harry Ed.
Publisher: Forum (Tor-1969)　　　　　　　　　　Note: 232p; R15; DL

Books Read, Enjoyed & Recommended

Philosophy & Science

A UNIVERSE FROM NOTHING* Krouse, L.
Publisher : Simon & Schuster (NY-2013) Not:e: 239p; R16, DL

BECOMING * Alpart, G.W.
Publisher: Yale U.P. (NJ-1955) Note: 105p; R80; DL

THE REBEL * Camus, A. (Trans A. Bower)
Publisher: Penguin Books (Lon-1953) Note: 265p; R80; DL

SCEPTICAL ESSAYS * Russell, Bertrand
Publisher: Allen & Unwin (Lon-1935) Note: 190p; R81;DL

AN INQUIRY INTO THE HUMAN PROSPECT * Heilbronner R.
Publisher: Penguin (Harms-) Note: 200p; R81,PG

STUDIES IN CRITICAL PHILOSOPHY * Marcusse, H.
Publisher: Beacon Pr (Lon-1972) Note: 225p; R82, PG

ESSAYS AND APHORISMS * Schopenhauer, A.(tr.Hollingdal
Publisher: Penguin (Lon-1851) Note: 235p; R82; DL

THE CONQUEST OF HAPPINESS * Russell, B.
Publisher: Allen & Unwin (Lon-1930) Note: 190p; R82; DL

HUSSERL AND THE SEARCH FOR CERTITUDE * Kolakowski, L.
Publisher: Yale U.P. (NY-1975) Note: 85p; R82;PG

CONCEPTS AND CATEGORIES – PHIL. ESSAYS * Berlin, Isaiah
Publisher: Viking Pr. (Lon-1979) Note: 213p; R83; CNC

THE CENTRAL TAXTS OF WITTGENSTEIN * Brand, G
Publisher: B. Blackwell (-1979) Note: 180p; R83; CNC

PRAISE OF FOLLY & LETTER TO MARTIN DORP
* Erasmus (trans. B. Ladice)
Publisher: Penquin (Harms-) Note: 260p;R83; DL

THE QUESTION CONCERNING TECHNOLOGY AND OTHER ESSAYS
* Heidegger, M.(tran Wlm Lovitt)
Publisher: Harper & Row (NY-1977) Note: 220p; R83; DL

DISCOURSE ON METHOD * Descartes, Rene
Publisher: Penguin (Harms-1637) Note: 130p; R83,DL

BY THE WAY...

THE LAW OF LOVE & THE LAW OF VIOLENCE * Tolstoy, Leo
Published 1909   Note: 107p; R84; CNC

ON THE HISTORY OF PHILOSOPHY * Copleston, F.
Publisher: Search Press (-1979)   Note: 160p; R84; CNC

EXISTINTIALISM AND HUMANISM * Sarter, Jean-Paul
Publisher: Mathuen (Lon-1948)   Note: 70p; R86; DL

MYTH AND REALITY * Eliade, Mircea (Tr W. Trask)
Publisher: Harper & Row (NY-1963)   Note: 212p; R87; DL

MY PHILOSOPHICAL DEVELOPMENT * Russell, Bertrand
Publisher: Unwin (Lon-1975)   Note: 200p; R87; DL

THE FEMALE EXPERIENCE & THE NATURE OF THE DEVINE
    * Ochshom, Judith
Publisher: Indiana U.P. (Bloom.-1981)   Note: 250p; R87; CNC

ON THE USE OF PHILOSOPHY * Maritain, Jacques.
Publisher: Princeton U.P. (Itacha-1961)   Note: 70p; R87; CNC

HAS MAN A FUTURE? * Russell, Bertrand
Publisher: Penguin (Balt.-1961)   Note: 125p; R87; DL

SAVING THE APPEARANCES : STUDY IN IDOLATRY*Barfield, Owen
Publisher: Harcourt Brace (NY-1983)   Note: 185p; R88; DL

SIX EXISTENTIALIST THINKERS * Blackham, H.J.
Publisher: Routhledge&Kagan (Lon-1961)   Note: 175p; R88; DL

LANGUAGE AND MYTH * Cassirer, E. tran Langer, S.K.
Publisher: Dover Publications (Dover-1946)   Note: 103p; R89; DL

LABRYNTHS OF REASON * Paunstone, William
Publisher: Anchor Books (NY-1988)   Note:270p;R90; DL

WHAT IS PHYLOSOPHY? * Ortego y Gasset, J
Publisher: Norton & Co (NY-1960)   Note: 252p; R91; DL

WELCOME TO PHILOSOPHY: A HANDBOOK FOR STUDENTS
    * Ginsberg, R.
Publisher: Freeman Cooper (SanFran-1977)   Note: 172p, R91, DL.

CONVERSATIONS WITH ISAIAH BERLIN * Jahanbegloo, R.
Publisher: Orion (Lon-1993)   Note: 208p; R93; DL

Books Read, Enjoyed & Recommended

BERLIN * Gray, John
Publisher: Harper Collins (Lon-1995) Note: 190p;R98;;DL

THE CROOKED TIMBER OF HUMANITY * Berlin, Isaiah
Publisher: Prinston UP (NJ-1990) Note: 275p; R98; DL

PHILOSOPHY, RELIGION, & CONTEMPORARY LIFE
   * Rouner & Langford Eds.
Publisher: U of Notre Dame Pr. (NDame-1996) Note: 245p;R99;DL

PHILOSOPHY & PHILOSOPHERS * Shand, John
Publisher: Penguin (Lon-1993) Note: 330P;R99;DL

THE MIND OF GOD * Davies, Paul
Publisher: Simon & Schuster (NY-1992) Note: 250p; R99; DL

TRUTH: A HISTORY * Arnesto, Filipe Fernandes
Publisher: Black Swan (Lon-1997) Note: 233p; R2000; DL

CONCISE ENCYCLOPEDIA: WESTERN PHILOSOPHY & PHILOSOPHERS
   * Rie & Ormson, Eds.
Publisher: Unwin & Hyman (Lon-1991) Note: 662p; R00; DL

REAL PRESENCES * Steiner, George
Publisher: UofChigPr (Chic.-1989) Note: 236p; R01; DL

THE WISDOM OF BERTRAM RUSSELL * Russell, B
Publisher: Citadel (NY-2002) Note: 170p; R04; DL

INTERPRETING THE UNIVERSE * Macmurray, John
Publisher: Faber & Faber (NY-1933) Note: 164p; R07; UNBC

ON HISTORICAL & POLITICAL KNOWING * Kaplan, Morton A.
Publisher: U of Chic. Pr (Chicago-1971) Note: 159p; R07; DL

HERETICS * Chesterton, G. K.
Publisher: Hendrickson (Peabody Mass-1905) Note: 179p; R07; DL

ON DECARTES * Thompson, Garrett
Publisher: Wadworth (Belmont-2000) Note: 91p; R2008; DL

LIFE AFTER THEORY * Paynes, M & Schad, J. Eds.
Publisher: Continuum (Lon-2003) Note: 196p; R09; DL

TRUTH: A GUIDE * Blackburn, Simon
Publisher: Oxford UP (NY-2005) Note: 238p; R10; S280; DL

BY THE WAY...

A DICTIONARY OF PHILOSOPHY * Flew, Anthony, Ed
Publisher: St. Martins Pr (NY-1984)   Note: 370p; R10; DL

IN PRAISE OF DOUBT * Berger, P. & Zijderveld A.
Publisher: Harper (NY-2009)   Note: 179p; R2011; DL

DISCOURSE ON THINKING * Heideger, Martin
Publisher: Harper (NY-1959)   Note: 93p; R11; DL

A BRIEF HISTORY OF THOUGHT * Ferry, Luc, Theo Cuffe tr.
Publisher: Harper (NY-2011)   Note: 282p; R2012; DL

IRRATIONAL MAN * Barrett, William
Publisher: Anchor Bks (NY-1958)   Note: 314p; R2012; DL

ESSAYS IN EXISTENTIALISM * Sarte, Jean Paul
Publisher: Citadel Pr (NY-1965)   Note: 431p; R2012; DL

FREE WILL * Harris, Sam
Publisher: Free Press (NY-2012)   Note: 83p; R13; DL

THE GOD ARGUMENT * Grayling, A.C.
Publisher: Bloomsbury Pr (NY-2013)   Note: 269p; R14; DL

PHILOSOPHY AT 3AM * Marshal, Richard,Ed
Publisher: Oxford UP (NY-2014)   Note: 296p; R14;DL

GOD IS NOT GREAT * Hitchins, Christopher
Publisher: Emblem, M & S (Tor-2007)   Note: 307p; R14; ;DL

EXAMINED LIFE * Taylor, Astra, Ed.
Publisher: New Press (NY-2009)   Note: 222p; R15; DL

PHILOSOPHY BITES BACK * Edmonds, D. & Warburton
Publisher: Oxford UP (Oxford-2012)   Note: 274p; R15; DL

THE PROBLEMS OF PHILOSOPHY * Russell, Bertrand
Publisher: Dover Pub (NY-1912)   Note: 121p; R15; DL

THIS IDEA MUST DIE * Brockman, John Ed.
Publisher: Harper (NY-2015)   Note: 568p; R15;DL

DEATH OF THE SOUL * Barrett, William
Publisher: Anchor Bks (NY-1986)   Note: 173p;R15; DL

Books Read, Enjoyed & Recommended

I AND THOU * Buber, Martin
Publisher: Touchstone (NY-1970)　　　　　　　　Note: 185p; R15; DL

KANT * Scruton, Roger
Publisher: Sterling (NY-2010)　　　　　　　　Note: 161p; R15; DL

MIND & COSMOS * Nagel, Thomas
Publisher: Oxford UP (NY-2012)　　　　　　　　Note: 130p; R15; DL

MODES OF THOUGHT * Whitehead, Alfred North
Publisher: Macmillan (NY-1938)　　　　　　　　Note: 179p; R15; DL

THE GENEALOGY OF MORALS * Nietzsche, Friedrich
Publisher: Dover Pub (NY-1913)　　　　　　　　Note: 118p; R15; ;DL

THINKING OF ANSWERS * Grayling, A.C.
Publisher: Walker &Co (NY-2010)　　　　　　　　Note: 338p; R15; DL

DIALOGUES-CHARMIDES, PHAEDOUS, CRITO, * Plato
Publisher: Great Books (NY-1952)　　　　　　　　Note: 162p; R86; DL

DIALOGUES-APOLOGY, TIMAEUS, 7th LETTER * Plato
Publisher: Great Books (NY-1952)　　　　　　　　Note: 109p; R86; DL

PLATO AND AUGUSTINE * Jaspers, Karl Prof.Ed Arend,H.
Publisher: Harcourt & Bros. (-1962)　　　　　　　　Note: 119p; R86; CNC

FIRST ENNEAD - TRACTATES 1-IX; SECOND ENNEAD I-IX;
    THIRD - V * Plotinus
Publisher: Great Books (NY-1952)　　　　　　　　Note: 160p;R87;DL

ON THE NATURE OF THINGS * Lucretius, Tr.Munro,H.A.J
Publisher: Great Books (NY-1952)　　　　　　　　Note: 194p; R87; DL

ARISTOTELIANISM * Stocks,John L.
Publisher: Cooper Sq. Pub. Inc. (NY-'63)　　　　　　　　Note:155p;R87,CNC

PLATONISM AND ITS INFLUENCE * Taylor, A.E.
Publisher: Cooper Sq. Publ (NY-1963)　　　　　　　　Note: 148p;R87;PG

ON THE NATURAL FACULTIES * Galen (130 - 200 A.D.)
Publisher: Great Books (Lon-1952)　　　　　　　　Note: 100p;R88;DL

THE STOIC PHILOSOPHY OF SENECA*Seneca Tr Hadas, M.
Publisher: W.W. Norton (NY-1958)　　　　　　　　Note: 262p; R88;CNC

BY THE WAY...

THE PHILOSOPHY OF SCIENCE * Bird, Alexander
Publisher : McGill UP, (Montreal 1998) Note : 324p;R16, DL

THE AGE OF GENIUS – THE 17th CENTURY, BIRTH OF THE HUMAN MIND – Grayling A.C.
Publisher: Bloomsbury (NY 2016) Note: 351p;R16,DL

SENECA, THE PHILOSOPHER & HIS MODERN MESSAGE * Gummere, R.M.
Publisher: Cooper Sq. Pub. (NY-1963) Note: 144p; R88; CNC

SENECA: LETTERS FROM A STOIC * Seneca; Radin,Betty Ed
Publisher: Penguin (Lon-1969) Note: 250p; R99; DL

SCIENCE & ITS LIMITS * Ratzsch, Del
Publisher: Inter Varsity Press (Ill-2000) Note: 189p; R16; DL

NOT OUT OF AFRICA * Lefkowitz, Mary
Publisher: Basic Bks (NY-1997) Note: 250p; R00; DL

CICERO: TUSCULAN DISPUTATIONS * Douglas, A, Ed & Tr.
Publisher: Aris&Phillips (Lon-1990) Note: 168p; R15; DL

THE ORIGIN OF KNOWLEDGE & IMAGINATION * Bronowski, J.
Publisher: Yale U.P. (NHaven-1978) Note: 140 p.; R80; DL

EARLY GREEK SCIENCE: THALES TO ARISTOTLE * Lloyd, G.E.R.
Publisher: Chatto& Windus (Lon-1970) Note: 152p; R89; DL

A BRIEF HISTORY OF TIME * Hawking, Steven W.
Publisher: Bantam Books (NY-1988) Note: 196p; R90;CNC

THE MYSTERY OF CONSCIOUSNESS * Searle, John R.
Publisher: NY Review of Bks (NY-1997) Note: 220p;R99;DL

BELIEF IN GOD IN AN AGE OF SCIENCE * Polkinghorne, J.
Publisher: YaleUP (Harms.-1998) Note: 133p ;R00; PGL

STRUCTURE OF SCIENTIFIC REVOLUTIONS * Kuhn, T. S.
Publisher: UofChigPr,3rd Ed (Chic-1996) Note: 212p; R00; DL

WHAT IS THIS THING CALLED SCIENCE? * Chalmers, A.F.
Publisher: U of Queensl.Pr (-1999) Note: 260p; R02; DL

THE DANCING UNIVERSE * Gleiser, Marcelo
Publisher: Penguin (NY-1997) Note: 338p;R03;DL

Books Read, Enjoyed & Recommended

THE WHOLE SHEBANG * Ferris, Timothy
Publisher: Touchstone (NY-1997)   Note: 393p; R03; DL

THE IMPACT OF SCIENCE ON SOCIETY * Russell, Bertand
Publisher: Routledge (Lon-1952)   Note: 127p; R03; DL

INTELLIGENT THOUGHT: SCIENCE Vs THE DESIGN MOVEMENT
    * Brockman, John Ed
Publisher: Vintage Bks (NY-2006)   Note: 256p; R08; DL

SCIENCE AND THE MODERN WORLD * Whitehead, Alfred N.
Publisher: Free Pr. (NY-1925)   Note: 212p; R12; DL

HUMAN EVOLUTION * Wood, Bernard
Publisher: Sterling (NY-2005)   Note: 167p; R2014; DL

Philosophy of Religion

ON CHRISTIAN DOCTRINE * Augustine
Publisher: Great Books (NY-1952)   Note: 158p; R88; DL

READING SCRIPTURE AS WORD OF GOD * Martin, George
Publisher: (Servant Books - 1975
    Note:188p; R80; DL

ON BEING A CHRISTIAN * Kung, Hans (Trans E. Quin)
Publisher: Collins (Lon-1979)   Note: 700p; R81; DL

INFALLIBLE? AN ENQUIRY * Kung, Hans
[Phil-R] Publisher: Doubelday (NY-1971)   Note: 260p; R83,DL

THE DEAD SEA SCROLLS -A REAPPRAISAL * Allegro, A.
Publisher: Penguin (Harms-1964)   Note: 205p; R83; DL

THE DEAD SEA SCROLLS IN ENGLISH * Vermes,G.
Publisher: Penguin (Harms-1975)   Note: 280p; R83; DL

KUNG IN CONFLICT * Swidler, L Ed
Publisher: Image Bks (-1981)   Note: 620p; R84; DL

THE RELIGIOUS RIGHT & CHRISTIAN FAITH * Facre, G
Publisher: Eardmans (-1982)   Note: 122p; R84; PG

BY THE WAY...

SPEAK OUT AGAINST THE NEW RIGHT * Vetter, H.
Publisher: (-1982)   Note: 190p; R84; PG

CHRISTIANITY & THE ENCOUNTER WITH WORLD RELIGIONS
   * Tillich, Paul
Publisher: Columbia UP (-1962)   Note: 99p; R84; PG

ISLAM * Guillanme, A.
Publisher: Penguin (Harms.-1966)   Note: 202p; R84; DL

THE CHRISTIAN NEW MORALITY * Barr, O.S.
Publisher: (-1969)   Note: 115p; R84; PG

A CHURCH WITHOUT GOD * Harrison, E.
Publisher: Lippincott (-1966)   Note: 150p; R84; DL

ACCORDING TO THE SCRIPTURES * Dodd, C.H.
Publisher: Fontana Bks (Lon-1952)   Note: 135p; R85; DL

TOLERANCE AND TRUTH IN RELIGION * Mensching, G.,Trans H.Klimkeit
Publisher: U of Alabama (Univ-1955)   Note: 200p; R85;DL

HOW THE POPE BECAME INFALLIBLE * Hasler, August
Publisher: Doubleday (-1979)   Note: 350p;R85, CNC

THE IDEA OF THE CHURCH * Butler, B.C.
Publisher: (-1962)   Note: 230p; R85; PG

TOWARDS A NEW CHRISTIANITY: READINGS- DEATH OF GOD
      THEOLOGY * Altizer, J.J. Ed
Publisher: Prentice Hall (-1967)   Note: 364p; R85;CNC

PAGAN & CHRISTIAN IN AN AGE OF ANXIETY* Dodds, E.R.
Publisher: Norton (Lon-1965)   Note: 140p; R86;DL

MORE EVIDENCE THAT DEMANDS A VERDICT*McDonald, Ed
Publisher: Here's Life P. (-1981)   Note: 300p; R86; DL

THE GNOSTIC GOSPELS * Pagels, Elaine
Publisher: Vintage (NY-1979)   Note: 220p; R86; DL

THEOLOGIANS IN TRANSITION * Wall, J.M. Ed
Publisher: (-1981)   Note: 205p; R86, CNC

THE CONFESSIONS * St. Augustine
Publisher: Great Books (NY-1952)   Note: 250p; R86; DL

Books Read, Enjoyed & Recommended

TRUTH AND IDEOLOGY * Barth, Hans
Publisher: U of Cal Press (Berkeley-1945) Note: 202p; R87; DL

CELIBACY IN THE CHURCH * Bassett W. & Huizing P. Eds
Publisher: Hardwin H. (NY-1972) Note: 150p;R87;DL

ST. PAUL AND HIS LETTERS * Beare, F.W.
Publisher: A.C. Black (Lon-1962) Note: 140p; R87;PG

PROPHECY & HERMENEUTIC IN EARLY CHRISTIANITY * Ellis, E. Earle
Publisher: Wlhm Erdmann (Mich-1978) Note: 260p;R87;PG

ECCLESIOLOGY OF VATICAN II * Kloppenburg, B.
Pub: Fransiscan Herald Pr. (Chic.-1974) Note: 370p; R87,CNC

EARLY CHRISTIAN WRITINGS *Clement,Ignatus, et al
Publisher: Penguin (Lon-1987) Note: 195p; R87; DL

SATAN: THE EARLY CHRISTIAN TRADITION * Russel, J.
Publisher: Cornell U.P. (Lon-1981) Note: 250p;R87;CNC

TRUTH, MYTH AND SYMBOL * Altizer,Beardslee&Young, Eds
Publisher: Prentice Hall (NY-1962) Note: 170p; R87; DL

THE RATZINGER REPORT: INTERVIEW ON STATE THE CHURCH
 * Ratzinger & Messori
Publisher: IgnatiusPr (SanFran-1985) Note: 190p; R87; PG

THE INTERPRETATION OF THE NEW TESTAMENT:
 1861-1961 * Neill, Stephen.
Publisher: Oxford U.P. (NY-1964) Note: 350p; R87;DL

WOMEN PRIESTS - A CATHOLIC COMMENTARY ON THE VATICAN
 DECLARATION * Swidler L.A. Ed
Publisher: Panlisth (NY-1977) Note: 300p; R87;PG

THE PENTATEUCH (OR THE TORAH) * The Jerusalem Bible
Publisher: Darton L (-1969) Note: 262p; R87;DL

CHURCH AS MORAL DECISION MAKER * Gustafson, James M.
Publisher: Pilgrim Pr. (Phil.-1970) Note: 163p; R87; CNC

PAUL * Bernkamm, G. Prof.Tr.Stalker
Publisher: H & R Pblsh (NY-1971) Note: 237p;R88;PG

BY THE WAY...

PHILOSOPHY AND RELIGIOUS BELIEF * McPherson, Thomas
Publisher: Huthinson U.L. (NY-1974)　　　　　　Note: 125p; R88;CNC

OUR CHRISTIAN FAITH: ANSWERS FOR THE FUTURE
  * Rahner, K. & Heinzwegen, K.
Publisher: Crossroad (NY-1981)　　　　　　Note: 180p; R88;CNC

THE CITY OF GOD * St. Augustine
Publisher: Great Books (NY-1952)　　　　　　Note: 490p; R88; DL

MULIERIS DIGNITATEM * John Paul II
Publisher: Vatican (Rome-1988)　　　　　　Note: 55p;R88;DL

ETHICAL PATTERNS IN EARLY CHRISTIAN THOUGHT * Osborn, E.
Publisher: Cambridge U.P. (Camb.-1976)　　　　　　Note: 227p; R89; CNC

THE WRITINGS OF ST. PAUL * Meeks, Wayne A. Ed.
Publisher: W.N. Norton & Co. (NY-1972)　　　　　　Note: 450p;R89;CNC

HISTORY & FAITH, A PERSONAL EXPLORATION * Brown, C.
Publisher: Academic Books (Mich.-1987)　　　　　　Note: 120p; R89,CNC

PAUL'S LETTERS (ROMANS TO PHILEMON)*Good News B.
Publisher: American Bible Society (-)　　　　　　Note: 67p; R89; DL

RELIGIOUS LANGUAGE & KNOWLEDGE*Ayers & Blackstone, Eds.
Publisher: U. of Georgia Pr (Athens-1972)　　　　　　Note: 150p; R89; DL

THE SECOND VATICAN COUNCIL: STUDIES BY 8 ANGLICAN
    OBSERVORS * Pawley, B. Ed.
Publisher: Oxford U..Press (Lon-1967)　　　　　　Note: 250p; R89;DL

GREEK THOUGHT & THE RISE OF CHRISTIANITY * Shiel, J.
Publisher: Barnes & Noble (NY-1968)　　　　　　Note: 160p;R89;CNC

THE CHRISTIAN AND THE WORLD: READINGS IN THEOLOGY
    * Auer, Rahner et al
Publisher: P.J. Kennedy & Sons (NY-1965)　　　　　　Note: 230p; R89; DL

THE LION & THE HONEYCOMB- RELIGIOUS WRITINGS OF TOLSTOY
    * Tolstoy, Leo; Wilson, A.L. Ed
Publisher: Collins, Wllmn (Lon-1987　　　　　　Note: 158p; R91; DL

PAUL AND HIS INTERPRETERS*Schweitzer, A; tr Montgomery
Publisher: Black, Adam & Chs (Lon-1912)　　　　　　Note: 260p; R91; PG

Books Read, Enjoyed & Recommended

MAN & HIS SALVATION: STUDIES IN MEMORY OF S. G. F. BRANDON
  * Shanon & Hinnells Eds
Publisher: Man U P (Manch.-1973)　　　　　　　　Note: 338p; R91; DL

ORWELLIAN WORLD OF JEH. WITNESSES * Botting, H & G
Publisher: U of T Press (Tor-1984)　　　　　　　　Note: 206p;R92;DL

CHRISTIAN DISCOURSE: SOME LOGICAL EXPLORATIONS * Ramsey, Ian J.
Publisher: Oxford U P (Lon-1965)　　　　　　　　Note: 90p; R92; CNC

ON RELIGIOUS FREEDOM * Newman, Jay
Publisher: U of Ottawa Press (Ottawa-1991)　　　　Note: 238p; R92; CNC

THE TWO-EDGED SWORD: AN INTERPRETATION OF THE OLD
  TESTAMENT * McKenzie, J. L.
Publisher: Image Books (Boston-1955)　　　　　　Note: 345p; R93; DL

RESCUING BIBLE FROM FUNDAMENTALISM * Spong, John H.
Publisher: Harper (SanFran-1991)　　　　　　　　Note: 260p; R93; DL

THE AUTHORITY OF THE BIBLE * Dodd, C. H.
Publisher: Collins (NY-1929)　　　　　　　　　　Note: 288p; R93; DL

FROM JESUS TO CHRIST * Fredrikson, Paula
Publisher: Yale U. P. (NewH-1988)　　　　　　　 Note: 250p;R93; DL

THE UNAUTHORISED VERSION: TRUTH & FICTION IN THE BIBLE
  * Fox, Robin Lane
Publisher: Penguin (Lon-1991)　　　　　　　　　 Note: 470p; R93; DL

BIBLICAL RELIGION & THE SEARCH FOR ULTIMATE REALITY
  * Tillich, Paul
Publisher: U of Chicago Press (Chic.-1968)　　　　Note: 85p; R93; DL

BORN OF A WOMAN * Spong, John S.
Publisher: Harper (SanFran-1992)　　　　　　　　Note: 240p;R93; DL

FOUNDATION OF N. T. CHRISTOLOGY * Fuller, Reginald H.
Publisher: Cha Scribners (NY-1965)　　　　　　　Note: 260p;R94;UNBC

RESURRECTION: MYTH OR REALITY? * Spong, John Shelby
Publisher: Harper (SanFran-1994)　　　　　　　　Note: 320p; R95; DL

HONEST TO GOD * Robinson, John A. T.
Publisher: Westminster Press (Phil-1963)　　　　　Note: 141p;R95;DL

BY THE WAY...

TWENTIETH CENT. FAITH, HOPE & SURVIVAL* Mead, M.
Publisher: Harper (NY-1972)　　　　　　　　　　Note: 170p; R95; DL

THE N. T: A GUIDE TO ITS WRITINGS * Bornkamm, Gunther
Publisher: Fortress Press (Phil-1973)　　　　　　Note: 157p; R95; DL

THE TRUING OF CHRISTIANITY * Meagher, John
Publisher: Doubleday (Tor-1990)　　　　　　　　Note: 380p; R95;CNC

KINGDOM AND COMMUNITY * Gager, John G.
Publisher: Englewood Cliffs (Cliff-1975)　　　　　Note: 160p;R95; DL

HAS THE CATHOLIC CHURCH GONE MAD? * Eppstein, J.
Publisher: Tom Stacy Ltd. (Lon-1971)　　　　　　Note: 167p; R95; DL

THE END OF CHRISTENDOM * Muggeridge, Malcolm
Publisher: Wllm Erdsman Pub. (GR-1980)　　　　Note: 62p; R95; DL

IUSTITIA DEI * McGrath, Alister
Publisher: Camb. UP (Camb.-1986)　　　　　　　Note: 250p; R96;DL

TRANSFORMATION OF THE CHRISTIAN RIGHT * Moen, M. C.
Publisher: U of Alab. Pr (Tuscal.-1992)　　　　　Note:204p;R96;UNBC

CHRISTIANITY AND HEGEMONY * Nederveen, Jan P.
Publisher: Berg Pub (NY-1992)　　　　　　　　　Note: 320p; R96;UNBC

SPIRITUAL WARFARE:POLITICS & THE CHRISTIAN RIGHT * Diamond, Sara
Publisher: Black Rose 00(Mont.-1990)　　　　　　Note: 290p; R96;UNBC

FOUNDATIONS OF RELIGIOUS TOLERANCE * Newman, Jay
Publisher: U of Tor. Pr. (Tor-1982)　　　　　　　Note: 184p; R96;UNBC

POSTMODERNISM, REASON AND RELIGION * Gellner, E.
Publisher: Routledge (Lon-1992)　　　　　　　　Note: 108p; R96;UNBC

NEOFUNDAMENTALISM: THE HUMANIST RESPONSE
　* Academy of Humanism
Publisher: Prometheus Books (NY-1988)　　　　　Note:185p; R96; UNBC

WORLD ORDER & RELIGION * Eds Wade Clark Roof
Publisher: State U. of NY Albany-'91)　　　　　　Note: 308p;R96;UNBC

THE ORIGIN OF SATAN * Pagels, Elaine
Publisher: Vintage Books (NY-1995)　　　　　　　Note: 200p;R96; DL

Books Read, Enjoyed & Recommended

THE IRONY OF THEOLOGY & THE NATURE OF RELIGIOUS
    THOUGHT * Wiebe, Donald
Publisher: McGill UP (LonOnt-1991)   Note: 250p; R96;DL

SOLLICITUDO REI SOCIALIS * John Paul 11
Publisher: Encyclical (-)   Note: 70p; R96;CNC

HANDBOOK OF MORAL THEOLOGY * Primmur, D. M.
Publisher: Mercio Press (Cork-1963)   Note: 493p; R96; DL

CHRISTIAN FAITH & SOCIETY * Harland, Gordon
Publisher: U. of Calgary Pr (Calg.-1989)   Note: 94p;R96;UNBC

DOCUMENTS - EARLY CHRISTIAN THOUGHT*Wiles, Santer Eds.
Publisher: Camb. UP (Camb-1975)   Note: 268p; R97; UNBC

ROMAN CATHOLIC MODERNISM * Reardon, Bernard, Ed.
Publisher: Stanford UP (Stan-1970)   Note: 250p; R97; UNBC

THE TWO CHURCHES:CATHOLICISM &CAPITALISM IN THE WORLD
    SYSTEM * Budde, M. L.
Publisher: Duke UP (Durham-1992)   Note: 170p;R97; UNBC

CHRISTIAN THEOLOGY: AN INTRO.* McGrath, A. E.
Publisher: Blackwell Pub. (Oxf.-1994)   Note: 500p;R97;UNBC

GOSPEL FICTIONS * Helms, Randel
Publisher: Prometheus Books (NY-1988)   Note: 155p; R97; DL

TWO TYPES OF FAITH * Buber, Martin
Publisher: Collier Books (NY-1951)   Note: 175p; R97; DL

LIBERATING THE GOSPELS * Spong, John Shelby
Publisher: Harper (SanFran-1996)   Note: 350p;R97;DL

PUTTING AWAY CHILDISH THINGS * Ranke-Heinemann U, P. Heinegg Tr
Publisher: Harper (SanFran-1992)   Note: 306p; R98; DL

JESUS AT 2000 * Borg, Marcus J. Ed
Publisher: Westview Press (Boulder-1992)   Note: 180p; R98;;DL

THE DOGMA OF CHRIST * Fromm, Eric
Publisher: Henry Holt (NY-1963)   Note: 212p; R98; DL

THE ART OF BIBLICAL NARRATIVE * Alter, Robert
Publisher: Basic Books (NY-1981)   Note: 195p; R98;DL

BY THE WAY...

EUNUCHS FOR THE KINGDOM OF GOD * Ranke-Heinemann, Uta, Tr P.Heinegg
Publisher: Penguin (Harms-1991)   Note: 360p; R98;DL

FOUR VIEWS ON HELL * Crockett, William Ed
Publisher: Zondervan Press (GRapids-1996)   Note: 180p; R98;DL

THE FIRST CHRISTMAS * Richards, H. J.
Publisher: Mowbray (Oxford-1973)   ote: 128p;R98;DL

THEIR KINGDOM COME: INSIDE THE SECRET WORLD OF OPUS DEI * Huthinson,Robert
Publisher: St. Martins Pr (NY-1997)   Note: 450p; R99;UNBC

THE SECRET SAYINGS OF JESUS * Grant & Freedman
Publisher: Barnes & Noble (NY-1959)   Note: 206P; R99; DL

RELIGIOUS TRUTH FOR OUR TIME * Watt,William M.
Publisher: One World (Oxford-1995   Note: 109P; R99; UNBC

FUNDAMENTALISM:HAZARDS & HEARTBREAKS * Evans & Berent
Publisher: Openlit (LaSalle-1988)   Note: 165p; R00; DL

THE SCEPTER & THE STAR * Collins, John J.
Publisher: Doubleday (NY-1995)   Note: 265p; R00;DL

THE CASE FOR CHRIST * Stroebel, Leo
Publisher: Zonderiun Pub. (GRapids-1998)   Note: 395p; R00;DL

HONEST TO JESUS * Funk, Robert W.
Publisher: Harper (SanFr-1996)   Note: 245P; R00;DL

THE AUTONOMY OF RELIGIOUS BELIEF * Crosson F. Ed.
Publisher: Uof NotreD Pr (NDame-1981)   Note: 162p; R00;DL

LUTHER * Grosshans, Hans-Peter
Publisher: Fount (Lon-1997)   Note: 100p; R00; UNBC

THE ESSENTIAL JESUS * Crossan, John Dominic
Publisher: Castle Bks (NJ-1998)   Note: 199p; R00;DL

SKEPTICS & TRUE BELIEVERS * Raymo, Chet
Publisher: Doubleday (Tor-1998)   Note: 280p; R01;DL

SCRIBES AND SCHOOLS * Davies, Philip R.
Publisher: Westm.JKnoxPr. (Louisville-1998)   Note:210p;R01;DL

Books Read, Enjoyed & Recommended

THE REAL JESUS * Johnson, Luke T.
Publisher: Harper (SFran-1996)   Note: 180p; R01; DL

ACCORDING TO THE SCRIPTURES * Van Buren, Paul M.
Publisher: Wm.B. Erdmann (Camb.-1998)   Note: 140p;R01;DL

A RADICAL JEW * Boyarin, Daniel
Publisher: UCLAPr (Berk.-1994)   Note: 360p; R01; DL

THE CONCISE GUIDE TO JUDAISM * Rosenberg, Roy
Publisher: Meridian Pr. (NY-1994)   Note: 255p; R01;DL

J. ISCARIOT & THE MYTH OF JEWISH EVIL * Maccoby, H.
Publisher: FreePress (NY-1992)   Note: 212p; R02;DL

THE SCAPEGOAT * Girard, Rene
Publisher: CBC (Tor-2001)   Note: 53p; R02;DL

JESUS AMONG OTHER GODS * Zacharias, Ravi
Publisher: WorldPub (Nash.-2000)   Note: 190p; R03; DL

THE PROPHETIC IMAGINATION * Bruggemann, Walter
Publisher: Methuen (Min.-2001)   Note: 146p; R2004; DL

NEW EVANGELIZATION OF CATHOLICS * MacGabhann, S.
Publisher: Trafford (Victoria-2008)   Note: 348p; R08; DL

FAITHS IN CONFLICT? * Ramanchandra, Vinoth
Publisher: Inter Varsity (DGrove-1999)   Note: 192P;R08;DL

MORAL PURITY AND PERSECUTION IN HISTORY * Moore, Barrington Jnr.
Publisher: Prinston UP (NY-2000)   Note: 158p; R09;DL

JOURNEYS TO THE HEART OF CATHOLICISM * Schmidt, T.
Publisher: Seraphim (Hamilton-2007   Note: 245p; R2010;DL

CONTESTING FUNDAMENTALISMS*Shick,J.&Watkinson,ed
Publisher: Fernwood (Ham-2004)   Note: 175p; R10;DL

THE RAGE AGAINST GOD * Hitchins, Peter
Publisher: Zondervan (G Rapids-2010)   Note: 224p;R11;DL

THE FUTURE OF BELIEF * Dewart, Leslie
Publisher: Herder (NY-1966)   Note: 223p;R11; DL

BY THE WAY...

THE REASON FOR GOD * Keller, Timothy
Publisher: Riverhead Bks (NY-2008) Note: 310p;R12;DL

GOD IN PAIN : INVERSIONS OF APOCALYPSE * Zizek, S & Gunjevic
Publisher: Seven Stories Pr. (NY-2012) Note: 285p: R12; DL

BETWEEN FAITH AND DOUBT * Hick, John
Publisher: Palgrave (Lon-2010) Note: 176p; R13;DL

ZEALOT * Aslan, Rega
Publisher: Random Hse (NY-2013) Note: 296p; R13; DL

THE JEWISH GOSPELS * Boyarin, Daniel
Publisher: New Press (NY-2012) Note: 222p;R13;DL

THE FUTURE OF CATHOLICISM * Coren, Michael
Publisher: Signal (Tor-2013) Note: 241p;R14;DL

IMAGINATIVE WORLD OF REFORMATION * Matheson, P.
Publisher: Fortress Press (Min-2001) Note: 153p;R14; DL

A THIRD TESTAMENT * Muggeridge, Malcolm
Publisher: Collins&BBC (Lon-1976) Note: 207p;R14;DL

GOD: AN INTINERARY * Debray, Regis -J Mcleman Tr.
Publisher: Verso (Lon-2004) Note: 307p; R14; DL

THE DAWKINS DELUSION? * McGrath, Alister & Joanna
Publisher: IVP Bks (Downers Gr.-2007) Note: 118p; R14;DL

THE BIBLE * Riches, John
Publisher: Sterling (NY-2010) Note: 225p;R15; DL

REVELATIONS * Pagels, Elaine
Publisher: Penguin (NY-2012) Note: 244p; R15; DL

PAUL & JESUS * Tabor, James D.
Publisher: Simon & Schuster (NY-2012) Note: 291p; R15; DL

IRRELIGION * Paulos, John Allen
Publisher: Hill&Wang (NY-2008) Note: 158p; R15; DL

THEOLOGY: VERY SHORT INTRODUCTION * Ford, D. F.
Publisher: Oxford UP (Oxford-2013) Note: 190p; R15; DL

Books Read, Enjoyed & Recommended

SWORD OF THE SPIRIT, SHIELD OF FAITH * Preston, A.
Publisher: Anchor Bks. (NY-2012)   Note: 815p; R15; DL

THE MYTH-MAKER: PAUL & THE INVENTION OF CHRISTIANITY
 * Maccoby, Hyam
Publisher: Harper (SanFran-1987)   Note: 225p; R97; DL

Political Science

BARBARISM WITH A HUMAN FACE. * Levy, Bernard H.
Publisher: Harper & Row (NY-1977)   Note: 210p; R80; DL

THE AGE OF ANXIETY. * Glasrud, C.A. Ed.
Publisher: Houghton & Mifflin (NY-1960)   Note: 210p; R80; DL

THE COLLAPSE OF DEMOCRACY * Moss, Robert
Publisher: Abacus (-)   Note: 250p; R80; DL

LETTER TO SOVIET LEADERS * Solzenitsyn, Aleksandr
Publisher: Harper & Row (NY-1974)   Note: 57p; R80; DL

THE REVOLT OF THE MASSES * Ortega y Gasset
Publisher: Norton (NY-1932)   Note: 220p; R80; DL

FROM UNDER THE RUBBLE * Solzenitsyn A., et al
Publisher: Little Brown (Boston-1974)   Note: 300 p; R81; DL

REVOLUTION IN THE THIRD WORLD * Chaliland, Gerard
Publisher: Penguin   Note: 200p; R81; CNC

THE SOCIALIST PHENOMENON * Shafarevich, I., (Tjalsma Tr.)
Publisher: Harper & Row (NY 1980)   Note: 320p; R81; CNC

THE REVOLUTIONARY ASCETIC – EVOLUTION OF A POLITICAL TYPE
 * Maglish, B.
Publisher: Basic Bks. (NY-1976)   Note: 250p; R82; CNC.

ON REVOLUTION * Arendt, H.
Publisher: Penguin (Harms-1965)   Note: 330p; R82; DL.

CIVILIZATION AND ITS DISCONTENTS * Freud, S.
Publisher: W.W. Norton (Lon-1930)   Note: 100p; R82; PG

BY THE WAY...

WESTERN POLITICAL THEORY IN THE FACE OF THE FUTURE * Dunn, J.
Publisher: Cambridge UP (-1979) Note:120p; R82; PG

TWO CHEERS FOR DEMOCRACY * Forster, E.M.
Publisher: Penguin (Harms-1951) Note: 340P; R82; DL

ON LIBERTY * Mill, J.S.
Publisher: Great Books (-1859) Note: 150p; R82; DL

MORTAL DANGER * Solzenitsyn, A. (Nicholson&Klimoff-tr)
Publisher: Harper & Row (NY-1981) Note: 130p; R82; DL

FOUR ESSAYS ON LIBERTY * Berlin, I.
Publisher: Oxford U.P. (Lon-1969) Note: 270p; R82;DL

THE POVERTY OF LIBERALISM * Wolff, R,P.
Publisher: Beacon (Lon-1968) Note: 200p; R83;PG

RELIGION AND THE RISE OF CAPITALISM * Tawney, R.H.
Publisher: Penguin (Harms-1926) Note: 334p; R83; DL

PUBLIC AFFAIRS * Snow, C.P.
Publisher: Macmillan (Lon-1971) Note: 224p; R83;PG

BETWEEN PAST AND FUTURE : EIGHT ESSAYS IN POLITICAL
     THOUGHT * Arendt, Hanna
Publisher: Penguin (Harms-1968) Note: 300p; R83; DL

ROADS TO FREEDOM * Russell, Bertram
Publisher: Chatto & Windus (Lon-1918) Note: 155p; R84; DL

THE PRINCE * Machiavelli, N
Publisher: Penguin (Harms.-1513) Note: 90p; R84; DL

NOTES ON BASIC POLITICAL THEORY * Preston, C.
Publisher: Forum House (-1969) Note: 192p;R84;DL

IDEOLOGY AND POPULAR PROTEST * Rude, George
Publisher: Lawrence&Wisbart (Lon-1980) Note: 170p;R84;PG

PROTESTANTISM, CAPITALISM AND SOCIAL SCIENCE: WEBER
     THESIS CONTROVERSY * Green, R. Ed.
Publisher: (1973) Note: 206p;R84;CNC.

THE NEW SOCIETY * Carr, E.H.
Publisher: Macmillan (Lon-1951) Note: 118p; R85; DL

Books Read, Enjoyed & Recommended

INTERNL RELATIONS BETWEEN TWO W.WARS*Carr E.H.
Publisher: MacMillan (Lon-1967)　　　　　　　　Note: 290p; R86; DL

STUDIES IN REVOLUTION * Carr, E.H.
Publisher: MacMillan (Lon-1950)　　　　　　　　Note: 228p; R86; DL

MEDIEVAL POLITICAL THOUGHT * Ullman, Walter
Publisher: Penguin (Lon-1975)　　　　　　　　　Note: 250p; R86; DL

THE ORIGINS OF SOCIALISM * Lichteim, George
Publisher: Weidenfeld (Lon-1972)　　　　　　　Note: 302p;R88;DL

THE SUBORDINATE SEX - A HISTORY OF ATTITUDES TOWARDS
　　　WOMEN * Bullough, Vern
Publisher: Univ. of Ill. Press (Chic.-1973)　　　Note: 360p;R87;PG

AN ESSAY ON LIBERATION * Marcuse, Herbert
Publisher: Beacon Press (Boston-1969)　　　　　Note: 91p;R88;DL

HISTORY AND SOCIAL THEORY * Heff, Gordon
Publisher: U of Alabama Press (1969)　　　　　Note: 235p; R88; CNC

PLATO: TOTALITARIAN OR DEMOCRAT? * Thorson, T.L.
Publisher: Prentice Hall (NJ-1963)　　　　　　Note: 184p; R89; DL

LIBERTY IN THE MODERN WORLD * Butterfield Herbert
Publisher: Ryerson Press (Tor.-1952)　　　　　Note: 60p; R89;DL

STATECRAFT OF MACHIAVELLI, THE * Butterfield, H.
Publisher: G. Bell & Sons (Lon-1940)　　　　　Note:167p; R89;CNC

POLITICAL IDEALS * Russell, Bertrand
Publisher: Allen & Unwin (Lon-1917)　　　　　Note: 80p; R89;DL

NECESSARY ILLUSIONS * Chomsky, Chomsky
Publisher: CBC Enterprises (Tor.-1989)　　　　Note: 422p; R89; DL

CLASS WARFARE * Chomsky, Noam
Publisher: New Star Books (Van.-1997)　　　　Note: 295p; R98; DL

LANGUAGE & POLITICS * Chomsky, Noam
Publisher: Black Rose (Mont.-1988)　　　　　　Note: 778p; R91;DL

MANUFACTURING CONSENT* Herman, E S &Chomsky N.
Publisher: Pantheon (NY-1988)　　　　　　　　Note: 390p; R92; DL

BY THE WAY...

PROGRESS AND THE CRISIS OF MAN*Gartz,Larson&Hassel
Publisher: Nelson Hall (Chic.-1976)   Note: 140p; R92; CNC

THE PATHOLOGY OF POWER * Cousins, Norman
Publisher: WW Norton & Sons (NY-1987)   Note: 210p; R92; DL

THE END OF HISTORY & THE LAST MAN * Fukuyama, F.
Publisher: Avon (NY-1992)   Note: 340p; R93; DL

BEYOND THE STORM * P. Bennis & M. Moushebek, Eds
Publisher: Olive Branh Press (NY-1991)   Note: 412p; R95; DL

ON HISTORICAL & POLITICAL KNOWING * Kaplan, M. A.
Publisher: U of Chicago Press (Chic.-1971)   Note:167p;R95;UNBC

ESCAPE FROM FREEDOM * Fromm, Eric
Publisher: Henry Holt (NY-1965)   Note: 318p; R96;DL

CHRONICLES OF DISSENT * Chomsky, Noam
Publisher: New Star Books (Van-1992)   Note: 290p; R98; DL

PROTAGONISTS OF CHANGE * Said, Abdul A.
Publisher: Prentice Hall (NJ-1971)   Note: 181p; R00; DL

LAND OF IDOLS: * Parento, Michael
Publisher: St Martins Pr (NY-1994)   Note: 201p;R00;DL

SLUMBING IT AT THE RODEO * Laird, Gordon
Publisher: Doug McIntyre (Van-1998)   Note: 200p;R00;DL

9-11 * Chomsky, Noam
Publisher: 7 StoriesPr. (NY-2001)   Note: 124p;R01;DL

FATEFUL TRIANGLE * Chomsky, Noam
Publisher: BlackRose (Mont.-1999)   Note: 578p;R01;DL

UNTO CAESAR: POLITICAL RELEVANCE OF CHRISTIANITY
   * McLillan, David
Publisher: U of N. Dame Pr. (ND-1993)   Note: 102p;R02; UNBC

THE END OF THE PEACE PROCESS * Said, Edward W.
Publisher: Vintage Bks (NY-2000)   Note: 388p;R02;DL

THE IRON WALL * Shlaim, Avi
Publisher: WWNorton (NY-2001)   Note: 670p;R03; DL

Books Read, Enjoyed & Recommended

HEGEMONY & SURVIVAL * Chomsky, Noam
Publisher: Henry Holt (NY-2004)   Note: 300p;R05;DL

COLOSSUS:RISE & FALL OF THE AM. EMPIRE * Ferguson, N.
Publisher: Penguin (NY-2004)   Note: 386p; R2006; DL

ISREAL LOBBY&US FOREIGN POL. * Meirshiem, J.& Walt, S.
Publisher: Farrar Strous (NY-2007)   Note: 482p; R2008; DL

EUROPEAN UNIVERSALISM * Wallerstein, Immannuel
Publisher: New Press (NY-2006)   Note: 94p; R09; DL

LIBERALS & CANNIBALS * Lukes, Steven
Publisher: Verso (Lon-2006)   Note: 180p;R09; DL

DREAMS OF PEACE AND FREEDOM * Winter, Jay
Publisher: Yale UP (NY-2006)   Note: 261p; R10; DL

MARX'S DAS CAPITAL * Wheen, Frans
Publisher: Atlantic Monthly Pr. (NY-2006)   Note: 130p;R10;DL

CONVERSATIONS WITH EDWARD SAID * Ali, Tarig
Publisher: Seagul Pub. (Oxf-2006)   Note: 128p;R11;DL

DEATH OF THE LIBERAL CLASS * Hedges, Chris
Publisher: Alfred A Knoph (Tor-2010)   Note:248p; R11;DL

THE HOLOCAUST INDUSTRY * Finkelstein, Norman
Publisher: Verso (Lon-2003)   Note: 286p; R2011;DL

SPEAKING OF EMPIRE & RESISTANCE*Ali,T.&Barsamian D.
Publisher: NY Press (NY-2005)   Note: 234p;R11; DL

FUTURE OF NATIONAL IDENTITY * Klafter C.E. et al, eds
Publisher: UBC Pr (Van-2007)   Note: 153p;R11;DL

WHEN ATHEISM BECOMES RELIGION * Hedges, Chris
Publisher: Tor Pr (NY-2008)   Note: 212p;R11;DL

THE WORLD AS IT IS * Hedges, Chris
Publisher: Nation Bks. (NY-2011)   Note: 350p;R12;;DL

PALESTINE: PEACE NOT APARTHEID * Carter, Jimmy
Publisher: Simon & Schuster (NY-2007)   Note: 270p;R13;DL

BY THE WAY...

AMERICAN FASCISTS * Hedges, Chris
Publisher: Free Press (NY-2006) Note: 274p;R13;DL

POWER SYSTEMS * Chomsky, Noam
Publisher: Met. Books (NY-2013) Note: 211p;R13;DL

BLOOD,CLASS & NOSTALGIA * Hitchins, Christopher
Publisher: Ferrar Strause (NY-1990) Note: 398p;R14;DL

DARK AGE AHEAD * Jacobs, Jane
Publisher: Vintage (Tor-2004) Note: 241p;R14; DL

BATTLE FOR JUSTICE IN PALESTINE * Abunimah, Ali
Publisher: Haymrkt Bks (Chic.-2014) Note: 292p;R15;DL

DON'T THINK OF AN ELEPHANT * Lakoff, George
Publisher: Chelsea Green (White Riv-2004) Note: 124p;R15;

THE POLITICS OF DISPOSSESSION * Said, Edward W.
Publisher : Vintage Boks (NY-1994) Note: 450p; R16; DL

Victorian History

VICTORIAN PEOPLE * Briggs, Asa
Publisher: UofChicPr (Chic.-1972) Note: 308p;R03;;DL

ENGLISH SOCIETY IN THE 18TH CENTURY * Porter, Roy
Publisher: Penguin (Lon-1990) Note: 420p;R03;DL

VICTORIAN ENGLAND: PORTRAIT OF AN AGE * Young, G.M.
Publisher: OxfordUP (Chic.-1972) Note: 218p;R03; DL

HISTORY IN OUR TIME * Cannadine,David
Publisher: Penguin (Lon-2000) Note: 313p;R03 DL

VICTORIAN DIARIES * Creaton, Heather Ed.
Publisher: MBazley (Lon-2001) Note: 144p;R03; DL

FAMILY,SEX & MARRIAGE ENGLAND 1500-1800 * Stone, L.
Publisher: Penguin (Lon-1979) Note: 445;R2003;DL

Books Read, Enjoyed & Recommended

A PRISON OF EXPECTATIONS: FAMILY IN VICTORIAN CULTURE
 * Mintz, Steven
Publisher: NY UP (NY-1983) Note: 234p; R03;UNBC

THE RISE OF RESPECTABLE SOCIETY * Thompson, FML
Publisher: Harvard UP (camb.-1988) Note: 375p;R03; UNBC

ARISTOCRATIC WONMEN & POLITICAL SOC. IN VICT. BRITAIN
 * Reynolds, K.D.
Publisher: Oxf UP (Oxford-1998) Note: 219p;R03; UNBC

VICTORIAN ESSAYS * Young, G.M.
Publisher: Ox. UP (Lon-1962) Note: 216p;R03;DL

CRUELTY & COMPANIANSHIP: CONFLICT IN THE 19TH CENTURY.
 MARRIED LIFE * Hammerton, A. James
Publisher: Routledge (Lon-1992) Note: 236p;R03; UNBC

FROM CASTLEREAGH TO GLADSTONE 1815-1885 * Beales, Derek
Publisher: WW Norton (NY-1969) Note: 320p;R03; UNBC

THE MAKING OF VICTORIAN ENGLAND * Clark, G. K.
Publisher: Methuen (Lon-1962) Note: 312p;R03;UNBC

THE AGE OF EQUIPOISE * Burn, W.L.
Publisher: WW Norton (NY-1964) Note: 340p;R04;;DL

EARLY VICTORIAN BRITAIN 1832-1851 * Harrison, J.F.C.
Publisher: Fontana (Lon-1988) Note: 192p;R04; DL

THE BEST CIRCLES * Davidoff, Leonore
Publisher: Cent. Hutchison (Lon-1986) Note: 127p;R04; DL

GLADSTONE * Birrell, Francis
Publisher: Collier (NY-1962) Note: 127p; R04; DL

MID-VICTORIAN BRITAIN 1851-1875 * Best, Geoffrey
Publisher: Fontana (Lon-1985) Note: 350p;R04; DL

THE VICTORIANS * Wilson, A.N.
Publisher: Arrow (LON-2003) Note: 738p;R04; DL

CONSCIENCE OF THE VICTORIAN STATE* Marsh, P. Ed
Publisher: Harvester Pr (NY-1979) Note: 257p;R04; DL

BY THE WAY...

THE VICTORIAN HOUSE * Flanders, Judith
Publisher: Harper (Lon-2003)   Note: 475p;R04; DL

VICTORIAN ENGLAND: ASPECTS OF ENGLISH & IMPERIAL HISTORY
* Seaman, L.C.B.
Publisher: Methuen (Lon-1973)   Note: 484p;R04; UNBC

REFORM & INTELLECTUAL DEBATE IN VICTORIAN ENGLAND *
Dennis,B & Skilton,D Eds.
Pub: Croom Helm (Lon-1987)   Note: 223p;R05; UNBC

THE VICTORIAN FRAME OF MIND 1830-70*Houghton, W.
Pub: Yale UP (New Haven-1957)   Note: 467p;R05; UNBC

VICTORIAN MINDS * Himmelfarb, Gertrude
Pub: ElephantPbacks(Chic-1968)   Note:392p;R05; UNBC

VICTORIAN DUKE * Huxley, Gervas
Publisher: Oxford UP (lon-1967)   Note:202p; R05; UNBC

MANNERS, MORALS & CLASS IN ENGLAND 1774-1858 * Morgan, Marjory
Pub: St, Martin's Pr (NY-1994)   Note: 195p;R05; UNBC

VICTORIAN PEOPLE AND IDEAS * Altick, D.
Pub: WW Norton (NY-1973)   Note: 337p;R05; UNBC

DAILY LIFE IN VICTORIAN ENGLAND * Mitchell, Sally
Pub: Greenwood Pr. (Westport, '96)   Note: 311p;R05;UNBC

1859: ENTERING AGE OF CRISIS *Applemann, &Wolff,Eds.
Pub: Indiana UP (Bloom-1959)   Note: 320p;R05;UNBC

THE ENGLISH GENTLEMAN * Castonova, David
Publisher: Ungar (NY-1987)   Note: 171p;R05; DL

WHEN PASSION REIGNED * Anderson, Patricia
Publisher: Basic Books (NY-1995)   Note: 204p;R05; DL

VICTORIAN VALUES * Marsden, Gordon Ed.
Publisher: Longmans (Harlow-1993)   Note: 232p;R06; DL

CONTEMPLATING ADULTERY: SECRET LIFE OF A VICTORIAN
WOMAN * Hamburger, L & J
Publisher: Fawcett (NY-1991)   Note: 314p;R07;DL

Books Read, Enjoyed & Recommended

KING LEOPOLD'S GHOST * Hochschild, Adam
Publisher: Haughton Mifflin (NY-1998)   Note:376p;R09;DL

BURY THE CHAINS * Hochschild, Adam
Publisher: Haughton Mifflin (NY-2005)   Note:467p;R09; DL

THE MAKING OF VICTORIAN VALUES * Wilson, Ben
Publisher: Penguin (NY-2007)   Note: 445p;R10 ; DL

A WORLD ON FIRE * Foreman, Amanda
Publisher: Random Hse (NY-2010)   Note: 958p;R11; DL

Jamaica & Latin America

A VOICE IN THE WORKPLACE * Manley, Michael
Publisher: Andre Deutsh (Lon-1975)   Note: 230p; R91; DL

THE POLITICS OF LATIN AMERICAN DEVELOPMENT * Wynia, Gary W.
Publisher: Camb UP (Camb.-1978)   Note: 330p; R97; DL

BRAZIL: ONCE AND FUTURE COUNTRY * Eakin, M. C.
Publisher: St. Martins Pr (NY-1997)   Note: 290p;R99;DL

SIXTY YEARS OF CHANGE:1806-1866 * Jacobs, H.P.
Publisher: Instof Jam. (Kin-1973)   Note: 122p;R01;DL

FREE JAMAICA: 1838-1865 * Hall, Douglas
Publisher: Carib. UP (Kin-1959)   Note: 280p;R01;DL

LATIN AMERICA * Chomsky, Noam
Publisher: Ocean Pr. (Melb.-1999)   Note: 116p;R01;DL

SIR JOHN PETER GRANT * Marsalla, V.J.
Publisher: Inst of Ja. (Kin-1972)   Note: 125p;R01;DL

JAMAICA * Henriques, Fernando
Publisher: MacGibbon (Lon-1960)   Note: 216p;R01;DL

A SHORT HISTORY OF THE WEST INDIES * Perry,Sherlock, Maingst
Publisher: Macmillan (Lon-1987)   Note: 330p;R02; DL

LADY NUGENT'S JOURNAL 1801-1805 * Wright, Philip Ed.
Publisher: Inst of Jam (Kin-1966)   Note: 331p;R03;DL

BY THE WAY...

A NARRATIVE OF EVENTS SINCE 1ST AUGUST 1834, Williams, Patton, Hope: Eds
Publisher: DukeUP (Lon-2001) Note: 129p;R03;DL

LETTERS FROM JAMAICA 1858-1866 * Penfield, T&S; Gosselink,ed
Publisher: Boat Hse Bks (NY-2005) Note: 226p;R10;DL

THE SACK OF PANAMA * Earle, Peter
Publisher: Thos Dunne Bks (NY-2007) Note: 291p;R10;DL

JESUITANA JAMAICA HISTORY. PROFILES 1837-1996 * McLaughlin, G.L.
Publisher: Arawack (Kingston-2000) Note: 78p;R11; DL

EXPLORING JAMAICA * Wright, Philip & White, P.
Publisher: Andre Deutsch (Lon-1969) Note: 254p;R13;DL

Modern Warfare

THE CRIMEAN WAR * Troubetskoy, Alexis
Publisher: Robinson Bks (Lon-2006) Note: 334p; R15; DL

PEASANT WARS OF THE 20TH CENTURY * Wolf, Eric
Publisher: Harper (NY-1969) Note: 340p; R80; DL

THE FIRST WORLD WAR * Keegan, Keegan
Publisher: Vintage (NY-1998) Note: 475p;R13; DL

THE FIRST WORLD WAR * Robbins, Keith
Publisher: Oxford UP (Oxford-1984) Note: 186p;R07;DL

THE RUSSIAN REVOLUTION * Smith, S.A.
Publisher: Sterling (NY-2011) Note: 217p;R13; DL

THE ILLUSION OF PEACE 1918-1933 * Marks, Sally
Publisher: Palgrave (NY-2003) Note: 214p;R12; DL

BLOODLANDS:EUROPE BETWEEN HITLER & STALIN * Snyder, Timothy
Publisher: Basic Bks. (NY-2010) Note: 543p;R13;DL

THE COMING OF THE THIRD REICH * Evans, Richard J.
Publisher: Penguin (NY-2003) Note: 620p;R08;DL

Books Read, Enjoyed & Recommended

THE ORIGINS OF THE SECOND WORLD WAR * Taylor, A.J.P.
Publisher: Penguin (Lon-1964) Note: 350p; R81; CNC

THE ORIGINS OF THE SECOND WORLD WAR-A.J.P. TAYLOR & HIS
CRITICS * Louis, R. Ed.
Publisher: Penguin Note: 150p.; R81; CNC

ORIGINS OF THE SECOND WORLD WAR * Robertson, E.M,Ed
Publisher: Penguin (Lon-1971) Note: 250p; R86; DL

THE SECOND WORLD WAR * Beevor, Anthony
Publisher: Back Bay Bks (NY-2012) Note: 863p;R14;DL

THE FALL OF FRANCE * Jackson, Julian
Publisher: Oxford UP (Oxford-2003) Note: 274p;R06;DL

1939 COUNTDOWN TO WAR * Overy, Richard
Publisher: Penguin (Lon-2009) Note: 159p;R11;DL

HITLER* Kershaw, Ian
Publisher: Penguin (Lon-2000) Note: 1115p;R02;DL

A WAR AGAINST TRUTH * Roberts, Paul W.
Publisher: Rain Coast Bks. (Vanc.-2004) Note: 352p;R05;DL

STATE OF WAR * Risen, James
Publisher: FP Free Press (NY-2006) Note: 214p; R06;DL

FATEFUL CHOICES * Kershaw, Ian
Publisher: Penguin (NY-2007) Note: 623p;R08;DL

CHOICES UNDER FIRE: MORAL DIMENSIONS OF WWII * Bess, Michael
Publisher: Vintage (NY-2006) Note: 395p;R09; DL

THE FALL OF BERLIN * Beevor, Antony
Publisher: Viking Pr (NY-2002) Note: 489p;R09;DL

ENDGAME, 1945 * Stafford, David
Publisher: Back Bay Bks (NY-2007) Note: 581p;R09;DL

TEN DAYS TO D-DAY * Stafford, David
Publisher: DaCapoPr (Camb. Mas.-2005)
  Note: 377p;R09;DL

AMONG THE DEAD CITIES * Grayling, A.C.
Publisher: Walker & Co. (NY-2006) Note: 361p;R09; DL

BY THE WAY...

THE BITTER ROAD TO FREEDOM * Hitchcock, William I.
Publisher: Free Press (NY-2008) Note: 445p;R09;DL

WITH WINGS LIKE EAGLES * Korda, Michael
Publisher: Harper (NY-2009) Note: 322p; R10; DL

ABSOLUTE WAR: SOVIET RUSSIA :WWII * Bellamy, Chris
Publisher: Macmillan (Lon-2007) Note: 814p; R10;DL

AMAZING AIRMEN * Darling, Ian
Publisher: Dunburn Pr. (Tor-2009) Note: 257p; R10;DL

GERMANY 1945: FROM WAR TO PEACE * Bessell, R
Publisher: Harper (NY-2009) Note: 522p;R10;DL

NO SIMPLE VICTORY * Davies, Norman
Publisher: Penguin (NY-2006) Note: 644p; R11;DL

THE END: DEFENSE & DESTRUCTION - HITLER'S GERMANY
  * Kershaw, Ian
Publisher: Penguin (NY-2011) Note: 564p;R13; DL

SAVAGE CONTINENT * Lowe, Keith
Publisher: St Martin's Pr (NY-2012) Note: 460p;R14;DL

DREAMING WAR * Vidal, Gore
Publisher: Nation Bks (NY-2002) Note: 197p;R14;DL

EMPIRE'S WORKSHOP: LATIN AMERICA, THE US & RISE OF
  IMPERIALISM * Grandin, Greg
Publisher: Owl Books (NY-2007) Note: 292p;R2007;DL

GEORGE BUSH'S WAR * Smith, Jean Edward
Publisher: Henry Holt (NY-1992) Note: 300p; R95; DL

DIRTY WARS: WORLD IS A BATTLEFIELD * Scahill, Jeremy
Publisher: Nation Bks. (NY-2013) Note: 642p;R15;DL

THE WAY OF THE KNIFE * Mazzetti, Mark
Publisher: Penguin (NY-2013) Note: 381p; R15; DL

DISCENT INTO CHAOS * Rashid, Ahmed
Publisher: Viking (NY-2008) Note: 484p;R08; DL

Bibliography, Sources & Endnotes

Mind & Cosmos

Nagel, Thomas – *Mind and Cosmos: Why the Materialist Neo-Darwinian Conception of Nature Is Almost Certainly False* Oxford UP, NY, 2012

Ferry, Luc – *A Brief History of Thought* - Theo Cuffe, Trans., Harper Perennial, NY, 200

Shand, John – *Philosophy and Philosophers*, Penguin Books, Lon., 1993

Whitehead, Alfred North – *Modes of Thought*, The Free Press, NY, 1938

Searle, John R. – *The Mystery of Consciousness*, NYREV Inc., NY, 1997

Flew, Anthony (Ed.) - *A Dictionary of Philosophy*, St. Martin's Griffin, NY, 1984

Cicero – *Tusculan Disputations II & V* -A. E. Douglas, (Ed & trans.) Aris & Philips, Warm., 1990

Decartes, Rene - *Discourse on Method and other writings* A. Wollaston (trans.) Penguin

Urmson J. O. & Ree, J. – *The Concise Encyclopedia of Western Philosophy and Philosophers*, Unwin Hyman, Lon., 1989

Brockman, John (Ed) – *Intelligent Thought : Science vs the Intelligent Design Movement*, Vintage Books, NY, 2006

Science & Its Limits

Ratzsch, Del *Science & Its Limits: the Natural Sciences in Christian Perspective*, InterVarsity Pr., 2nd edition, Downers Grove, Il., 2000

Acton, H.B. *Concise Encyclopedia* of *Western Philosophy & Philosophers*, J. Urmson & J. Ree - Eds. Unwin Hyman, Lon. 1989

Shand, John *Philosophy & Philosophers*, Penguin Books, Lon. 1996

Grayling, A. C. *The Age of Genius (for Isaac Newton quotation)*

BY THE WAY...

Kuhn, Thomas S. *The Structure of Scientific Revolutions*, Third Edition, University of Chicago Press, Chic. 1996

Bird, Alexander *The Philosophy of Science*, McGill UP, Montreal, 1998

Those Social Animals

Hobbes, Thomas *Leviathon*, Great Books of the Western World

Rousseau, Jean-Jacques *The Social Contract*, Great Books of the Western World

Lenin, V. *Selected Essays of Lenin*, Philosophical Library, NY 1970

Arendt, Hannah *Between Past and Future*, Penguin, Harms., 1980

Heidegger, Martin *The Question Concerning Technology and Other Essays*, W. Lovitt- trans., Harper Colophon, NY, 1977

A Rose by Any Other Name

For insights into the Cathars, I am indebted to:

Moore, R. I. – *The Origins of European Dissent*, Toronto, 1994

Cohn, Norman - *Europe's Inner Demons*, Pimlico, London, 1975

Bredero, Adrian H. - *Christendom & Christianity in the Middle Ages*, Mich. 1994

Russell, Jeffrey - *Satan: The Early Christian Tradition*, Ithaca, 1981

Note: Umberto Eco, author of *The Name of the Rose*, was one of Italy's leading intellectuals. He was professor of semiotics at the University of Bologna, with several philosophical works and historical novels to his name.

The Company We Keep

Gower, L. C. B.- *The Principles of Modern Company Law*, Stevens & Sons, Lon., 1969

Report of the Company Law Committee: *Jenkin's Report*, 1962

Schmitthoff & Thompson - *Palmers Company Law*

Touche, **A. G.** - *Accounting Requirements of the Companies Acts* - Butterworth & Co., London, 1967

Institute of Chartered Accountants in En – Institute of Chartered Accountants in *Company Legislation in the 1970's* - Institute of Chartered Accountants in England and Wales

1973 White Paper - U.K. Department of Trade & Industry,

The Community and the Company - U. K. Labour Party – 1974 Green Paper

Laws of Jamaica - Government of Jamaica

Articles on Company Law 1960-1974, Accountancy magazine

The Jamaica Stock Exchange Review 1969 - 1973

Christianity From Below

Pagels, Elaine *The Gnostic Gospels*, Vintage Books, NY 1981

Subliminal Contradictions

Gilbert, Arthur - *The Second Vatican Council and the Jews* – World Publishing Company, Cleveland, 1968

Shlaim, Avi – *The Iron Wall: Israel and the Arab World* - W.W Norton & Co, NY, 2001

Rodinson, Maxime – *Israel and the Arabs*, M. Perl - Trans., Penguin, Harms., 1970.

The Israeli-Arab Reader – Seventh Edition, Laqueur, W. & Robin, B. Eds., Penguin, NY, 2008

Said, Edward W. – *The Politics of the Dispossessed: the Struggle for Palestinian Self-Determination 1969-1994*, Vintage Books, NY, 1994

Sand, Shlomo – *The Invention of the Land of Israel*, Geremy Forman - Trans., Verso, Lon., 2012

Omer-Man, Michael S. - *972mag.con*, 20/06/2016

Abunimah, Ali - *The Battle for Justice in Palestine* - Haymarket

BY THE WAY...

Books, Chicago, 2014. Whole-heartedly recommended, this book as an up to date account of what is happening inside and outside of Israel, regarding the plight of Palestinians.

Youse, Bilal, *Going against the Grain*, Al Jazeera *World*, uploaded to You Tube, February 2013

Macmillan, Margaret – *Paris 1919*, Random House, NY, 2001

Thatcher's Enduring Legacy

Harding, Herschel *The Privatization Putsch* Institute For research on Public Policy, Halifax, 1989

Feigenbaum, Henig & Hamnett *Shrinking the State*, Cambridge UP, Camb. 1999

Judt, Tony *Postwar: A History of Europe Since 1945*, Penguin, NY, 2006

The Pre-Vatican II Church

1. Manuel de los inquisidores - Nicolau Eymerich: quoted by Jean-Pierre DeDieu in The Inquisition Error! Bookmark not defined. and Popular Culture, from *Inquisition and Society in Early Modern Europe* – Stephan Halizer, Ed. & Tran., Barnes & Noble, 1987, Totowa, NJ, p.143
2. ibid. Virgilio Pinto Crespo - *Thought Control in Spain*, p.180; the author elaborates on this obsession in reference to a country where in the 16th & 17th centuries it became "a sort of cultural no phobia" against foreign publications.
3. This development spilt over into the secular realm as well. In his *Literature and the Sixth Sense*, Philip Rahv, writing in 1950, makes the point concerning literary discourse, that "there is far too much manipulation of the notions of guilt, evil and sin, notions drawn from theological sources....and converted, under cover of the religious revival, into a kind of aesthetic demonology...." Boston, Haughton Mifflin Co.,

1969, pg. 174

4. Dostoyevsky, Fyodor *The Brothers' Karamazov*, David Magarshack, Trans., Harmondsworth, 1958, pgs. 288 et sec

5. Rahv, ibid., opines that the Grand Inquisitor realizes the three forces: miracle, mystery and authority - found within totalitarian systems, from Communist to Catholic, "for holding captive the conscience and loyalty of mankind." pgs. 172-173

6. Dostoyevsky, ibid.

7. Brooke, Christopher N. L. - *The Medieval Idea of Marriage*, Oxford University Press, 1991 p. 128

8. Ibid see pgs.139 et sec - an illuminating discussion of the issues involved.

9. Paragraph notations are from: The *Handbook of Moral Theology*, 3rd edition, by Dominic M Prummer (G.W. Shelton, Trans.), Mercier Press, Cork, 1963

10. Quotations from reports December 1, 2015, by Stoyan Zaimor of *The Christian Post*; and Sarah Bailey of *The Washington Post*

In Deference to Mark

Crossan, John Dominic – JESUS*: a Revolutionary Biography*, Harper, NY, 1994

Spong, John Shelby – *Born of a Woman*, Harper, NY, 1992

Helms, Randel – *Gospel Fictions*, Prometheus Bks, NY,1988

Marcus J. Borg & N.T. Wright– *The Meaning of Jesus: Two Visions* Harper, San Francisco, 1999

Women Priests?

Fredricksen, Paula – *From Jesus to Christ*, Yale UP, NH, 1998

Bammel & Moule, Eds. – *Jesus and the Politics of His Day*, especially papers by E. Bammel and F.F. Bruce

BY THE WAY...

Brandon, S.G.F. – *Jesus and the Zealots*, Manchester UP, Man.,1967

Crossan, J.D. - The Birth of Christianity, Harper, NY, 1998

Josephus, New Complete Works-W. Whiston-trans; P.L. Maier-commentary, Kregel Pub., Grand Rapids, MI, 1999

The Auditors' Responsibilities: the Gathering Storm

1. U.S. News and World Report - *Accountants: Cleaning up the Mystery Profession*, December 1977 (editorial)
2. Ibid.
3. The Economist, circa December, 1977
4. Brown, Richard (Ed) - *A History of Accounting and Accountants* (1905), Frank Cass & Co Ltd. (1968)
5. Ibid., p.178 - Earliest state-protected accounting body was founded in Venice, 1581
6. Ibid, p. 75
7. Ibid, p.79
8. Ibid p 90, from Lecky's *"England in the Eighteenth Century"*
9. L.C.B. Gower's *Modern Company Law* (3rd Edition) Stevens & Sons (Lon.), 1969, pgs. 48-49. Mandatory audits became optional in 1856, & remained until 1900
10. History, ibid., p. 318
11. Gower, ibid., p.470
12. J.R. Edwards - *The Accounting Profession and Disclosure in Published Reports*, Accounting and Business Research, Autumn 1976,
13. View expressed by Society of Incorporated Accountants – reported by Edwards
14. Research by Barbara D. Marino for the *Cohen Commission*
15. Montgomery, R. H. - *Auditing, Theory and Practice*, Ronald Pr. Co, 1912
16. Samuel, H. B. - *Shareholder's Money* Pitman 1933, by Edwards

Bibliography, Sources & Endnotes

17. Dickenson, R.W.V. – Rex vs. Kyslant & Morland: *Accountants and the Law of Negligence*, 1966, p. 488.
18. *The Future of Auditing* (Anonymous) – The Accountant, January 1942.
19. Previts, Gary – *The Accountant In Our History, a bicentennial overview*: Journal of Accountancy, July 1976, p. 50
20. Carey, John L. – *Organization and Activities of the Accounting Profession in the US* – an address before ICAEW Oxford Summer Course, 1953
21. Burton, J.C. & Roberts, William - *A Study of Auditor Changes*, Journal of Accountancy, April 1967, p.32
22. Edwards, James – *History of Public Accounting in the US*, 1960, p.206
23. *History of the Institute of Chartered Accountants in England & Wales 1880-1965*, (1966), p.137
24. *Commission on Auditors' Responsibilities* - Report, Manuel F. Cohen, Chair, NY, 1978, p. 86
25. Ibid, *History of ICAEW*, p.195
26. Buckley & McKenna–*The Practicing Chartered Accountant: Job Attitudes & Values*, A & BR, Summer 1973, p.199
27. Picking, Bruce C. - *Auditing Standards*, Accountancy and Business Research, Winter 1973, p. 60
28. Ibid, Cohen, p. 59 et sec.
29. Beck, G. W.- *The Role of the Auditor in Modern Society: An Empirical Appraisal*, Accountancy and Business Research, Spring, 1973
30. ibid., Cohen, p. 2
31. *Corporations & Their Outside Auditors*, Journal of Accountancy, July 1972, p.29
32. Woolf, Emile - *Lesson of Equity Funding: the ultimate indictment*, Accountancy, January 1977, p.30

BY THE WAY...

33. Rankin, Deborah – *How CPAs Sell Themselves*, N. Y. Times, September 1977
34. Metcalf, Lee – *The Accounting Establishment*, 1976
35. Editorial - *CA Magazine*, December, 1976

About the Author

Dereck C. Sale spent nine years under Jesuit tutelage as a youth before undertaking his professional education in the UK. His life experiences include years in Canada, England, Sweden, and Jamaica where he grew up. Once the youngest partner in a Big Eight international firm of Chartered Accountants, he served as president of a national institute of CAs, and was governor of the South Florida District of Serra International - aspects of a career spanning five decades of public practice that included teaching at professional, university, and college levels. His publications include two books - *Testament of the Third Man,* and *Exiles at Home,* as well as many articles on professional and world affairs that have appeared in magazines and newspapers in three countries. Sale and his Swedish wife make their home in British Columbia, Canada.

CPSIA information can be obtained
at www.ICGtesting.com
Printed in the USA
LVOW12s0258090118
562311LV00001B/2/P